UNDER CONSTRUCTION

DANIEL MAINS

UNDER CONSTRUCTION

Technologies of Development in Urban Ethiopia

Duke University Press Durham and London 2019

Printed in the United States of America on acid-free paper ∞
Designed by Courtney Leigh Baker
Typeset in Whitman and Helvetica by Copperline Books

Library of Congress Cataloging-in-Publication Data
Names: Mains, Daniel, [date] author.
Title: Under construction : technologies of development
in urban Ethiopia / Daniel Mains.
Description: Durham : Duke University Press, 2019. |
Includes bibliographical references and index.
Identifiers: LCCN 2018061093 (print) | LCCN 2019010350 (ebook)
ISBN 9781478007043 (ebook)
ISBN 9781478005377 (hardcover : alk. paper)
ISBN 9781478006411 (pbk. : alk. paper)
Subjects: LCSH: Cities and towns—Ethiopia—Growth. | Infrastructure
(Economics) —Ethiopia. | Economic development projects—Ethiopia—
Planning. | Ethiopia—Economic policy. | Community development—
Ethiopia—åAwasa. | Community development—Ethiopia—Kefa Kifle Håager.
Classification: LCC HT384.E8 (ebook) | LCC HT384.E8 M35 2019 (print) |
DDC 307.760963—dc23
LC record available at https://lccn.loc.gov/2018061093

COVER ART: Cobblestone road construction, Jimma.
Courtesy of the author.

FOR ALISE

CONTENTS

ACKNOWLEDGMENTS

Nothing is constructed without the work of many people, and this book is certainly no exception. In Jimma I relied heavily on the friendships I have developed over the years. I thank these friends for always welcoming me with coffee and conversation. I thank the Anthropology Department at Hawassa University for supporting me during my research from 2013 to 2014. Walelign Tadesse, Mellese Madda, Mesganaw Andualem, and Dubale Gebeyehu were particularly great companions for discussing anthropology over beers at "The Pentagon."

I was extremely fortunate that I met Eshetayehu Kinfu during my first weeks in Hawassa. Eshetayehu was an outstanding research collaborator and I have learned a lot from working with him. Eshetayehu shares my love for good food and coffee, and our fieldwork was always punctuated by long discussions over gomen besiga, goden tibs, kitfo, and fried fish. I look forward to following Eshetayehu's exciting work on the politics of urban planning and informal settlements in periurban areas.

My colleagues at the University of Oklahoma Honors College provided critical feedback on much of this book. Ben Alpers, Marie Dallam, Julia Ehrhardt, Rich Hamerla, Brian Johnson, Bob Lifset, Mandy Minks, Carolyn Morgan, Andreana Prichard, and Sarah Tracy are wonderful readers and pushed me to improve my writing and conceptual thinking. I've been fortunate to work with multiple writing groups at OU. Lucas Bessire, Miriam Gross, Jessica Pearson, Erika Robb-Larkins, Emily Rook-Koepsel, and Noah Theriault all helped me refine chapter drafts. I discussed every chapter in this book with Pete Soppelsa, often while cooking or tossing a Frisbee. Pete is an endless source of ideas and a wonderful brainstorming partner. Outside of OU, Jed Stevenson and Marco Di Nunzio were particularly generous in reading chapter drafts and offering critical feedback.

The University of Oklahoma's Humanities Forum sponsored a manuscript development workshop that was essential for reshaping this book. Brenda Chalfin, Suzanne Moon, Charlie Piot, and Erika Robb-Larkins all participated in what for me was an amazing day of pulling apart the text and putting it together again. A special thanks to Erika for sitting down with me after the workshop and helping me process all of the feedback I received. Charlie Piot's ongoing support of the book after the workshop was essential for connecting me with Duke University Press and keeping the project moving forward. Charlie has a rare talent for offering both critique and enthusiastic support. Thanks to Janet Ward, director of OU's Humanities Forum, for facilitating the entire process.

The final round of revisions on this project took place in Berlin, Germany, where I was based at Leibniz-Zentrum Moderner Orient (ZMO). Leibniz-ZMO provided an ideal combination of vibrant intellectual discussion and space for quiet writing. André Chappatte, Paolo Gaibazzi, Judith Scheele, Samuli Schielke, and Abdoulaye Sounaye all participated in a critical discussion of the book's introduction. There was a wonderful convergence of Ethiopianists at Leibniz-ZMO in 2017, and I benefitted from a number of productive discussions with Katrin Bromber, Izabella Orlowska, and Julian Taddesse. Particular thanks to Katrin Bromber for doing everything necessary to make my time at Leibniz-ZMO possible.

Thanks to Elizabeth Ault and Kate Herman at Duke University Press for making the review and production process move as smoothly as possible.

I am grateful for invitations to present portions of this project at Oxford University's Horn of Africa Seminar, Humboldt University's Institute of Asian and African Studies, Hawassa University, Free University of Brussels, Leibniz-ZMO, KU Leuven, Bayreuth Academy of Advanced African Studies, University of Florida's Center for African Studies, and University of Chicago's African Studies Workshop. In each case I received feedback that was valuable in shaping the book.

Portions of this book have appeared previously in *American Ethnologist*, *Cultural Anthropology*, *Focaal*, and the *Journal of Modern African Studies*. Research and writing for this book were supported by the Alexander von Humboldt Foundation, the University of Oklahoma (arts and humanities faculty fellowship and junior faculty fellowships), a Fulbright Research and Teaching Grant, and the National Science Foundation (award ID 0717608). Financial support was provided from the Offices of the Provost and Vice President for Research at the University of Oklahoma.

Finally, I thank my family. My parents, Tom and Kathy Mains, have always encouraged me to wander and trusted that I would eventually arrive somewhere. My wife, Alise Osis, and our kids, Iris and Gus, have been with me for every stage of this journey. We made many amazing memories and friends during our years in Hawassa and Berlin. Without their willingness to continually uproot our lives and explore something new, this book would not have been possible. I look forward to our next adventure, wherever that may be.

INTRODUCTION. Foundations for Development

Infrastructure, the State, and Construction

The Ethiopian state is investing more than $5 billion in the Grand Ethiopian Renaissance Dam (GERD) on the Blue Nile River. It will be the largest hydroelectric project in Africa and generate six thousand megawatts of electricity, enough to power a light bulb for most of Ethiopia's more than 100 million residents. In both journalistic and scholarly accounts, Ethiopia is often held up as an example of one of the new "African Lions," on the leading edge of an Africa that is "rising" and changing its place within the global economy (Radelet 2010; Schuman 2014). With its name alone, the Grand Ethiopian Renaissance Dam implies not only that Ethiopia is rising, but that it is returning to greatness through infrastructural development. In Amharic, Ethiopia's national language, the term for infrastructure, *meseret limat*, translates literally as "the foundation for development." Like the English *infrastructure*, meseret limat refers to a foundation or base, but it is necessarily connected to development. Dams, roads, and other forms of infrastructure are the foundation from which the Ethiopian state seeks development and hopes to reach the status of a middle-income country by 2025.[1] Ethiopia had one of the fastest-growing economies in the world between 2007 and 2017, and much of that growth resulted from high levels of state investment in infrastructure (World Bank 2013; World Bank Group 2017). In many ways Ethiopia is an infrastructural state.

A poster produced by the Ethiopian government in celebration of Nations, Nationalities and Peoples' Day in 2013 featured a collage of images—high-rise apartment buildings, a bullet train, a power plant, propellers for generating wind power, and perhaps most importantly, a hydroelectric dam. At the base of all of this and emanating rays of light is the Ethiopian constitution. The poster announces, "Our Constitution for Our Renaissance" (see figure I.1). The constitution was introduced when the Ethiopian People's Revolutionary Democratic Front (EPRDF) came to power in the early 1990s, and the creation of Nations, Nationalities and Peoples' Day is specifically associated with the EPRDF. The poster implies that the particular laws and forms of governance implemented by the EPRDF are supporting the development of spectacular new infrastructural technologies. The EPRDF is leading the country toward a bright future, a renaissance, represented by bullet trains and massive dams. Infrastructures often support movement and connections across space, but it is this symbolic temporal movement that is perhaps most important for the politics of infrastructure. The dam has the potential to transform the nation's economy, but for many Ethiopians the technology itself symbolizes modernity and state-led development. As fast as possible, the Ethiopian state pushes forward with construction of infrastructure not only to support growth, but to secure legitimacy through images of progress and modernity.

The images of infrastructure depicted in state propaganda obscure the process of construction. It is easy to forget that infrastructures are planned, built, and paid for by people with very different interests—urban residents, laborers, engineers, and government administrators. In contrast to state propaganda, the messiness of construction is striking. Roads peeled back and dug up, rivers diverted, houses bulldozed, people at work—it is in the process of construction that contingency is revealed and simple temporal narratives are unsettled. Weather, soil conditions, friendships, corruption, international financing, and local politics are among the many factors that complicate plans and cause construction projects to succeed or fail. Infrastructural development is a continual struggle, and progress is neither inevitable nor impossible. In this book I take the process of construction as a site for exploring everyday encounters between citizens, the state, and infrastructural technologies.

In the city of Jimma, where I have worked intermittently since the early 2000s, people were highly enthusiastic about asphalt road construction, and in 2009 they willingly donated money to support the project (figure I.2). Five years later, with work still unfinished, Jimma residents claimed, "We don't have roads, we have mud." Old asphalt was scraped away from roads, but for many years the resurfacing was not finished. Heavy rains brought

FIGURE I.1. “Our Constitution for Our Renaissance.” Poster from Nations, Nationalities, and Peoples Day. Photo by the author.

erosion and further complicated construction. Many roads were blocked to vehicles and people moved through the city on foot, carefully negotiating each step through the sticky red mud. It is in the construction of urban infrastructures that abstract citizen/state relations materialize. Jimma residents blamed ethnic politics and a corrupt city government for the failed construction. They claimed they would never again give their money to support such a project. Rather than the renaissance associated with the dam, in Jimma roads evoked a sense of being mired in the muddy present. When I visited Jimma at the time of the 2015 national election, talking politics and infrastructural development was a way of catching up with old friends. "Satan is better than the EPRDF," claimed a friend I have known since the early 2000s. "We have no infrastructure, the cost of living is constantly going up, and the government is intruding into everything we do, even our religion." I replied that the EPRDF has certainly accomplished some things, and I pointed out the example of a new asphalt road that connected his neighborhood with the city center. "This kind of development is meaningless if people cannot eat," my friend responded. "The government sells all of our food to Saudi Arabia and Sudan, and now we cannot even afford to buy lentils." Others in Jimma made similar statements that contrasted new roads and buildings with empty stomachs.

Government administrators, however, blamed Jimma's soil type, rain, and insufficient funds. The road construction company that had been awarded the lucrative contract for renewing Jimma's roads claimed that old, densely constructed housing in the city center caused the delays. Construction was not easy, and even when it was successful urban Ethiopians did not easily accept the association between the EPRDF and the images of a renaissance displayed in state propaganda. In building infrastructure the state seeks to establish its own legitimacy, but the process of construction is very messy, and the building of roads and dissent cannot be separated.

In contrast to Jimma, in the city of Hawassa, where I conducted research in 2013 and 2014, asphalt roads were quickly built and provided a foundation for economic growth. The benefits of Hawassa's new roads, however, were not distributed equally. Even when it is successful construction is inseparable from certain types of destruction. With the coming of asphalt roads, many inner-city residents were forced to give up their homes as they were resettled to the outskirts of the city to make way for commercial interests. In urban Ethiopia, construction was a continual process of contestations between citizens and state over access to imagined futures.

FIGURE I.2. Road construction in Jimma. Photo by Alise Osis.

Such tensions became particularly apparent in October 2016. Just days after announcements that Ethiopia had overtaken Kenya as the largest economy in East Africa, the government declared a six-month state of emergency. After months of peaceful public demonstrations against the ruling EPRDF party, to which the state consistently responded with violence, protestors focused their attention on private interests and attacked and destroyed foreign-owned factories and flower farms south of Addis Ababa. The same factories that were generating growth and creating jobs were attacked because of their relationship with the Ethiopian state. The state's rapid push to construct an Ethiopian renaissance resulted in destruction. Hundreds of protestors have been killed since 2015 (Horne 2018), and it is unclear whether the EPRDF regime will survive to see the renaissance it has proclaimed.

Construction offers both a theory and methodology for exploring the relation between state-led development and destruction that is emerging globally in places such as Turkey, China, and Vietnam. As methodology, the process of construction is a site for ethnographic research in which states, citizens, materials, markets, labor, and plans for the future continually encounter each other. Construction sites can be dangerous, and they are ideal places for exploring conflict. It is during the process of construction that labor, materials, and the state collide. This collision is highly unstable, but among other outcomes it produces roads, dams, and transportation networks.

Construction offers an analytical framework for understanding temporal change that is very different from conceptions of abjection or rising that have recently been used in relation to development in Africa. Construction necessarily involves long-term plans for the future and expectations of growth, as well as change and instability. Life is uncertain, and yet plans are important, even when they are not fulfilled. Because construction builds at the same time that it destroys, it offers a sense of direction without directionality. The process of construction reminds us that movements and transformations may occur in multiple directions that are in no way linear, and yet conceptions of progress remain important. Expectations of modernity (Ferguson 1999) shape urban Ethiopians' evaluations of state interventions, but their desires for progress and growth are rarely satisfied. It is through the process of construction that articulations between multiple temporalities are made visible. At the moment of construction there is potential for spatial and temporal movements to occur in multiple directions, and it is in this sense that the time of construction is also a time of destruction.

Some of this temporal movement occurs within the lives of the people who do the physical work of constructing infrastructure. In contrast to the images of infrastructure in state propaganda, construction sites are filled with people. Construction depends on labor. Although anthropologists have embraced AbdouMaliq Simone's (2004) conception of people as infrastructure, they rarely discuss the people who actually construct material infrastructures. I initially became interested in infrastructural development when I observed many of the unemployed young men who were involved in my research in the early 2000s (Mains 2012b), working for international companies to build infrastructures. For the equivalent of around $150 per month, many young men from Jimma worked for Salini Impregilo to build a twenty-six-kilometer power tunnel for the Gibe II hydropower project. They spoke of the heat and the stifling air inside the tunnels of the $500 million project. Jimma was a long day's journey from the construction site, and the workers lived in camps. When the project wound down most of the construction workers returned to Jimma and searched for new jobs, usually building infrastructure. Some of them ended up building urban cobblestone roads. Although the jobs created by dam construction are certainly important, they pale in comparison to the more than hundred thousand young people who have found work building cobblestone roads in the past decade. Cobblestone is a new technology in urban Ethiopia, and it has been adopted with the support of the German government. In contrast to dams, cobblestone roads are not monumental infrastructures associated with modernity. Images of cobblestone are not common in state propaganda, but cobblestone road construction is very important for the Ethiopian state for the simple reason that it creates jobs. Infrastructural technologies resonate with different temporalities and ideologies of development. Cobblestone is slow infrastructure. Locally quarried rock is chiseled and set by hand (see figure I.3). Where contracts for dams are worth billions of dollars, associations of neighborhood youth compete for $20,000 cobblestone contracts managed by municipal governments.

Cobblestone and hydropower dams are very different technologies, but in both cases to be under construction is to engage in a tense encounter between materials, labor, and the state. Both discursively and materially, Ethiopians experience the state through specific infrastructural technologies that are associated with distinct ideologies of development—hydroelectric dams, asphalt roads, three-wheeled motorcycle taxis, and cobblestone roads. My research engages with construction workers, engineers, residents of rapidly changing neighborhoods, government administrators, and taxi drivers in two Ethiopian cities. It is the process of construction that brings together so many different people, things, and places. Each chapter examines a particular form of urban infrastructure to advance arguments about encounters between citizens, states, and materials that emerge through the construction process and the struggle for a desirable future.

What does it mean to live in a time of construction? In the following sections I outline four major arguments that emerge from a close analysis of the construction process. These arguments are based in the Ethiopian case, but they may be applied globally in the numerous places where state plans for development simultaneously build and destroy.

1. Although states have withdrawn from many areas of governance, they maintain a selective engagement in the field of construction. Ethnographic research on the process of construction is essential for understanding the contemporary state.
2. The regulations associated with state planning interact with the precarious improvisations of urban life to build infrastructures and inequalities.

FIGURE I.3. Cobblestone construction. Photo by the author.

3. Urban residents' affective relationships with the construction of infrastructures shape the legitimacy of the state.
4. The politics of infrastructural development is best understood through a synthesis of historical and vital materialisms.

Absent States, Africa Rising, and Infrastructural Development

Ethiopia demonstrates the problems of conceptualizing the withdrawal of the state in relation to narratives of abjection or rising. States are certainly absent in many areas, but they often continue to maintain strong presences through construction. Beginning with the structural adjustment policies of the 1980s and 1990s and the end of the Cold War, African states have been in retreat and abandoned much of the work of governance (Ferguson 1999, 2006; Larkin 2008; Piot 2010). Regarding Africa, Charles Piot wrote that the absence of international aid after the end of the Cold War forced "the state to withdraw from social and development fields and to turn its back on the large-scale, top-down development projects (and the linear teleologies that accompanied them)" (2010, 15). Rather than pursuing projects in the interest of the public good, the primary function of African states has been to provide the legal authority to "legitimate the extractive work of transnational firms" (Ferguson 2006, 207). In this context abjection and economic decline became key elements of people's experiences of day-to-day life (Ferguson 1999; Mains 2012b).

In contrast, journalists and scholars have begun advancing a narrative of Africa rising. Proponents of the Africa rising narrative celebrate the withdrawal of the state as an opportunity for economic growth that is not stifled by an inefficient and often predatory state. One of the most insightful of these analyses is journalist Dayo Olopade's book, *The Bright Continent*. Olopade examines the relationship between what she calls "fail states" and entrepreneurship. When states fail to provide basic services, entrepreneurs step in with market-based solutions to development problems (Olopade 2014, 143). Steven Radelet claims that there is a direct relationship between downsizing states, democratic governance, and economic growth (2010, 2016). Radelet argues that austerity policies and forced elections created more pluralistic and democratic regimes, which in turn support economic growth (2010, 17). Radelet's evidence connecting austerity to democracy is unclear, and as he acknowledges (Radelet 2016), Ethiopia's rapid growth has occurred in the absence of democratic reforms. Vijay Mahajan's optimism in *Africa Rising* (2009) borders on absurd. In his opening chapter Mahajan explains that frequent power outages are good news for African entrepreneurs. He offers the example of the South Africa–based Innscor, owner of restaurant chains such as Steers, Pizza Inn, and Bakers Inn, and claims that during the power outages that plague many African countries, it is difficult for people to cook at home and thus they are more likely to eat out at fast food restaurants, thereby generating economic activity. Aside from my family, I never observed anyone in our shared compound going to a restaurant as a result Hawassa's frequent power outages in 2013 and 2014.

Abjection and decline certainly do not describe Ethiopia's rapid economic growth, but at the same time, optimistic Africa rising narratives do not fit the daily struggles of many urban Ethiopians to access electricity, water, and other basic services. The Ethiopian state's investment in infrastructure takes place within a peculiar context of unprecedented economic growth and daily struggles to access basic needs. On one hand, a recent *Time* magazine article announced, "Forget the BRICS [Brazil, Russia, India, and China]; Meet the PINES [the Philippines, Indonesia, Nigeria, and Ethiopia]!" (Schuman 2014). Ethiopia's GDP grew at a rate of more than 8 percent annually between 2001 and 2010 (*Economist* 2011), and growth occurred at a rate of more than 10 percent from 2010 to 2015 (Africa Development Bank n.d.). On the other hand, beginning in 2008 the cost of staple foods rose dramatically, forcing many families to skip meals (Ulimwengu et al. 2009), rates of unemployment among urban youth are still quite high, particularly for women (Broussard and Tekleselassie 2012), and high levels of inflation have made life very difficult for government workers and pensioners. Very few of the urban Ethiopians I know feel they have benefitted from recent growth in GDP, and most complain of a rising cost of living that makes purchasing basic necessities increasingly difficult.

Although there is certainly much evidence that African states have withdrawn from some aspects of governance, in Ethiopia state-led development and narratives of progress have not been abandoned. The Ethiopian state retracted after the sprawling bureaucracy of the Marxist Derg regime (1974–91), in which every secondary school graduate was guaranteed a government job. However, a state that wages a war with Eritrea, establishes nearly thirty new federally run universities in less than fifteen years, and relocates hundreds of thousands of people in the name of avoiding famine is certainly not absent. Writing about twentieth-century Nigeria, Brian Larkin explains, "Infrastructures were the promise a state made to its citizenry. In return for political support, the state claimed to provide citizens with the infrastructural path to the future" (2016, 47). The Ethiopian case demonstrates that similar promises are still being made, but within the peculiar context of the twenty-first century. The EPRDF party that has ruled since the early 1990s defines itself as a developmental state (Lefort 2012; Vaughan 2011) and maintains a highly selective presence as it invests massive amounts of resources in the construction of infrastructure. The Ethiopian state has withdrawn, and yet it asserts itself quite forcefully in building and regulating infrastructures. It is this construction that produces economic growth as well as destruction and instability.

The Ethiopian government has sought to define itself in opposition to what former Prime Minister Meles Zenawi called the neoliberal "night watchman state" (Zenawi 2011b, 140). Rather than standing aside to make way for private enterprise, the state actively intervenes in Ethiopia's economy. For the EPRDF, investing billions of dollars in hydropower projects and asphalt roads has been a key strategy for achieving a hegemonic developmental state. Will Jones and his colleagues write, "The idea of omniscient, enlightened mandarins using 'sacred' knowledge to guide the backward masses is an enduring one, recently recycled in institutions such as Ethiopia's Office of the Prime Minister, the Rwanda Revenue Authority and Sudan's Dam Implementation Unit (DIU)" (2013). In Ethiopia, however, the developmental state is not an anachronism. It is specifically intended to counter the dangers and failures of African states that do not provide basic public services for their citizens. Former mayor of Addis Ababa, Arkebe Oqubay (2015), has argued for an "activist state" that avoids the failures of the "Washington consensus" structural adjustment policies of the 1980s and 1990s. The twenty-first-century developmental state looks not to the West, but to models from the East, particularly China (Mosley and Watson 2016).

Struggles over dams, roads, and public transportation are not unique to Ethiopia. Across the African continent states seek to advance visions of growth and modernization through infrastructural development. The Grand Inga Dam that is being planned in the Democratic Republic of Congo would be the world's biggest hydropower project, cost more than $80 billion, and generate forty thousand megawatts of electricity. Dakar residents debate the merits of road construction and struggle with various forms of "bottlenecks" as their city is transformed (Melly 2017). In Kinshasa residents imagine spectacular futures in relation to large-scale construction projects (De Boeck 2011). Kenya seeks to define itself as a "silicon Savannah" at the center of Africa's expanding digital technology sector (Poggiali 2016). Beyond Africa, construction mediates citizen/state relationships in many urban areas. In Turkey "bulldozer capitalism" creates rapid cycles of state sponsored construction and destruction (Evrem forthcoming). The construction/destruction relationship in Ho Chi Minh City has created a world of "luxury and rubble" (Harms 2016). In urban China redevelopment is inseparable from "disrepair" (Chu 2014). Taken together, these cases suggest that much of the world is under construction, both figuratively and literally, and the Ethiopian case is particularly instructive in illuminating this process.

The proliferation of construction is in part due to China's emergence as a source of funding and labor for infrastructural development in Africa. With growth slowing in China, accumulated Chinese capital and expertise can be put to use in Africa (Tilt 2015, 182–83). China's emergence has pressured the World Bank to return to large-scale infrastructural development. Under structural adjustment, the World Bank and the IMF forced African nations to downsize in order to receive loans. Quality of life suffered as states cut back on funds for health care, education, and public services and abandoned large investments in infrastructures (Ferguson 1999; McMichael 1996). At the beginning of the twenty-first century the debts of African nations began to be forgiven under the World Bank and IMF's Highly Indebted Poor Country (HIPC) initiative. Structural adjustment policies were replaced with Country Led Poverty Reduction Strategies that gave individual nations somewhat more autonomy in determining their strategies for development. Aid to African countries has also begun to increase from its post–Cold War low in 1999, and this has freed up funds to invest in infrastructural projects that were largely abandoned during the structural adjustment era (Radelet 2010). These factors have contributed to a relative boom in construction, particularly large projects related to infrastructural development.

Despite these shifts, the Ethiopian state still faces financial constraints on its ability to build. The state seeks to establish its legitimacy through investment in infrastructure and public services, but it often lacks the funds to provide for the basic needs of its citizens and actualize its vision of developmental hegemony.[2] Its access to loans and aid packages is far less than in the Cold War years of the mid-twentieth century. As a result the state has forced government employees to donate portions of their salaries to projects ranging from the GERD to Jimma's road construction. Infrastructure often depends on complex relationships between public and private interests. The three-wheeled motorcycle taxis that provided nearly all public transportation in Hawassa were entirely owned and operated by private interests, but the state determined taxi routes and passenger fares. Drivers eventually refused to work when state-mandated fares were so low that it was impossible to maintain a livelihood. The state's limited resources to advance its vision of development have created much of the tension that drives the construction/destruction relationship. As the state builds it extracts labor, wages, and resources from its citizens. The protests that eventually culminated in the 2016 state of emergency began with the expansion of Addis Ababa's administrative boundaries and fears of expropriation of land from Oromo farmers. Protestors had multiple complex motivations, but opposition to state planning was certainly one of the reasons they took to the streets.

To construct an Ethiopian renaissance, the state also depends heavily on international capital. Much of this investment comes from China, but companies from around the world are involved in constructing Ethiopia. Salini Impregilo has built many of Ethiopia's dams, including the multibillion dollar GERD. In some cases Salini has been awarded no-bid contracts, meaning that there is very little transparency and numerous opportunities for corruption. The Ethiopian state's dependency on international companies adds one more source of instability to the process of construction.

It is partially the nature of Ethiopia as an extreme case of state-led development that makes it so valuable for understanding other cases of construction. Ethiopia is not a typical state in the developing world. It was never colonized. Different Ethiopian regimes have excelled at manipulating foreign alliances to maintain regional power. Beginning in the twentieth century under Haile Selassie, the state has invested significant resources in top-down development projects. Under the EPRDF, the central government allocates virtually all fiscal resources and nominates all key regional personnel (Hagmann and Abbink 2013, 5). The Ethiopian case offers a particularly intense contrast between state-led development and ongoing poverty. However, rather than arguing for Ethiopian exceptionalism, I believe Ethiopia has great value as an extreme exemplar for understanding the selective engagement of states in construction that is also found elsewhere. In recent years Ethiopia has had one of the highest rates of public investment in infrastructure in the world. State investment is combined with collaboration with private construction companies, both national and international. The Ethiopian case clarifies contestations surrounding development, governance, and technology that are certainly present elsewhere but may not be immediately apparent.[3]

Regulating and Improvising Construction

A key project for this book is to implode the opposition between the simplified generalizations associated with state planning and the particularities of local practices, environmental conditions, and human relationships. I argue that regulations and improvisations represent distinct ways of engaging with the future, but they are not necessarily opposed.[4] Rather, regulations and improvisations interact to construct infrastructures and shape relations of power and inequality. An illustration comes from the three-wheeled motorcycle taxis—referred to by their brand name, Bajaj—that provided nearly all of the public transportation in Hawassa. The Bajaj was at the center of conflicts between the top-down state regulation associated with planning and large-scale infrastructure, and the irregular economic and social relationships that are of great importance in urban Ethiopia. Bajaj owners generally leased the vehicles to drivers who earned an income based on the number of passengers they carried throughout the day. The state controlled passenger fares, Bajaj routes, and license distribution. Drivers consistently violated state regulations to meet the needs of passengers and maximize their incomes. A functional urban transportation system depended on state regulations and driver improvisations. Although the tension between the two was certainly important, it was the interaction between regulation and improvisation that allowed people to move through the city.

In the mid-twentieth century states assumed that they could use expert knowledge and planning to serve the public good and attain imagined futures. Critical development scholars questioned the legitimacy of these projects during the 1980s and 1990s. Among other critiques, they highlighted the problems that occur when those who are affected by projects have no voice in the planning process (Ar. Roy 2001; Scott 1998). Particularly influential was James Scott's (1998) critique of state-led planning that relies on "radical simplifications" and ignores localized knowledge and practices in favor of singular solutions intended only to increase production. Critiques of development were also based on the "knowledge problem" addressed by Austrian economists Friedrich von Hayek and Ludwig von Mises (Elyachar 2012). From this perspective, similar to Scott's (1998) view, top-down planning is destined to fail because of a lack of knowledge regarding on-the-ground conditions. In contrast to Scott's attention to practice, however, "Protagonists of the calculation debate set up a structured opposition between two ideal types: the entrepreneurial individual subject of the free market, on the one hand, and the public sector of the totalitarian state, on the other. There was no consideration of other kinds of subjects and other forms of property" (Elyachar 2012, 119). The arguments of Austrian economists have increasingly been incorporated into development schemes that avoid large-scale projects and instead distribute funds to individuals with the hope of creating entrepreneurs who can pull themselves out of poverty (Caldeira and Holston 2005; Ferguson 2015; Hanlon et al. 2010). Scholars have celebrated improvisations in the absence of planning as paths to almost utopian future cities (Gandy 2005). Even the World Bank has called itself "anti-development" in order to distinguish between the megaprojects it financed in the past and its increasing support for microfinance initiatives (Elyachar 2002).

Specific infrastructural technologies are associated with these competing ideologies of development. The hydroelectric dam, for example, modifies the environment and depends on state planning and expertise to generate and distribute power. In contrast, the flexibility of the Bajaj enables individual drivers to function as entrepreneurs who make decisions in response to changing market conditions. One technology uses generalizable expert knowledge to change the environment, whereas the other facilitates the use of localized knowledge to respond to a changing context.

Shifts among competing ideologies and technologies of development have occurred simultaneously with the changing roles of states described above. As AbdouMaliq Simone (2004) explains, when states fail to provide basic public services, people and their social networks often function as infrastructure, delivering the services necessary to sustain urban life. For example, in 2014 when water ceased to flow from faucets in Hawassa neighborhoods, boys carrying jerry cans of water on handmade wheelbarrows filled the streets, delivering it to households for a small fee. Neighborhoods without piped water continually relied on boys using donkey carts to deliver water. These networks of people generally lack the centralized organization that is associated with state-led projects and technologies such as piped water. Instead, networks organized on the basis of gender, ethnicity, and kin used flexible technologies such as donkey carts to respond to possibilities for earning incomes.

Social scientists often categorize these networks that are not regulated by the state as informal economic activity—in some cases they are explicitly illegal and in others they are not connected with a codified set of laws.[5] In many African countries the bulk of economic activity occurs in the informal sector. It is partially for this reason that the formal/informal binary is problematic—it does not make sense to call the most pervasive types of economic activities "informal" (Ferguson 2015, 94). Perhaps even more importantly, "informal" categorizes a highly variable set of activities, and even when clear definitions are offered, such as defining informality in terms of a lack of state-issued documentation, it is not clear that this is relevant for maintaining a livelihood.[6] For example, the dependence of Bajaj drivers on violating laws is no more important for their livelihood than state regulations. Water delivery boys fill their jerry cans from state-provisioned faucets. State regulation of the transportation sector and water delivery is often shaped by bribes and other seemingly informal practices. Many livelihoods encompass both regulated and unregulated activities. Regarding urban infrastructures, contrasting types of practices are clearly at play, but their qualities are not usefully captured by the informal/formal distinction.

Scholars have used a variety of terms to get to the heart of the qualitative differences that are missed by the formal/informal dichotomy. Scott (1998) contrasts complexity with simplifications that are based in a singular evaluative hierarchy that is applied to variable contexts. Anna Tsing's (2015) distinction between scalable and unscalable also differentiates between practices in terms of their potential to be applied across a wide range of contexts. In their analysis of road construction, Hannah Knox and Penny Harvey contrast the "systemic stabilization" of roads with an unstable world (2011, 145). Ferguson draws on AbdouMaliq Simone's work to suggest that many economic activities should be considered "improvisation under conditions of adversity" (2015, 94).[7] Improvisation may be usefully contrasted with a more rigid pattern of behavior in which uniform practices are applied regardless of context. Simplification versus complexity, stability versus instability, scalable versus unscalable, rule-bound rigidity versus improvisation—in each case the distinction is between a regularized pattern of behavior and practices that are flexible and change depending on context.

Improvisations are specific to particular times and places. This does not mean that improvisation is somehow instinctive or free from past experience. Improvised practices draw on past experiences to develop solutions for changing conditions encountered in the present. These temporal dynamics are not captured with the informal/formal dichotomy. Just as jazz musicians do not improvise alone, and in some cases, like Sun Ra's Arkestra (Szwed 1997), they play and improvise together for more than thirty years, the improvisations of urban Ethiopians are based in long-term relationships. People learn to improvise together, and that practice plays out at particular points in time. In the process of provisioning infrastructure, certain people tend to play with others, and the relationships that are formed through this practice may reinforce or subvert power hierarchies. Each time a Bajaj driver chooses to leave his assigned route and alter the price from the state-mandated fare, he is improvising in a way that is based on relationships with the passenger, other drivers, and traffic police.

It is through construction that regulations and improvisations interact to build and destroy. It is the willingness of Bajaj drivers to improvise and violate transportation regulations that enables Hawassa residents to move effectively through the city. State-led development interventions also depend on improvisation. In chapter 2, I describe how government administrators in Hawassa used extralegal improvisations to construct asphalt roads in a timely manner. The improvisations of government administrators and Bajaj drivers were based in long-term relationships and social networks. They collaborated with others to respond to precarious conditions. However, not all improvisations are created equally. The improvisations of government administrators constructed asphalt roads that transformed neighborhoods and lives—houses were bulldozed and their occupants were resettled to the edge of the city. The power of particular improvisations generates construction's destructive potential. The improvisations of elder, male government administrators built roads that destroyed the precarious improvisational livelihoods of inner-city residents. This tension has been a key factor in destabilizing the state. To the extent that improvisations support successful construction, they also generate resistance.

Constructing Legitimacy and the Affective Politics of Infrastructure

Construction is as much about building images and feelings as it is about building things. The EPRDF is heavily invested in discourses of development, and the provision of infrastructure is key to the maintenance of its legitimacy in terms of popular acceptance of its authority. The symbolic dimensions of infrastructure are particularly important. In discussing the "poetics of infrastructure," Brian Larkin explains, "in the case of infrastructures, the poetic mode means that form is loosened from technical function. Infrastructures are the means by which a state proffers these representations to its citizens and asks them to take those representations as social facts" (2013, 335). For the Grand Ethiopian Renaissance Dam, the title alone provides a taste of the poetics of infrastructure. Although the technical function of the dam is certainly important, the dam is also a powerful symbol that Ethiopia's ruling political party invokes to advance a particular narrative about the future and the passage of time. The degree to which Ethiopians embrace the concept of renaissance and the complex feelings that it evokes partially determines their relationship with the state.

Poetry, however, does not simply rely on direct representations, in the sense that the GERD symbolizes modernity or an asphalt road symbolizes movement. Poetry works by evoking sensory experience, emotion, human relationships, and complex feelings such as nostalgia or loss. The poetics of infrastructure are grounded in the sense of fantasy and desire associated with specific infrastructural technologies (Larkin 2013). "How can I express it in words?" asked a woman regarding a newly constructed asphalt road in Hawassa. "It is like the feeling after your child is wed." Urban Ethiopians experience layers of feelings and attachments for places, things, and the state that may be partially understood in terms of Kathleen Stewart's notion of ordinary affects, which "happen in impulses, sensations, expectations, daydreams, encounters and habits of relating, in strategies and their failures, in forms of persuasion, contagion, and compulsion, in modes of attention, attachment, and agency, and in publics and social worlds of all kinds that catch people up in something that feels like *some*thing" (2007, 2; emphasis in the original). Affect feels like something, but that something is very difficult to articulate.

For many theorists, affect exists precisely in the gap between sensation and cognition (Gregg and Seigworth 2010).[8] Affect is intensity (Massumi 1995, 2002). It is fleeting but also extremely powerful. The value of affect as an analytical tool is that it describes the multiple overlapping resonances and feelings that people associate with objects, images, or experiences. Affect explains much of political life—people often support a party, leader, or regime because something about it feels right. A successful politician is often like a poet, able to convey feelings of fear, unity, or passion by manipulating images and language. The challenge for an analysis of affective politics is to connect the fleeting impulses and sensations of affective experience with the legitimacy of the state.[9] A direct causal relationship between affective experience and legitimacy is very difficult to identify, and yet the two are inseparable.

Sasha Newell's (2018) analysis of what he calls the affectiveness of symbols offers a helpful path for connecting the affective poetics of infrastructure with the politics of legitimacy. Newell argues that "affective force can also be found lodged in signs and that this is actually the principal manner in which affect transmits between bodies. Furthermore, it is precisely this semiotic transmission of affect that allows the social to permeate the thinking of persons without their conscious awareness" (2). Newell challenges us to consider how affect enables things to communicate. Such communication does not rely on representational language. In the context of a developmental state, infrastructures are particularly charged signs that connect citizens and states through affective communication. Urban Ethiopians feel the state through infrastructures that have multiple meanings and intensities. The experience of construction and urban transformation is a form of affective communication in which citizen/state relationships are continually remade.

I examine sensation, temporal experience, and intimate relations of exchange as three key elements of affective communication through which infrastructures create complex feelings for the state. Each area offers a loose foundation from which to explore the affective politics of infrastructure. In articulating affective politics in terms of these categories, I necessarily simplify and obscure portions of what is felt. However, it is only through a degree of simplification that it is possible to analytically engage with the affective politics of infrastructure.

Urban Ethiopians sense infrastructure through the intense smells from a failed sewage system, the noise of a gas-powered generator, the cooling breeze that comes with a ride in the back of a three-wheeled motorcycle taxi, or the dust from a dirt road that irritates one's eyes and nose. These sensations generate feelings about the developmental state that has staked so much of its legitimacy on the construction of infrastructure.[10] A smooth ride on a newly paved road and an hour of inhaling dust as one bounces over potholes produce very different affective relationships with the state. As I explore further in chapter 3, sensations of infrastructure are processed through discussion and conversation, which then further shape perceptions of infrastructures and the state.

Affective attachments also form on the basis of specific infrastructural temporalities that are connected with ideologies of development (Redfield 2016). For example, in chapter 1 I explore how hydropower projects are imagined in relation to particular models of development and temporal narratives that are associated with dammed and undammed rivers. Specific things, the dam and the river, signify complex affective attachments to the passage of time. Bodies feel particular ways of moving through time differently. For some there is the headache-inducing stress of change and a life that is continually unsettled. For others, a life without change produces feelings akin to boredom in which the body is physically tired (Mains 2015). Urban Ethiopians often struggle with the feeling of waiting as construction projects stretch on without end. People's relationships to infrastructure and the state are caught up with these complex temporal experiences of change. As Peter Redfield explains in his discussion of the LifeStraw, feelings for certain technologies are connected with a state's "failure to ensure proper material conditions for modern experience" (2016, 174). While massive hydropower projects represent state attempts to secure a modern future, privately owned three-wheeled motorcycle taxis are a result of the state's failure to provision urban transportation. Desires for a specific type of state and temporal experience are inseparable from feelings for particular infrastructural technologies.

In constructing large-scale infrastructures, states redistribute resources. Infrastructures benefit some more than others on the basis of ethnicity, class, gender, age, and location of residence (Harvey 1985; Klineberg 2006; Mains and Kinfu 2016; Squires and Hartman 2006). Protests against the EPRDF that began in 2014 and culminated in the 2016 declaration of a state of emergency were based in part on the perception that government plans and projects benefitted some ethnic groups at the expense of others. The affective politics of legitimacy, however, go beyond a rational calculation of the distribution of resources. They are shaped by exchange and intimate relationships. Throughout the African continent love, intimacy, and friendship have been inseparable from exchange (Cole and Thomas 2009). To have a close relationship with another person is to give and receive. Similarly, relations between citizen and state are based in affective attachments that emerge from the exchanges and redistributions of wealth associated with the construction of infrastructure. This dynamic is embedded in norms surrounding relations of power and exchange that are specific to Ethiopia.

Affect brings together the construction and destruction of the state's legitimacy. The state seeks to secure legitimacy through the construction of infrastructure, but this process destabilizes attempts to manipulate the poetics of infrastructure. When Jimma residents felt ongoing road construction through mud instead of asphalt, it drove a wedge between citizens and state. In the context of the failed infrastructural development that I discuss in chapter 3, urban Ethiopians sometimes used metaphors of kinship to frame their relationship with the state. Feelings of rejection and betrayal were common. Infrastructures are evocative partially because they are so caught up within intimate relationships between citizen and state. To the extent that the poetics of infrastructure have the potential to bond citizen and state in the common project of working together for an Ethiopian renaissance, it may also pull them apart and leave lasting feelings of animosity.

Technology, Development, and Multiple Materialisms

The anthropology of development has had a peculiar relationship with technology. Based in mid-twentieth-century modernization theory, development interventions have consistently offered technical solutions to the problem of poverty.[11] In the mid-twentieth century W. W. Rostow (1960) confidently argued that impoverished, newly independent nations in the global south would rapidly modernize by borrowing technology from more developed nations. The claims of modernization theorists rested on the assumption that a technology that is successful in one context will also work in another. Their faith that the introduction of new technologies could rapidly alleviate poverty led states and international organizations to make massive investments in infrastructure. Among the most visible—and controversial—of these projects were the construction of hydroelectric dams in places as different as Egypt, Mozambique, India, and Brazil. Development practitioners argued that technologies such as these could raise all boats. Echoes of modernization theory are common in contemporary analyses of international development. In his influential book *The End of Poverty*, Jeffrey Sachs describes the transmission of technologies as the "single most important reason why prosperity spread, and why it continues to spread" (2005, 41). As I detail in chapter 1, the Ethiopian state is investing billions of dollars in dams partially because of the faith that hydropower technology will support prosperity by generating power and irrigating plantations.

In the case of the Gilgel Gibe III project in the lower Omo Valley, however, the project threatens the livelihoods of nearly 500,000 seminomadic people who rely on the Omo River for water for cattle, fishing, and flood plain farming. The Ethiopian people will ultimately pay the more than $1 billion that the project will cost, but it is unclear whether they will see any benefits. The bulk of the electricity generated will probably be exported or used in large factories. The dam will also enable the irrigation of monocrop plantations owned by the state and private investors. Land appropriated for the plantations has caused further displacement.

As Karl Marx (1976) explained in his analysis of the commodity fetish, when humans grant power to things, relations of exploitation between people are masked.[12] This is often the case with technologies of development. The Gibe III dam can be read as a case in which the technical solutions to the problem of poverty displace attention from a politics that is concerned with the "means by which certain classes and interests attempted to control the behavior and choices of others" (Ferguson 1994, 237). Marxian scholars of underdevelopment, such as Walter Rodney (1981), argue that technological interventions essentially function as masks for accumulation by dispossession. A classic example is the railroad constructed in Congo under King Leopold's bloody rule. The railway, justified in terms of providing transportation and supporting the growth of markets, in fact was used to export massive amounts of rubber out of the country (Hochschild 1998). In other cases technology was not used specifically with the intent to achieve dispossession, but it obscured the need for redistribution of resources. Randall Packard (1997) describes Western faith in the power of technology to wipe out malaria in sub-Saharan Africa. The belief that pesticides could eliminate malaria distracted attention from the need to alleviate poverty and build up a public health infrastructure to combat malaria and other illnesses. At the time of this writing, the Gates Foundation has invested well over $1 billion in eradicating malaria through technological innovation, but it generally does not consider structural economic inequalities, such as those associated with the extraction of resources, in relation to health. Investments in the development of new drugs to block the transmission of malaria are technical solutions to a problem that might also be addressed in political and economic terms.

Cases such as these lead to a great deal of suspicion among scholars of development. When I encounter promises that technology will alleviate poverty, I immediately want to dig deeper, suspicious that there are structural inequalities to be uncovered. Jane Bennett (2010) explains that this desire to "demystify" has its roots in Marxist historical materialism. For historical materialists, technology is significant largely in relation to production and in shaping inequalities in power over the product of one's labor (Donham 1999a). For Bennett (2010, xv), "demystification tends to screen from view the vitality of matter and to reduce political agency to human agency." The problem of the Marxist conception of the fetish is that it ignores the very real power of things to attract and engage humans, a power that is no less real than the human relations that produce things (Donham 2018).

Bennett argues that demystification always leads to critique rather than the "possibility of positive formations" (2010, xv), and therefore she pursues a "vital materialism" that distributes agency among a wider field of actors. Attention to the political agency and vitality of things has been a key contribution from the growing number of social scientists studying infrastructure (Anand 2011; Barry 2013; Larkin 2008, 2013; Latour 1993; Mitchell 2002; Truitt 2008; von Schnitzler 2008, 2013). As Andrew Barry explains, "No longer can we think of material artifacts and physical systems such as pipes, houses, water and earth as the passive and stable foundation on which politics takes place; rather, it is argued, the unpredictable and lively behavior of such objects and environments should be understood as integral to the conduct of politics" (2013, 1–2). Vital materialism necessarily gives serious attention to the opportunities and limits created by specific materials and technologies. For example, citizens in Hawassa encounter the state as they use public transportation to move through the city. As I detail in chapter 4, it is through the particular technology of the three-wheeled motorcycle that struggles take place over transportation and the right to the city. Technology does not mask politics; rather, technology is politics. Dams, for example, do not simply push water in different directions to serve the whims of government officials and owners of capital. Both water and the physical structure of the dam act in ways that are outside of human control and produce unexpected outcomes. This was apparent when, shortly after its inauguration in 2010, a tunnel that was part of the Italian-built Gibe II hydropower project in southern Ethiopia collapsed. A given technology pushes and pulls humans in directions that are quite distinct from anything that its creators intended.

I combine vital materialism's attention to particular qualities of technology with a historical materialism that emerges out of neo-Marxist critiques of development. Bennett certainly offers an important contribution in drawing attention to the vitality of things, but this must be complemented with attention to the class relationships and regimes of labor that are essential for building infrastructure. Bennett (2010, 38) asks, "Should we acknowledge the distributive quality of agency to address the power of human–nonhuman assemblages and to resist a politics of blame? Or should we persist with a strategic understatement of material agency in the hopes of enhancing the accountability of specific humans?" This is a false opposition. There is no reason that one should come at the expense of the other. Combining vital and historical materialism reveals the complex intersections between the agency of humans and technologies, and their implications for different forms of inequality.

More specifically, historical materialism draws attention to labor and relations of production that are essential for provisioning infrastructure. The recent explosion of anthropological work on infrastructure insightfully examines the relationship between technology and politics, but it rarely explores the importance of labor for building and maintaining infrastructure. For example, a special section of the website for the journal *Cultural Anthropology* offers a "toolbox" of concepts to help anthropologists analyze infrastructure (Appel et al. 2015). The toolbox includes important concepts such as data, finance, and materials, but for the most part the people who actually carry a toolbox with them to work—the laborers—are absent. Anthropologists have done well to explore the particular qualities and histories of infrastructural technologies, but they must not ignore the people who build and provision infrastructures.

Developmental states such as Ethiopia depend on inexpensive labor to construct infrastructure, move people through the city, and in some cases deliver basic goods such as water. The state generates conflict as it demands more from human infrastructure, partially in the interest of maintaining its legitimacy. At the same time, the people who function as infrastructure depend on specific materials and technologies that create limits on and opportunities for provisioning basic services. Technologies such as the three-wheeled motorcycle taxi and cobblestone only became widespread in urban Ethiopia at the beginning of the twenty-first century. They carry specific histories that interact with contemporary labor regimes though the construction process (Redfield 2016; von Schnitzler 2013). Particularly in chapters 4 and 5, I draw on Donald Donham's (1999a) exploration of anthropology and Marxist theory to articulate a historical materialism that understands conflict in terms of control over the product of one's labor. I argue that the politics of urban infrastructure must be understood in terms of encounters between productive inequalities and vital technologies.

Research Sites and Methodology

Under Construction is about two cities, Jimma and Hawassa. Both are secondary cities, much smaller than Addis Ababa, but still among the largest cities in Ethiopia. The cities are not far from each other in southern Ethiopia. However, without an asphalt road connecting them, it is necessary to first pass through Addis Ababa, and the journey takes two days by bus. Jimma and Hawassa are both ethnically diverse. In terms of religion, Jimma is split almost evenly between Muslims and Orthodox Christians, whereas Hawassa is split between Protestant and Orthodox Christians. Both cities experienced significant urban development and road construction between 2005 and 2015.

Hawassa is located on the banks of a picturesque Rift Valley lake, and at an altitude of around 5,600 feet, the climate is nearly ideal. It seems that the sun is always shining and a cool breeze is continually blowing in off the lake. I first visited Hawassa in 1999. At that time it was a sleepy town populated by government administrators and a handful of tourists visiting the lake. When I came back in 2001, looking for a research site for my dissertation project concerning urban youth, Hawassa still did not fit with how I imagined a real city should feel. There were few people and markets and little vibrant life, and I soon learned that the city had been founded only around forty years earlier. Instead, I chose to conduct my research in Jimma, a city that had been a regional crossroads and market center for hundreds of years. However, I returned to Hawassa a third time in 2013 to teach at the university and start a new research project, and I found the city transformed. The number of asphalt roads in Hawassa doubled between 2005 and 2015. It had a population of nearly 250,000, a significant increase from my first visit almost fifteen years earlier. As the capital of the Southern Nations, Nationalities, and Peoples' Region (SNNPR), Hawassa had received significant public investment. With its palm-lined asphalt boulevards, bustling shopping districts, growing university, and ethnic diversity, the city of Hawassa attracted migrants from every corner of Ethiopia who were looking for something better. Multistoried buildings housing clothing and appliance shops filled the commercial districts, and Italian-run pizzerias and gelato shops catered to wealthy NGO employees in the posh lakeside neighborhoods. Unlike many Ethiopian cities, beginning in the early 1960s Hawassa developed on the basis of a formal urban plan that organized neighborhoods into large grids.

This was not the sort of Ethiopian city that I was accustomed to—and it was not the image of urban Africa that one generally finds in Western journalistic or scholarly accounts, including my own.

Jimma, however, attracts few expats and tourists. Without a lake or other major attraction it is not a destination for weekenders from Addis Ababa. Jimma is in the Oromia region, on the border of the SNNPR, and unlike Hawassa, it is not a regional capital. This means fewer government and NGO offices. That said, from my first short trip to Jimma in 2001, I have been drawn to its vibrant city center with its views of the surrounding mountains. More than anything, it is the people of Jimma that keep me coming back. Jimma residents seem to have a particular talent for *chewata*, the playful conversation that Ethiopians use to pass the time. In contrast to Hawassa, Jimma was very walkable and during my research in the early 2000s; I used daily walks through the city as a way to meet new people and experience chance encounters with acquaintances. Jimma was not, however, a comfortable place to live between 2010 and 2015, largely because of failed road construction. As I will detail in chapter 2, road construction in Jimma was plagued by delays and setbacks. Asphalt roads were torn up but it was years before they were replaced. In the meantime, moving in the city became difficult, as roads were impassable for vehicles and pedestrians had to negotiate mud and gaping ditches. Although struggles with infrastructure make for interesting conversations, I selected Hawassa as a research site in part because it would be far more comfortable for my wife and two small children who were accompanying me to the field. The strong anthropology program at Hawassa University, where I could teach master's students, was also a factor in bringing me to Hawassa. For the most part, my analysis is not structured around a comparison of the two cities, but their contrasting experiences provide insights into the intersection between development, infrastructure, and governance.

I have conducted research intermittently in Jimma since 2002, and for this project I spent extended periods of time with individuals with whom I have developed close relationships over the years. My first book examined unemployed young men in Jimma, many of whom spent years struggling to find work after finishing secondary school (Mains 2012b). It was returning to Jimma throughout the years and watching these young men find jobs in the construction of infrastructure that led me to this project. In Jimma I developed detailed longitudinal case studies of people whose lives have become increasingly intertwined with infrastructural development.

Research in Hawassa was conducted over ten months in 2013 and 2014 and during short periods of follow-up in 2015 and 2017. I engaged closely with government officials, urban planners, road construction engineers, construction company leaders and laborers, Bajaj drivers, leaders of taxi associations, and residents in rapidly changing neighborhoods, including those who had been displaced by new roads. The Ethiopian government permits only limited access to hydroelectric dams and the surrounding communities. Therefore I focused my research on dams on everyday conversations among urban Ethiopians and state discourse (billboards, speeches, and official documents) promoting the dams. I also examined an anti-dam activist organization, International Rivers, based in Berkeley, California.

I collaborated with Eshetayehu Kinfu, an urban planner and faculty member at Hawassa University, on nearly all of the formal interviews that I conducted in Hawassa. Eshetayehu played an essential role in providing access to government administrators and many of the others we interviewed. Conversations with Eshetayehu were also important for shaping my understanding of the Ethiopian state. Eshetayehu and I have coauthored two articles together (Mains and Kinfu 2016, 2017). When I describe interviews in the text I seek to make clear when Eshetayehu was present and when I was working alone. I did not have a collaborator or research assistant for my work in Jimma.[13]

Structure of the Book

Each of the chapters explores a particular infrastructural technology: hydroelectric dams, asphalt roads, three-wheeled motorcycle taxis, and cobblestone roads. The one exception is chapter 3, which examines the affective experience of urban change and infrastructural development in relation to the state's legitimacy. In each case the encounter between the specific qualities of infrastructural technologies, labor, and the state both builds and destroys. The chapters explore these encounters to advance specific arguments. I begin the book with an analysis of hydroelectric dams in chapter 1 to demonstrate both the economic and symbolic dimensions of the Ethiopian state's vision of development through infrastructure. For both critics and proponents of dams, policy positions are based in emotional attachments to technologies and their associated temporalities. Chapter 2 examines the relations between asphalt road construction, regulation, and improvisation. Improvisation by engineers and administrators is essential for constructing asphalt roads, and these roads produce regularities that disrupt the improvisations of inner-city residents. In chapter 3, I explore what urban development feels like and how this shapes affective attachments to the state. Feelings about the state are based in part on how the construction of infrastructures is physically felt through materials such as mud, dust, and water. In chapters 4 and 5, I use a synthesis between vital and historical materialisms to understand tensions between states and the people who provision urban infrastructures. Chapter 4 explores the politics of urban public transportation through the case of the Bajaj (three-wheeled motorcycle taxis). Chapter 5 examines cobblestone roads and the role of infrastructural development in creating jobs for youth. In both cases infrastructural technologies mediate the relationship between the state and the people who provision infrastructure. Finally, in the conclusion I argue that construction as an analytical framework emphasizes both progress and instability, and is essential for understanding temporal experiences in places such as urban Ethiopia that are experiencing rapid transformation.

ONE. Constructing a Renaissance

Hydropower and the Temporal Politics of Development

What does hydropower have to do with renaissance, rebirth, and reawakening? The Grand Ethiopian Renaissance Dam (GERD) represents a new start for many Ethiopians who feel that their nation has slumbered for too long. The $5 billion GERD is easily Ethiopia's largest hydroelectric project, but it is part of a much wider national boom in dam construction that began in the twenty-first century. From the years 2000 to 2015, Ethiopia increased tenfold its capacity to generate hydropower—a key component of the state's strategy to become a middle-income country by 2025.

In connecting hydropower with renaissance, the Ethiopian state is telling a story about the past and the future.[1] Ethiopians are well aware of their nation's past glories—the magnificent stelae of Axumite civilization, the rock-hewn churches of Lalibella, and the defeat of the Italians in the Battle of Adwa. Then many years of stagnation and decline, with the nation perhaps reaching its lowest point in the 1980s when Ethiopia became not an emblem of African independence, but a global symbol for poverty, famine, and international aid. A renaissance is something that many Ethiopians have desired for decades. In contrast to Africa Rising narratives, a renaissance clearly brings something new but also captures the glories of the past. Renaissance excites the imaginations of Ethiopians and international funders, and support from both is absolutely necessary for constructing large dams.

International scholars and anti-dam activists have specifically attacked this narrative of renaissance through hydropower. It is in this battle over renaissance, narrative, and dams that the intrinsic instability of the construction process emerges. Dams are monumental infrastructures that require billions of dollars to build, funds that come primarily from international lenders. Critics of dams ask whose past, whose renaissance, and whose future do dams support? Ethiopian leaders referenced the example of the Hoover Dam and economic growth in the US, arguing that the GERD will be their Hoover and promote rapid modernization (Tadesse 2013). In contrast, International Rivers (IR), an NGO based in Berkeley, California, is devoted to preventing the construction of large dams in the global south and has been particularly vocal in opposing dams in Ethiopia. Lori Pottinger (2013), an IR employee,[2] explicitly drew on the Hoover/GERD comparison as a point of critique: "The Hoover Dam was built in a time when we didn't fully understand the dire consequences of damming off major rivers. Today we do, and large dams such as Hoover would never be built in the US today. In fact, we're taking down dams to help restore rivers and the communities they support. The megadam model is a dinosaur. Ethiopia would be better off leapfrogging[3] over it to a more modern and efficient system, and find less provocative ways to assert its interests over the Nile waters."

In other words, the engine for generating Ethiopian renaissance and modernization is "a dinosaur." IR essentially flips the script, placing dams in the past and rejecting the association between big dams and a desirable future. IR's counternarrative drew harsh critiques from the Ethiopian government that reveal the importance of the technology/modernity relationship for the developmental state.

At one level, Ethiopian state discourse draws on mid-twentieth-century modernization theory to argue that big dams are technical solutions to the problem of poverty. However, this is not simply a case of the state adopting outdated models of development. As I explain in the first half of the chapter, government leaders argue that state-led technological interventions are an alternative to dominant modes of twenty-first-century development that assume that downsizing the state brings economic growth. The Ethiopian developmental state invests in large-scale infrastructure projects to promote development. Opposing this perspective is an argument rooted in anthropological critiques of development that interprets technological interventions as a mask for underdevelopment. From this perspective, depoliticized technical interventions distract attention from inequality and a need to redistribute resources. I connect this critique with a reading of Ethiopian history in which the center benefits at the expense of the periphery. Both of these perspectives evaluate big dams in terms of their implications for economic development and inequality, but whereas the first perspective understands modernization as benefitting the nation as a whole, the second claims that technologies such as dams benefit a few people at the expense of many. Distinct narratives about the relationship between the past, present, and future shape the legitimacy of construction. For critics of Ethiopia's dams, a history of center/periphery exploitation raises questions about the desirability of a renaissance.

In the second half of this chapter I explore what dams mean for their opponents and proponents in terms of conceptions of the future and ideologies of development. Each of the forms of infrastructure that I examine in this book has important symbolic dimensions, but dams are particularly potent in their power to generate emotional attachments. For both their proponents and opponents, dams signify particular ideologies of development and ways of moving through time. For the Ethiopian state, dams are singular technologies that can drive economic growth, and it is precisely this belief that attracts criticism from organizations such as International Rivers. Emotional attachments to particular imagined futures and modes of experiencing change over time are at the heart of debates between the Ethiopian state and IR. I argue that the symbolic temporalities of big dams are intertwined with the spatial dynamics of development and underdevelopment. International Rivers and the Ethiopian government each used spatial arguments to undermine the other's position. Their respective temporal narratives were rooted in particular conceptions of the nation and spatial relations of inequality. In contrast to the technologies of development that I discuss in other chapters, critiques of dams have come primarily from outside Ethiopia. This is partially because those who are negatively affected by dams already exist on the margins of power, making national identity a particularly salient issue in debates over dams. Dams are so contentious because they represent different conceptions of the passage of time and they concretely manifest contrasting spatial distributions of power and resources. It is these competing temporal and spatial narratives that often destabilize the construction of dams.

Dams and the Developmental State: Technical Solutions for Eradicating Poverty

The construction of large dams as a development strategy in Ethiopia is a distinctive characteristic of the current regime. When the EPRDF came to power in the early 1990s, Ethiopia had only four major dams that together generated less than 250 megawatts of power. In the early 2000s, the Ethiopian government began building more dams. The first of these, Gibe I, is located near one of my research sites, Jimma. The construction of Gibe I was funded by the World Bank and cost around $330 million. When it came on line in 2004, Gibe I generated 180 megawatts of power, increasing Ethiopia's total supply of hydropower by nearly 75 percent. However, Gibe I would be dwarfed by the megadams that soon followed. By 2016 Ethiopia had finished construction on ten new dams that generated an additional 1600 megawatts of electricity. The two dams that I focus on in this chapter are scheduled to generate 1,870 megawatts (Gibe III) and 6,000 megawatts (GERD). Gibe III dams the Omo River in southern Ethiopia and the GERD dams the Blue Nile River, near the Ethiopia–Sudan border. These projects have generated a great deal of controversy, and as a result many multilateral funding organizations have withdrawn their support, forcing the Ethiopian government to rely on internal funding through the sale of bonds[4] and loans from state-owned Chinese banks. An Italian company, Salini Impregilo, is constructing both these projects. If successful, Gibe III and the GERD would generate enough power to make electricity Ethiopia's top export, replacing agricultural products such as coffee, khat, and oilseeds. In areas with functional electric grids, hydropower will provide electricity for businesses, schools, hospitals, and private residences. The Gibe III dam will also support irrigation for large-scale plantations, and therefore its impacts may extend even farther than those of the larger GERD.

Achieving economic growth through investment in hydropower is a strategy that was widely deployed internationally during the mid-twentieth century, and it fits well with classic modernization theory. From New Deal projects in the United States to postcolonial nation building in the global south, national leaders sought to use dams to generate the energy necessary to fuel growth (Ekbladh 2010). Dams facilitate the stage of growth that W. W. Rostow (1960) labeled the "take-off," providing the energy and distribution of water to support advances in agriculture and industry.[5] At first glance it seems that Ethiopia is simply adopting a development strategy from the past and applying it to the present. Given that modernization theory and dam construction have been heavily critiqued, it is legitimate to ask why Ethiopia has adopted such a dated strategy.

Although the Ethiopian state has historically sought to achieve development through high modernist planning and investments in technology (Fantini and Puddu 2016), big dams are not an anachronism. Ethiopia's twenty-first-century dam boom is supported by a specific political ideology that is directly opposed to the downsizing that many African governments experienced at the end of the twentieth century. The dam boom is also connected to the emergence of a strong relationship between Ethiopia and China, particularly in the aftermath of Ethiopia's contentious 2005 election. Investment in infrastructure as a means of attaining economic development is a lesson learned directly from the successful Chinese example (Fourie 2015, 306). Like China (Tilt 2015), Ethiopia is increasingly a nation led by engineers who are confident in their ability to transform the environment in ways that support development. In this sense Ethiopia is an example of what Walter Mignolo calls "de-Westernization," a process in which states reject Western models of economic growth and their associated human rights discourses (2011, 182–83). De-Westernization is, however, like Westernization in that it maintains a "type of economy in which life is subservient to economic growth and political power" (Mignolo 2011, 183).

Constructing large dams is central to the broader political economic philosophy that guides the Ethiopian state's development interventions. Meles Zenawi led the resistance fighters who overthrew the Marxist Derg regime in 1991. He became Ethiopia's first prime minister during the EPRDF era, and he ruled until he passed away in 2012. Meles[6] was not only the face of the EPRDF; he provided much of the intellectual energy for the government's policies. Meles articulated some of his ideas concerning development in a chapter titled "States and Markets: Neoliberal Limitations and the Case for a Developmental State," published in 2011 in an edited volume on good growth and governance in Africa. The chapter is specifically concerned with political and economic techniques for bringing about an "African renaissance." Although scholars of Ethiopia have debated the degree to which Meles's ideas were actually put into practice (De Waal 2013; Lefort 2013), it is clear that heavy investment in big dams by the state coheres with his broader vision of political economy.

Meles was highly critical of what he called the neoliberal paradigm in which "the smaller the role of the state, the better" (2011b, 140). He argued that neoliberal political economy is based in rational choice theory, in which all individuals are independent, self-interested actors. Neoliberal theory falters if the necessity of collaboration and cooperation is acknowledged. Meles explains: "If rational choice theory is wrong and people are not solely self-interested maximizers, the question of whether the state should be a nightwatchman state or not would become an empirical rather than a theoretical question" (2011a, 144). Meles uses the term *nightwatchman state* to reference the minimal role of the state within neoliberal theory and the neoliberal belief that decision making should be left to markets populated by self-interested individuals. Meles suggests that once assumptions regarding rational choice theory are thrown out and other motivations for human behavior are acknowledged, the neoliberal model of the nightwatchman state must be reassessed on the basis of how it actually functions in practice.

Despite this critique, Meles draws a key insight from the neoliberal paradigm that the only source of continued increase in per capita income is technological change (2011b, 149). However, Meles points out that neoliberal models do not actually explain how technological change will occur. The neoliberal assumption that it will occur naturally as a result of market incentives and relations between developed and undeveloped nations has not played out in practice. Meles argues that because technology is a public good, the market alone cannot be relied on for innovation and provision. There is no incentive for the market to introduce technologies that have public value but are not directly profitable. Therefore, governments must take the lead in introducing technologies that support development and the public good (2011b, 149–51).

For Meles, big dams are just such a technology. They provide electricity, irrigation, and flood control. In the Ethiopian case, much of the electricity generated will be exported rather than used domestically. The revenues gained from the export of electricity will be invested in public projects, a process that would be impossible if the introduction of hydropower technology was left to private companies. Of course, questions remain regarding the state's ability to select appropriate technological interventions that will advance public interests. Given the critiques made by activist organizations such as International Rivers, why should one assume that the state will advance the public good? Meles argues that, first, the developmental state must be autonomous from the private sector. It is only through this autonomy that the developmental state is able to discipline the private sector and support activities that are in the public interest. Second, "the development agenda must be hegemonic if successful development is to take place and if a developmental state is to be established" (2011a, 168). When the development agenda is hegemonic, millions of people willingly act in the interests of development. Meles is clear that while the developmental state's actions must reflect a national consensus, the state need not be a democracy. Meles explains that "the developmental state, however, has the motivation [to promote growth-enhancing activities] because its purpose is to accelerate growth and it can do so—and maintain its legitimacy—only by rewarding growth-enhancing activities and restricting and penalizing socially wasteful activities" (169). In other words, the developmental state must act in the interests of the public, because this is the only way it can maintain its legitimacy.

Meles's argument here is circular: the developmental state promotes growth because this is the purpose of the developmental state; the developmental state has legitimacy because it must be legitimate to promote growth. Rather than critique Meles's use of logic, my interest is in understanding how his political-economic ideology supports the construction of big dams. Meles's theory of the developmental state becomes a sort of faith. Development must occur because that is what a developmental state does. Problems regarding the use of public funds to hire private companies to build dams of questionable economic value are erased. The decisions of a developmental state cannot be questioned unless one questions the alleviation of poverty more broadly. Gibe III and the GERD must be in the interest of the public because supporting the public good is implicit in the definition of a developmental state.

This is a logic that occasionally occurs during casual discussions of dam building among urban Ethiopians. I was surprised to hear friends who were normally very cynical regarding state-led development argue that the GERD would be successful. They claimed that the EPRDF had failed in its previous political and economic initiatives and had staked everything on successfully completing this massive dam project. If the GERD fails, then the EPRDF will also fail, and this seemed to be inconceivable. Again, this is teleological: For a developmental state to exist, the development agenda must be hegemonic. For the development agenda to be hegemonic, the state must succeed in implementing growth-enhancing projects. Therefore the presence of a developmental state necessarily implies the success of growth-enhancing projects.

The fact that an argument is teleological does not necessarily render it false. Large-scale technical infrastructures, such as dams, can potentially function as a particular form of redistribution that is essential for alleviating poverty. Gibe III was financed primarily by loans, whereas the GERD has been supported largely by bonds purchased by Ethiopian citizens. In some cases the purchase of bonds has been voluntary, but there was a great deal of pressure for government employees to direct one month of their annual salary toward the bonds. The state also pressured large private businesses to make significant purchases. Payment for big dams comes from the public, but some citizens contribute more than others, particularly salaried government workers and successful companies in the private sector. It is certainly possible that the benefits from the dams will be distributed in a way that directly addresses poverty. To the extent that electricity is made available to households, it will clearly transform people's lives. Cheap energy will also support manufacturing, which creates jobs. Using irrigation to support large-scale agribusiness has the potential to do the same. It is not yet clear how the funds from the sale of electricity will be distributed, but investing them in schools, health care, and similar institutions will have significant benefits for the poor.

Deconstructing a Renaissance: Center/Periphery Exploitation and Hydropower

In the mid-twentieth century dams were frequently used as technical solutions to the problem of poverty. Critical scholars of development responded to these projects by arguing that such technical solutions depoliticize poverty (Escobar 1995; Ferguson 1994; Mitchell 2002). Investing in dams implies that poverty can be eliminated if the right technology is introduced, and this shifts attention away from systemic changes aimed at addressing inequality (Ar. Roy 2001). Proponents of dams do not acknowledge the possibility of underdevelopment, in which one group of people benefits at the expense of another. In advancing an Ethiopian renaissance the state assumes that dams will benefit all Ethiopians. Scholars and activist organizations have critiqued Ethiopia's dam boom and related development interventions by noting that they take resources from already marginalized peoples and put them in the hands of the state and economic elites. The environment that people in the Omo Valley depend on for their livelihood is heavily degraded to support economic growth in other parts of the country. Such a critique builds on long-standing center/periphery dynamics in Ethiopian political economy. To politicize poverty and development, I explain in this section how inequality in Ethiopia has historically been organized in terms of center/periphery relations that shape contemporary dam construction.

In connecting dams with the concept of renaissance, the Ethiopian state suggests that hydropower will bring the past into the present. However, attention to historical center/periphery dynamics raises the questions of whom the renaissance is for and which aspects of the past will shape the future. As

Erdem Evren (forthcoming) has suggested in relation to dam construction in Turkey, considering histories of violence has great value when examining futures that are constructed through infrastructure. In the Ethiopian case critics have argued that dams reproduce inequalities between center and periphery and support a renaissance that is based in a history of expropriation.

Beginning in the mid-nineteenth century, the core areas of the old Orthodox Christian Abyssinian kingdom, in what is now northern Ethiopia, were unified, and new territories in the south were conquered to form the modern Ethiopian state. Especially in the highland areas of what are now southern and western Ethiopia, the local populations lost large amounts of their land and were subjected to the often harsh rule of northerners (Donham 1986; Markakis 2011; Zewde 1991). The dynamics of northern rule in the south shared many similarities with the European colonial empires that were established elsewhere in Africa at that time (Markakis 2011, 5). The northerners who participated in the southern expansion were predominantly ethnically Amhara, but they also included significant numbers of Tigreans, Oromo Christians, and Gurage.[7]

Beginning during this period of northern expansion and continuing to the present, Ethiopia has been shaped by relations of expropriation and dependency between center and periphery. By the late nineteenth century, population growth and land degradation resulting from centuries of cultivation had left northern farmers in an increasingly precarious situation. At the same time rinderpest decimated cattle herds, leading to widespread famine. These forces were compounded by the presence of European powers competing with the Abyssinian empire for control over the Horn of Africa. Expansion into the south eased population pressure and provided access to significant resources and sources of revenue. Whereas the north had almost no production for a regional market, the southern and western highlands brought access to salt, gold, civet, ivory, coffee, and slaves. All of these goods became taxable as the areas were incorporated into the Ethiopian empire. It was also common for the conquering armies to engage in slave and cattle raiding. Perhaps even more important, northern expansion brought access to fertile land. Military leaders were given rights to both land and labor as tributes from the conquered southerners. In contrast to the north, where peasants were often able to limit their exploitation by local lords, in the south differences in culture and language made resisting northern exploitation very difficult (Donham 1986).

From the late nineteenth until the mid-twentieth century a dynamic emerged in which power hierarchies in the center were legitimized through rulers' ability to redistribute resources to their underlings from the newly conquered peripheries. Exploitation in the periphery decreased tensions between elites and a growing middle class. Following the brief Italian occupation of Ethiopia (1936–41), soldiers, police, civil servants, and families of veterans from the north all received land grants in the southern and western highlands. By this point individual land plots in the northern highlands were extremely small (Markakis 2011, 118–19), and opportunities for accumulating wealth were increasingly located in southern and western Ethiopia.

In 1974 Haile Selassie and the imperial regime were overthrown in a military coup and replaced by a Marxist military dictatorship known as the Derg (Amharic for "committee"). For most of its rule (1974–91), the Derg was plagued by insurgencies and resistance movements, and there was not a major redistribution of resources from periphery to center. Instead the meaning of the center gradually shifted. Despite the land reform that occurred under the Derg, Amhara cultural and political dominance was left basically unchanged (Clapham 2002). Amharic was still the language of governance throughout the country, and even at the local level political power was largely in the hands of the Amhara. However, the famines of the 1980s in northern Ethiopia made it clear that although northerners maintained a great deal of political power, the northern highlands were certainly not the economic center of the country. In contrast to the north, which was not suitable for growing Ethiopia's major cash crops, the former highland periphery in southern and western Ethiopia became the economic center through the production of coffee and khat. Furthermore, because of movements of people, both from the north and within the rest of the country, the ethnic makeup of southern and western Ethiopia changed dramatically. Particularly places such as my research sites, Hawassa and Jimma, became multiethnic urban centers.

The Ethiopian People's Revolutionary Democratic Front (EPRDF) drove the Marxist military regime from power in 1991 and quickly implemented a system of ethnic federalism. The EPRDF decided to enact this system because it recognized the diverse needs of Ethiopia's more than seventy ethnic groups. Under ethnic federalism, Ethiopia is divided into eleven states—two cities and nine regions—that are based primarily on historic ethnic boundaries.[8] States have a broad range of power covering education, economic development, health, police forces, and legal courts. Regions may conduct government business and education in the language of their choice, and in theory they have the right to secede and form their own nation, although it seems unlikely that this would actually occur peacefully.

Although urban Ethiopians often discuss divisions within the country in terms of ethnicity, a more important distinction may be the split between the highlands, including both the north and the more resource-rich south, and the lowlands, occupied largely by mobile pastoralists and shifting agriculturalists (Markakis 2011). Very real conflicts exist within highland Ethiopia, often along the lines of ethnicity, but in general most highlanders participate in formal education and rely on wage labor and intensive sedentary agriculture for their livelihoods. Although they often oppose the ruling party, there is no doubt that the state has a strong presence in the lives of highlanders. In contrast, the more mobile lowlanders have little engagement with formal schooling and less direct contact with the Ethiopian state. With southern and western Ethiopia relatively incorporated into the political and economic center of the nation, under the EPRDF wealth has been increasingly extracted from the lowland periphery. In Ethiopia, the federal government owns all land, and as a strategy for generating revenues it has begun leasing land in the lowland periphery to private investors, many of them based outside the country. Investors are establishing large-scale monocrop plantations to produce rice, sugar, and palm oil. Lowland residents in Gambella and the Lower Omo have been forced off their land and made to resettle in villages, often with the expectation that they will earn a living as laborers on the newly established farms (Stevenson and Buffavand 2018). With little education and access to state representation, those living in the lowland periphery have very little ability to protect their interests (Gebresenbet 2016; Oakland Institute 2011).

For the most part, Ethiopia's big dams are being constructed in these same lowland peripheral areas. Gibe III is located in the culturally diverse South Omo Valley, a UNESCO World Heritage Site. Activist groups have claimed that it will destroy the livelihoods of up to 500,000 pastoralists and fisher people in southern Ethiopia and across the border in Kenya (Hathaway 2008). Affected groups such as the Hamar, Mursi, Bodi, Kara, Chai, Kwegu, Nyangatom, and Dasanetch rely on multiple subsistence strategies including pastoralism, shifting agriculture, hunting, fishing, and occasional wage labor. They have had little access to education and they are not well represented in the government at either the local or national level. Human rights–based opposition to dams is often concerned with displacement, and although this in an issue in the case of Gibe III, more important is the disruption of livelihoods (Turton 2010). The Gibe III dam will block downstream movements of sediment and prevent the annual flooding that many people rely on to fertilize flood plains that are used for farming (Turton 2010). The Ethiopian government and Salini (the Italian company constructing Gibe III) claim that artificial floods will be created, but it is unclear whether this will adequately replace the natural floods that people have come to depend on. Dam opponents also question the likelihood that these artificial floods will in fact be implemented (International Rivers 2013; Turton 2010). The dam and the reservoir will also affect access to water for livestock and land for grazing, which is already a source of tension in this region. Many of the men in this region are armed with automatic rifles, and outbursts of violence occur periodically. There is evidence that displacement because of plantations and decreased access to necessary resources has already increased violence (Oakland Institute 2014).

Although initial government statements regarding Gibe III focused on the value of hydropower, it has become increasingly clear that one of its main effects is to support irrigation in the region. It is partially Gibe III's potential to support irrigation that makes its impacts so severe. Water from the dam will be channeled to plantations, some owned by the state and others by private investors (Oakland Institute 2011). Many of the plantations will produce cotton and sugarcane, both notoriously thirsty crops. The loss of water for irrigation and 320,000 hectares of land (Kamski 2016) for the plantations will put increasing pressure on the people in the South Omo region. The creation of plantations has also led to the forcible resettlement of pastoralists in villages, a process that in the past has had significant negative impacts on the health and livelihoods of people elsewhere in East Africa (Fratkin and Roth 2005) and is already disrupting lives in the Lower Omo Valley (Stevenson and Buffavand 2018).

Ethiopia's big dams seem to reproduce long-standing inequalities between center and periphery. Anthropologist Will Hurd provocatively calls Gibe III and its associated industrial plantations the "second conquest," after Emperor Menelik's nineteenth-century invasion (Hurd 2016). In this sense Ethiopia's dams may be contributing to a renaissance, but not one that is universally desirable. Like Menelik's invasion, exploitation in the periphery benefits those living in the center. This process eases class-based tensions and legitimizes relations of power between elites and the politically active urban Ethiopians living in the central highlands.

Gibe III has attracted the most attention from international activists, but not all of Ethiopia's new dams fit easily into the narrative of a second conquest. For example, the Tekeze Dam is located in northern Ethiopia, near the border of the Amhara and Tigray regions, and it has significantly displaced people and disrupted their livelihoods (Gizachew 2014). The Gibe I dam, near Jimma, has also caused displacement, though for much fewer people (Kebede 2009). Although Gibe I is within the vast area conquered by Menelik, today it is very much part of the highland center rather than the lowland periphery. One reason for the relative lack of attention given to these dams is their fit within established narratives. For example, Survival International seeks to protect "tribespeople" and "indigenous" people from the "catastrophic" impacts of Gibe III (Survival International 2016). It seems that sedentary Oromo, Amhara, and Tigrean farmers do not fit into these categories and therefore are not of interest to organizations such as Survival International. That said, International Rivers has mounted smaller campaigns against dams including the Tekeze and Gibe I. Part of the reason for their relative focus on Gibe III is that the impacts of these other dams are limited because they do not support massive irrigation schemes for large plantations that increase displacement and villagization.

Beyond national center/periphery dynamics, critics of Ethiopia's dams, such as International Rivers, have raised issue with the process for awarding contracts to construct dams. Salini received no-bid contracts for Gibe III, worth more than $2 billion, and for the GERD, worth more than $5 billion. Salini has a long history of winning construction contracts from the Ethiopian government, and in some previous projects, such as Gibe II, the Italian government actually provided loans to finance the work (Fantini and Puddu 2016).[9] Although the Italian government has shied away from the much bigger Gibe III and GERD projects, financing in other cases included loans amounting to hundreds of millions of dollars (Hathaway 2008). Gibe IV, a $1.7 billion project that has been contracted to Salini, is being supported by an Italian export credit agency. International Rivers argues that a lack of transparency in contracts and the high potential for corruption are general problems with big dam technology. These projects typically go over budget, and with such large sums of money being tossed around, careful accounting is difficult.

In contrast to state claims that Ethiopia's big dams will promote a distribution of resources that combats poverty, it is possible to read Gibe III as a classic case of underdevelopment organized in terms of relations between center and periphery. Marginalized peoples in Ethiopia's periphery had almost no voice concerning the construction of Gibe III or other dams in the region. To the extent that big dams demand the sort of top-down planning associated with a developmental state, there is often little room for the voices of those impacted by the dam to be incorporated into the planning process (Fisher 1997; Isaacman and Isaacman 2013; Ar. Roy 2001). It is common for dams to transfer resources from a marginalized periphery to a more developed center (Tilt 2015). In the Ethiopian case, people in the lowland periphery are forced to sacrifice their livelihoods to support these dams, and they receive little to nothing in exchange. In contrast, state officials, international construction companies, and investors all stand to reap benefits. Those living in Ethiopia's center might also gain numerous indirect benefits in the form of access to cheap electricity and reduced prices on manufactured goods and commodities such as sugar that are grown in the newly irrigated plantations. Specific center/periphery dynamics differ in the cases of urban infrastructure I examine in later chapters, as particular infrastructural technologies reshape the distribution of resources within cities.

In the following section I add another layer of analysis through attention to the process of construction. Construction is not only the physical process of building; it is the marketing of a project in order to access funding. It is here that narrative becomes so important. The Ethiopian state and international activist organizations tell competing stories about dams that are intended to sway public opinion. This aspect of advancing a narrative is essential for the construction process, but it also introduces tensions that may be highly destructive.

Renaissance and Modernity: The Poetics and Temporalities of Dams and Rivers, Part I

Arguments in favor of Gibe III and the GERD go well beyond their implications for economic growth and are often based in the symbolic dimensions of objects and their associated temporalities. As Sarah Pritchard (2011, 8–9) explains in relation to dams on the Rhone River in twentieth-century France, dams concretely reshape the environment at the same time that they produce and signify the state. It is partially through the structure of the GERD that the Ethiopian state is imagined by both citizens and the government administrators who form the state. In contrast to infrastructures that I examine in later chapters, dams are rarely experienced directly. Instead, people know dams through their impressive physical dimensions. The GERD will be 155 meters tall and 1800 meters in length—the seventh largest dam in the world (Salini Impregilo, n.d.). Millions of cubic meters of concrete will be used in its construction. Although dams are rarely visited, their size allows them to function as monumental infrastructures.

Ethiopians almost never see images of the actual dam and the construction process, but a particular digitally constructed image of the future dam is everywhere. I first saw this image of the GERD on a mobile phone recharge card in 2012. At that time all recharge cards had images of the GERD, creating an implicit link between mobile telecommunications technology, which had only recently become widespread in Ethiopia, and the dam. This image of the dam often forms the backdrop for the newscasters on ETV, the state-run television station that is the only viewing option for television owners who cannot afford a satellite dish. The dam also makes frequent appearances in posters and billboards that support the ruling EPRDF party.

In May 2015, at the time of Ethiopia's national elections, a large billboard in Jimma's city center featured an image of Ethiopia's late prime minister Meles Zenawi, a group of young children, and a digital image of the dam (figure 1.1). A child's gaze follows Meles's raised arm, which is pointing toward the horizon. The Amharic text translates roughly as "Our great father advised us and we kept the promise." A friend in Jimma offered a more poetic interpretation—"We will not forget the dreams of our great father." The dam represents the dream and the advice—a path to a desirable future. The dam is not the only object that is doing symbolic work in this image. Meles is the father, but importantly he is the deceased father whose dreams still remain. In Ethiopian cities, the number of images of Meles on billboards, posters, and the walls of government offices exploded after his death. In these images, Meles represents himself, the revolutionary leader and head of state for nearly twenty years. He also signifies the state more broadly. Even three years after his death, both opponents and proponents of the EPRDF commonly referred to it as the "Meles regime."

The billboard was located in front of Jimma's municipality building, thus connecting Meles with the local city government. Meles's raised arm and finger point not to a particular place, but a time—the future. These are promises that must be kept in the days and years to come. They are the dreams of a particular person and the state more broadly. Meles signifies the unity between the patriarch and the state. In the same manner, the children in the billboard represent Ethiopia's citizens. The children are the urban residents who will view the sign as they go about their day-to-day lives, and

FIGURE 1.1. "Our great father advised us and we kept the promise." Poster in Jimma. Photo by author.

in this sense they are the "we" who will keep the promise. The children also represent the future, and it is important that one child holds a pen and appears to be seated at a desk, signifying the modernizing institution of formal schooling. To the extent that the children represent Ethiopian citizens, they are fortunate to have received advice from a wise and great father, and it is now their responsibility to follow this advice, build the dam, and achieve an Ethiopian renaissance.

Nothing particular about this digitally constructed image of the future GERD indicates its location or power, but no Ethiopian should have any doubts about these details. This is the GERD, the ever-present image of development and the future. The case of the GERD contradicts Star's (1999) claim that infrastructure only becomes visible when it breaks down. In fact, a range of possibilities exists regarding visibility and infrastructure (Larkin 2008, 2013; Schwenkel 2015b). The GERD resonates with Larkin's (2008) discussion of the colonial sublime. For Larkin, the sublime involves "an appreciation of something so great it overwhelms our power to comprehend it" (35). In connecting the sublime to power, Larkin explains, "if one vests an idea of the sublime in the greatness of technology, this necessitates technologically ranking and ordering society and culture. It means dividing what is great from what is worthless" (36). The repeated display of the digitally constructed image of the GERD adds to its power. It is a technology that represents astounding sums of money and offers the potential to harness the power of the Blue Nile (*Abay*) River—a river that Ethiopian musicians have often sung about. It is a technology that promises modernity and a bright future. It is the EPRDF/Meles/Father that will deliver this gift. It is the EPRDF that is shepherding the nation into a new and modern future. As the billboard implies, the GERD represents the dreams of the country's leaders, and it is up to the people, represented as children, to make those dreams a reality.

This reading tells us far more about what the state seeks to signify with images of the GERD than how urban residents interpret these images. It takes a great deal of work to continually remind people of the significance of a dam that they neither see nor experience. A friend of mine, a university student, explained, "At first we were amazed by this dam. We would get a very good feeling every time we heard about it. But that changed. We have become used to it. We see the same image every day and it's like we don't even see it anymore. Maybe that will change when it begins generating electricity." Despite its ever-present image, unless I directly asked about the GERD, it was rare for friends to mention it in casual conversation. My friend's comment about having a "good feeling" about the dam connects with my analysis of affective politics and infrastructure that I raised in the introduction and expand further in chapter 3. An infrastructure must be felt in order for it to convey a deep sense of meaning that overpowers comprehension in the manner of the sublime. In contrast to the daily experience of road construction, urban Ethiopians generally did not feel dams. When Ethiopia was experiencing rolling blackouts in 2009, hydropower and its absence were sensed through the absence of light, and in Jimma there were frequent discussions of the nearby Gibe I dam (Mains 2012a). Although power outages continued to be an occasional issue, discussions of the dam gradually faded away. The technological sublime is highly ephemeral. It is continually threatened by invisibility and a loss of its power.

Although images of the GERD may have become invisible to many urban residents, the state clearly believes that the GERD has the power to communicate meaning. These attempts at communication tell us something of the poetics of dams for government leaders. As I discuss below, for International

Rivers dams represent obstructed flows and movement, but for the Ethiopian state the beauty of dams is precisely associated with the movement they facilitate. Most importantly, dams support movement through time. Dams represent a future that is better and more desirable than the present, and the dam itself takes on this value. The dam is not simply a tool for attaining modernity; the dam *is* modernity. In constructing dams, the state advances a temporal vision in which the nation moves forward through time, following Meles's outstretched hand toward the bright horizon.

Meles Zenawi's speech at a 2011 Pastoralist Day celebration in Jinka, a town in the Lower Omo Valley near the area affected by the Gibe III dam, demonstrates the values that drive dam construction in Ethiopia. Meles (2011a) stated:

> Our efforts to build a dam on the Omo River to eliminate the flood, to create a huge irrigation system and give pastoralists a sustainable income and a modern life, are facing roadblocks. Our limited capacity to execute this work, and limited financial aid, did not allow us to go as fast as we wanted to. There are some people who want to block our freedom to use our rivers, and to save our people from poverty. They just want to keep the pastoralists as a tourist attraction and make sure no development happens in pastoral areas. They team up with the people who don't want us to use our rivers to broadcast their propaganda. There can't be anyone more concerned for our environmental conservation than we are. We are determined to speed up our development in an environmentally friendly way. We want our people to have a modern life and we won't allow our people to be a case study of ancient living for scientists and researchers.

Meles constructs a clear opposition. On one hand, dam technology could be used to create a "modern life" and eliminate poverty. On the other hand, some individuals believe the lifestyles of pastoralists should be preserved for study or tourism. In juxtaposing "modern life" with people who are a case study for "ancient living," Meles constructs a dichotomy between the lives of pastoralists and modernity. He implies that pastoralists and others who depend on the Omo River are a relic of the past and that their lifestyles cannot be maintained if poverty is to be eliminated. In encouraging villagization and sedentary farming, the state forcibly institutes a lifestyle that has long been common in other parts of the country.

Meles advanced a developmental vision in which the state organizes technological interventions to bring about rapid and significant changes.

Technology and the expertise of engineers are used to transform the Omo River, and through villagization the state forces the people of the region to conform to their new environment (Stevenson and Buffavand 2018). This is not the gradual transition associated with the temporality of flow, which is discussed below. Instead, water is controlled and directed to support irrigation and the generation of hydropower. Engineers eliminate the element of chance from seasonal floods, controlling both the volume and timing of floods. Movement of water is an essential aspect of the Gibe III dam, but that movement is based on plans and engineering rather than the chaotic mix of weather, water, and sediment.

Katrin Bromber and her colleagues explain that the temporality of big dams is closely connected with hope, transformation, and promise for the future (2014, 290). The power of dams to transform lives has sometimes taken on an almost spiritual quality. Jawaharlal Nehru famously called dams temples of modern India (Nehru 1958), and Kwame Nkrumah claimed that the Volta Dam should be a site for pilgrimage (Miescher 2014, 342). In discussions of dams, emotion and faith are linked to normative expectations for the passage of time and attaining a desirable future. For the Ethiopian state, dams have specific practical implications regarding power generation, irrigation, and flood control, but equally important is their symbolic power.

Critics of dams use the attachment of leaders to the symbolic dimensions of dams to undermine the relationship between dams and modernization. For example, anthropologists working in Ethiopia often reference Meles's Pastoralist Day speech, quoted in part above, to illustrate the modernizing ideology of the Ethiopian state (Abbink 2012; Fratkin 2014). Critics use these statements to demonstrate that dam construction is based in a kind of blind faith in modernization. Dams have become such powerful symbols of modernity that their actual practical impacts are ignored. The logic of dam building is undermined when states invest billions of dollars in largely symbolic structures that have massive consequences for people who depend on rivers. Meles, however, offers a counterpoint to this position when he characterizes dam opponents as preservationists attached to ancient modes of living. If dam opponents are driven by emotional attachments to particular ways of life and environmental forms, they are no more rational than those who worship modernity. In the following section I argue that although it is not accurate to characterize dam critics such as International Rivers as preservationists, their position is still connected to a poetics of infrastructure (Larkin 2013). If dams represent transformation through modernization for their proponents, for their opponents they symbolize the destruction of an essential aspect of life: flow.

Flow: The Poetics and Temporalities of Dams and Rivers, Part II

International nongovernmental organizations that have directly opposed the Gibe III dam include Survival International, Human Rights Watch, and International Rivers (IR). I examine IR as a case study because the organization advances a particular vision of development and ecological change that directly opposes big dams. Essentially their mission is to support human rights and maintain the health of rivers by opposing the construction of large dams. IR was founded in 1985 as International Rivers Network, and since its inception it has focused its attention on Africa, Latin America, and Asia, because these are the regions where most large dams are being constructed.

Flow is a key term for IR and other critics of dams. *Flow* represents a particular vision of development and the passage of time, and it is sometimes connected with conceptions of "living waters" (Strang 2013). In IR's discourse the health of a river and the broader watershed ecosystem, including humans, depend on "flow." Dams disrupt flow. IR argues that protecting rivers is a sort of "health insurance policy," intended to support the long-term well-being of humans and ecosystems in a "climate-challenged future" (International Rivers, n.d., "Healthy Rivers"). Large dams fragment habitats, isolate species, interrupt the exchange of nutrients, and cut off migration routes (International Rivers, n.d., "Rivers and Biodiversity"). Dams have "choked" Earth's rivers (International Rivers, n.d., "Problems with Big Dams"). IR contrasts dams that fragment, isolate, interrupt, cut, block, and choke with free-moving rivers that are associated with flow, movement, and connection. Dams block and disrupt, whereas rivers need to flow. It is both the patterned and chaotic nature of flowing rivers that distributes sediment and water in a way that is necessary for regenerating life.

The Omo River, where Gibe III has been constructed, flows into Lake Turkana in northern Kenya. Largely on the basis of Sean Avery's (2012) research, IR claims that Lake Turkana is the world's largest desert lake and receives nearly 90 percent of its annual water inflow from the Omo River (International Rivers 2013, 2). This inflow from the Omo's annual floods maintains a balance in the lake and prevents a concentration of salts that would destroy the lake's biodiversity. The floods also bring sediment and nutrients from upstream and raise the level of the lake, thereby releasing nutrients from the shoreline into the lake. This process supports microscopic plants that are at the base of the lake's food chain. Plants and algae support fish that breed near the lakeshore; those fish are eaten by birds, humans, and crocodiles. IR argues that in blocking the flow of sediment, Gibe III will undermine downstream agriculture that depends on flooding to maintain the fertility of the land. From this perspective, flow supports an entire cycle of life. Change occurs from year to year, based on weather and the unpredictable combination of earth and water, but that change does not move in a single direction. Over time change is gradual and ecosystems are reproduced. When flow is blocked, this cycle is disrupted and change begins to occur rapidly in a single direction. IR argues that when the Gibe III dam interrupts the Omo River, Lake Turkana will ultimately dry up, much like the Aral Sea (International Rivers 2013).

Anti-dam activists are motivated partially by an attachment to the particular temporality of flow. IR claims that dams disrupt river flows in ways that damage ecosystems. This is an important argument, but something else is going on here. Critics of dams are attached to rivers, flow, and the chaotic movement of water. They oppose dams partially because that technology represents a very different ideology of development. Dams signify development and change through massive investment in a singular technology that replaces the chaotic patterning of flow with linear progress. As a temporal narrative, flow is directly opposed to the visions of modernity and engineered change associated with dams. The chaos of flow is a form of change that is beyond the control of humans; it cannot be engineered. To oppose dams is to advance a vision of development and change that is rooted in flow.

Richard Bangs, a former board member of International Rivers, wrote in his book *Rivergods*,[10] "Wild rivers are earth's renegades, defying gravity, dancing to their own tunes, resisting the authority of humans, always chipping away, and eventually always winning" (quoted in International Rivers, n.d., "Rivers and Biodiversity"). IR's communications director, Sarah Bardeen (2016), also connects rivers with dance in an essay written in honor of Earth Day in 2016: "Dancing is mastery without domination—a way of being in the world that works with the world, and doesn't bend it, contort it or kill it to conform to the shape of our will. That is the dance of life. Many people still believe in dominating rivers through dams and diversions. But rivers, like nature, bat last. They are powerful, sometimes unpredictable. They are, in fact, very much like life in that way."

Dams contain and control; they do not dance. This is a vision of development in which the chaotic flows of the river are prioritized over carefully engineered plans. In this conception water is granted agency, and if water is allowed to move without hindrance, it benefits all living things, including humans. Ecological relationships are maintained by avoiding ruptures in natural movements. Many, though not all, of these relationships and movements are cyclical. Just as a flowing river gradually carves a path in stone, change occurs slowly, over time. This is a form of gradual development that embraces movement and builds on preexisting connections and patterns. It is an ideology of development that is directly opposed to the technology of big dams.

Space and Legitimacy in Debates over Dams and Development

Returning to the dispute between IR and the Ethiopian state with which I began, it should be clear that much more is at stake in this debate than the efficacy of big dams in generating economic growth. Dams are the object of intense feelings of love and hate because they represent highly specific temporal narratives and visions of the future. When IR employee Lori Pottinger called big dams "dinosaurs" and suggested that Ethiopia take a more modern approach, she destroyed the temporal narratives advanced by the Ethiopian state. Pottinger and IR created a hierarchy that is not only temporal but spatial by emphasizing that large dams are not built in the US because they are no longer modern. The hierarchy of modernization is not rejected; instead it is extended to the twenty-first century, and importantly, the US is ahead of Ethiopia because it avoids the outdated technology of big dams. Such a critique goes right to the heart of the ways that the Ethiopian state symbolically deploys dams. Just as the state advanced the Gibe III dam in opposition to the backwardness of the pastoralists of the South Omo Valley, IR suggested that it is actually dams that are backward.

Ethiopian leaders have not been pleased with IR's opposition to the dams, which are such a major aspect of their plans for development. In a document specifically responding to IR's critiques of the GERD, a panel of experts[11] writes: "For these 'backward' countries, IRN [International Rivers] is the high priest that communes with God the Almighty and determines what is the most environmentally appropriate, most efficient and economical, and most beneficial for local, national and regional not only flora and fauna but also human communities too. What paternalism!!" (GERD National Panel of Experts 2014, 1). Later, in the same document, the panel writes, "The IRN! The IRN that resides in California, USA, whose activists never have endured or experienced what it means to go thirsty or hungry for days; the IRN, if it had all the power to do so would have halted all water resources development projects all over the developing world" (9). These are powerful attacks based in complex interpretations of neocolonialism and modernity. Both IR and the panel of experts advance narratives regarding dams, modernity, and place. They not only wish to tell stories about dams and the future; they seek to legitimize their right to tell these stories.

The GERD National Panel of Experts deploys critiques of colonial and neocolonial discourse that an international audience, including the well-educated liberals who support and work for IR, is familiar with. In this case, Ethiopian leaders put the word *backward* in the mouth of IR, claiming that it is because organizations such as IR are able to label Ethiopia as backward that they can justify offering prescriptive advice concerning dam construction. IR is also accused of paternalism, which further emphasizes how IR positions itself as temporally advanced in relation to Ethiopia. In contrast to much Ethiopian state discourse, it is unlikely that IR would ever actually use the term *backward* to characterize the Ethiopian government, or make an explicitly paternalistic statement such as the state's reference to the advice of "our great father" on the billboard in Jimma. For IR to do so would smack of neocolonialism and quickly erode its legitimacy. However, the GERD National Panel of Experts highlights the paternalism that is implicit in the guidance that IR gives to developing countries.[12]

The Panel's attack on IR's right to debate Ethiopia's dam construction is not only temporal but spatial. The authors of that paper construct a powerful image. The life of the comfortable activist in Berkeley, California, who can turn on a tap and drink glass after glass of clean, safe water is opposed to the thirst and hunger that many Ethiopians experience daily. Even the wealthy government administrators and engineers who are building the dam have probably experienced struggles with accessing adequate water and food at some point in their lives. Just as IR discredits the Ethiopian state's attempts to modernize as behind the times, IR is discredited as being too comfortable and too far from the realities of life in the developing world to have any legitimate voice in Ethiopia's policy decisions. The Panel of Experts constructs

IR as the postmodern Western activist, picking and choosing lifestyles and technologies for others on the basis of aesthetics, whereas the Ethiopian state is concerned with the hard work of modernization and alleviating poverty. Flow appears as a luxury rather than a legitimate temporal narrative. The decision to embrace this luxury is directly connected to the great distance between Ethiopia and "California, USA."

Although I have argued that IR partially conceives of dams in relation to the temporal narrative of flow, in my conversations with IR employees, they consistently framed their critiques of dams in terms of social justice. IR employees directly rejected the spatial dynamics assumed by the GERD Panel of Experts. I had the opportunity to spend three days at the International Rivers office in Berkeley, California, in April 2016. I asked IR employees to respond to the critiques raised by the GERD Panel of Experts, in particular the claims that IR was engaged in a kind of neocolonialism in its attempts to influence Ethiopia's programs for development. Pottinger responded:

> Certainly there's neocolonialism and colonialism and I would say that the Ethiopian government was engaging in colonialism of an internal sort when they decided that whole tribes and swaths of people were not allowed to determine their own fate and their own methods of livelihood and their own lives. That plus the fact that the Ethiopian government was using first world companies and Italian money and Chinese money and all the rest, this is not a simple argument that the Ethiopians are determining what they want to do and you should leave us alone. This is a very small elite in a very dictatorial kind of government determining what indigenous people can and cannot do with their lives. The consequences were very harsh if people tried to reject that paradigm and those sorts of very persuasive arguments on the part of their government and it got ugly very fast.

In Pottinger's response it is not IR that is forcing an external agenda on Ethiopia. Rather, it is some Ethiopians who are working with international elites to prevent others from controlling their own futures and livelihoods.

I suggested to Pottinger that the strong response from the Ethiopian government might result from a deep attachment to a narrative of modernization through big dam construction. Government officials may have been truly bothered by IR's unsettling of their conceptions of modernity and the implicit labeling of their plans for development through hydropower as backward. Pottinger acknowledged that this was certainly possible, but that in addition to any attachment to symbols of modernity, the government had a great deal at stake in the Gibe III and GERD projects. My meeting with Pottinger came a few weeks after Honduran dam critic and human rights activist Berta Cáceres was murdered, and Pottinger noted that severe attacks on those who stand in the way of big dams are common. Dams represent huge amounts of money and opportunities for graft for both construction companies and government administrators. Big dam projects frequently take ten to twenty years to complete, and those who stand in their way represent barriers to massive wealth.

Rather than an ideology of development as flow, Pottinger and others at IR repeatedly claimed that development projects should help the poor. They argued that big dam technology concentrates wealth in the hands of the privileged while the poor pay the price. This critique resonates with the center/periphery dynamics I described above relating to conceptions of big dams as underdevelopment. IR employees working in Latin America, Africa, and Asia voiced similar perspectives, noting that they came to this work not because of a particular connection with rivers, but because they were concerned with social justice and in many cases had a strong interest in the regions where they worked. Brent Millikan, IR's Amazon Program Director, argued that accusations of neocolonialism are an intentional attempt to confuse public opinion and create a false dichotomy between development and the environment. Millikan acknowledged that some environmental groups can be neocolonial in imposing their own agenda, but IR is different in that it specifically connects "human rights to the environment." He claimed that IR works with local partners to strengthen their voices rather than imposing its own agenda. Millikan contrasted the needs of those who are impacted by dams with those who promote their construction. "Dam projects make lots of sense when one thinks about the interests of the one percent.[13] I think that explains this obsession with repeating the same mistake." He argued that in Brazil, where he is based, construction companies and high-level government administrators stand to reap significant financial benefits through the distribution of contracts. Other IR employees made similar claims about the regions where they work.

The contrasting positions advanced by IR employees and the GERD Panel of Experts are based in very different understandings of who has a legitimate voice in decisions regarding Ethiopia's development. For the Panel of Experts, the right to determine development policy is based in part on nationality. As an organization based outside of Ethiopia, IR is not a legitimate participant in this debate. Personal experience is also important. The Panel of Experts implies that one cannot understand the need for development without having first experienced poverty and the absence of food and water. Like Meles Zenawi in his statement on Pastoralist Day, the Panel of Experts claims that a certain level of comfort leads activists to romanticize the lives of pastoralists.

In contrast, Pottinger questions whether Gibe III should rightfully be classified as an Ethiopian project. She focuses on the process of construction and draws attention to the involvement of Chinese and Italian interests to support her claim that the dam only helps government elites. Like other IR employees, Pottinger reframed the conflict, claiming that Ethiopians are not a homogenous group and that some are benefitting at the expense of others. If Gibe III is an international project with parties supporting and opposing construction both within and outside of Ethiopia, then there is no reason to exclude IR from the debate. IR employees distinguished corporations, governments, and lobbyists from those who would suffer the consequences of dam construction. They framed their work in terms of human rights and social justice, and claimed to act on behalf of marginalized people who had been denied a voice by their own government. When Millikan argues that dams primarily benefit the world's wealthiest 1 percent of people, he makes an argument for global solidarity that contradicts the assumptions about shared national interests that are at the foundation of the state's Ethiopian Renaissance discourse.

The voices that are notably absent from this debate are those of the people of the Omo Valley who are directly affected by Gibe III. In contrast to other parts of the world where IR employees coordinate directly with people affected by dams, in Ethiopia the government prevents IR and other organizations from accessing the Omo Valley, and in some cases IR employees have not been able to enter the country at all. Given their education status and lack of access to international media, the people of the Omo Valley have little ability to participate in international debates over their future. The few people who speak English and have international connections, such as Mursi filmmaker Olisarali Olibui, are often under government surveillance. It sometimes falls to the few international researchers and activists with significant experience in the area to help people affected by dams to be heard internationally, but even when this occurs their voices are often ignored or obscured. Will Hurd, who is fluent in Mursi, connected DFID/USAID representatives with Mursi people, who told of the atrocities they had experienced during the resettlement process, but agency representatives ignored their stories (Hurd 2015). Hurd has made a full transcript of these interviews available through the Oakland Institute (n.d.). The battle over who has a legitimate voice in dam policy will continue, but in Ethiopia the people affected by dams will be given little space to participate in this debate.

Conclusion

Throughout this book I explore how different technologies are intertwined with the politics of development and the distribution of resources. Dams, however, are distinctive in their symbolic power. It is partially their scale that makes dams particularly spectacular forms of infrastructure, worthy of being represented on billboards and political posters. Descriptions of big dams nearly always make note of their size—the biggest in Africa, the tallest in the world, the seventh largest. . . . Although urban Ethiopians rarely see actual dams, they are continually reminded of their scale. The size of dams also means that their economic and environmental implications are unparalleled. To build the GERD the state will pay well over $5 billion—more than 10 percent of Ethiopia's annual GDP at the time construction began. If successful, the GERD will provide public revenues that could transform the capacity of the Ethiopian state.

I have argued that dams generate such high levels of conflict because they bring together competing temporal and spatial narratives. The Ethiopian state conceives of dams as technologies of modernization that can be utilized by a developmental state to promote economic growth. Dams are the foundation for constructing a renaissance. This position is based in the notion of Ethiopia as a singular and homogenous space. A unified and self-contained nation uses hydroelectric technology to move from one stage to another. From this perspective, when properly managed by a developmental state dams help the nation advance, with benefits accruing to all citizens. It is therefore Ethiopian citizens who have a rightful voice in decisions about planning dams. This vision is essential to the conception of a national renaissance: the renaissance depends on a nation with unified interests.

IR's vision is far messier than this, with multiple competing interests that sometimes overlap and sometimes are directly opposed. Perhaps it is no accident that IR's conception of flow as a form of temporality is equally messy. Flow is a distinctly nonlinear process of change over time. Flow creates change through connections and movements. IR's notion of flow contrasts with the progress-based temporality of the Ethiopian state, but in some ways it also describes the complex connections between the multiple interests that are caught up in dam construction. Just as currents of water, rocks, and earth collide within rivers to create patterns and carve out new paths, something similar seems to be happening in the actual process of dam construction. It is in this sense that flow disrupts renaissance.

Chinese banks provide half-billion-dollar loans so that Ethiopia can hire Chinese contractors, Salini Impregilo has won multibillion-dollar dam construction contracts, and Saudi Star has leased thousands of acres of land for agriculture that will be supported by irrigation from dams. In undermining Ethiopia's spatial unity, IR's critique simultaneously raises questions about the potential for dams to support linear progress. The notion of a nation's citizens moving in a single direction is nonsensical when one group is benefitting at the expense of another. IR's critique draws attention to some of the contradictions between practice and Meles Zenawi's theory of the developmental state. Although Meles claimed that in order to serve the public good, state-led technological development must remain independent from private interests, multiple international actors are clearly caught up in Ethiopia's dam boom. Ethiopia's developmental state is inextricable from private interests. Like the flow of the river, these interests interact in the construction process—not to create linear growth, but certainly to transform the landscape.

IR's critiques of dams are intended to disrupt the process of construction, which is expensive. Partially as a result of IR's campaigning, major funders such as the World Bank and the African Development Bank have refused to support Gibe III and the GERD. Thus the state has been forced to improvise. A key source of funds for dam construction is the sale of bonds. These bonds are guaranteed by the state and sold only to Ethiopian citizens and those of Ethiopian descent. Bonds have guaranteed interest rates of 1.2–2 percent plus Libor, but assuming that rates of inflation in Ethiopia remain high,[14] the return on these bonds is questionable. Government employees told me that during the early stages of construction for the GERD they were required to invest a portion of their salary in GERD bonds. To the extent that Ethiopia can rely on its citizens to pay for dams, IR's critiques are ineffectual—there are no international donors who need to be convinced to pull their funds from the dam project. IR employees told me that this is one of the reasons that they have not mounted a large campaign against the GERD (in contrast to Gibe III). Through the sale of bonds the state reduces its dependence on the whims of international funders, but it must continually entice and coerce its citizens to purchase bonds. In February 2017 the Ethiopian government announced a celebration of "bond week" to encourage sales. The repeated use of the image of the GERD in state propaganda is in part a reminder to citizens that the construction of this symbol of modernity can be actualized only with their support.

In the following chapters I gradually shift the scale of my analysis to move from an examination of international debates over dams to struggles to secure funds for roads and to negotiate the challenges associated with actually building infrastructure. As I descend into the process of construction I increasingly move from an analysis of images to one of physical materials. The case of megadams is a reminder that even though large-scale infrastructures such as dams are built from concrete and steel, their construction would not be possible without the dissemination of images and narratives. It is the contrasting symbols and stories advanced by the Ethiopian state and International Rivers that ultimately determine the ability of engineers and laborers to construct massive dams such as the GERD. In the chapters to come, tensions with the Ethiopian state regarding the construction of infrastructure are with local urban residents rather than international critics.

TWO. Asphalt Roads, Regulating Infrastructures, and Improvised Lives

In 2014, five years after road construction vehicles paraded through central Jimma in celebration of beginning work to renew and widen asphalt roads, the project was still a year from completion. The asphalt in a once thriving city had been torn up to reveal sticky red dirt. A haze of dust hung in the air, and rickety wooden bridges spanned deep drainage ditches that separated businesses from the road. The road construction frequently cut off power and water supplies to neighborhoods. Without the possibility of easy movement, the city was changing, morphing into something far from Jimma residents' visions of a future city—a vision that had motivated them to donate money to the road construction effort in 2009.

Where Jimma declined, road construction in Hawassa transformed the city into a vibrant business center. Smooth, palm-lined asphalt avenues facilitated comfortable travel throughout the city. A Hawassa city administrator explained that "asphalt roads increase the value of land. They create opportunities for business. Asphalt brings commerce." DMC Construction, the company that built Hawassa's wide avenues, roughly between 2007 and 2009, was contracted to renew Jimma's roads. While DMC's work in Hawassa was generally a success and provided the foundation for future growth, in Jimma the company was unable to complete the roads. In fact, a protracted legal battle occurred between the city and the company, DMC equipment was temporarily seized, and the work was left unfinished.

Roads support temporal and spatial connections.[1] In cities roads connect and disconnect neighborhoods, people, and things. Roads remake urban residents' relationships with imagined futures. People ask themselves what a road will bring and where might it take them. Roads push and pull people and things to transform neighborhoods (Melly 2013, 2017). City planners imagine roads increasing commerce and the value of land, and these imagined futures support speculation. Even the possibility of a new road transforms a place, makes it into something new—something made more vibrant through its imagined future connections with other places (Dalakoglou and Harvey 2012).

For city planners and government administrators in Ethiopia, building asphalt roads was a necessary step in connecting the present to a desirable future. They were, however, aware that actualizing their progressive plans for the future was not guaranteed. In Jimma the road to the future crumbled, leaving residents without a city. In Hawassa, new asphalt surfaces throughout the city supported movement toward a vision of modern prosperity. Asphalt roads are paths to possible futures, but reaching a desired future requires negotiating the balance between improvisation and regulation. Asphalt road construction is an encounter between plans and contingency, simplification and complexity, the scalable and unscalable. As Hannah Knox and Penny Harvey explain, "the project of building a road is itself a process that aims to produce a systematic stabilization from an unstable social and material world" (2011, 145).

It is in the process of construction that asphalt roads encounter challenges from the irregularities of urban life—politics, weather, preexisting settlements, religion, and interpersonal relationships, to name a few. Road construction therefore requires a high degree of improvisation and flexibility. In Hawassa, improvisations based in social relationships were utilized to tame contingency (Bromber et al. 2015), and to overcome the irregular conditions that disrupt infrastructural development and the production of possible urban futures.

The balance between improvisation and regulation determines how roads affect lives. The regulatory effects of asphalt roads are partially based in their advancement of a single primary goal—increasing speed. As motorized vehicles increase their velocity the street shifts from a place for social life to one of rapid movement (McShane 1994; Wells 2012, 13). Asphalt roads are not a particularly flexible technology. They depend on conditions that are regular and generalizable to other places. They are an expensive technology that draws its value primarily from enabling the rapid movement of motorized vehicles, and they may become worse than useless when they fail. Less than ten years after the Jimma–Addis Ababa asphalt highway was completed in the early 2000s, potholes and washouts had broken it in many places, forcing vehicles to slow almost to a stop in order to proceed and presenting a significant danger to anyone traveling at night. A broken asphalt road ceases to facilitate speed and is less functional than a smooth gravel road.

Asphalt roads introduce a kind of regulatory stability when they are built in Ethiopian cities. They push out precarious livelihoods and settlements that are improvisational in the sense that they exist without permission from the state and do not function in accordance with state regulations. Improvised livelihoods are in a process of continual change, sometimes rapid and sometimes slow, that occurs in response to shifting environmental, political, and economic conditions (Simone 2004). Asphalt roads often replace these precarious improvisations with residences and businesses that conform to government regulations. These new businesses tend to operate with much higher levels of capital. They are investments that depend on relatively rigid long-term plans for the future.

In road construction the encounter between material and human infrastructures shapes the balance between regularization and improvisation. The notion of people as infrastructure emerges from AbdouMaliq Simone's analysis of African cities. Simone writes that "African cities are characterized by incessantly flexible, mobile, and provisional intersections of residents that operate without clearly delineated notions of how the city is to be inhabited and used. These intersections, particularly in the last two decades, have depended on the ability of residents to engage complex combinations of objects, spaces, persons, and practices. These conjunctions become an infrastructure—a platform providing for and reproducing life in the city" (2004, 407–8). Simone offers the example of the urban African bus station to demonstrate how people may function as infrastructure. At the bus station services are provided through multiple layers of collaboration that do not adhere to specific rules. Instead, practices and expectations shift on the basis of changing conditions and the needs and interests of specific individuals. In this sense, human infrastructures are improvised. The relationships that function as infrastructure are constantly in the process of reorganizing themselves, but the individuals in these relationships have shared histories that shape the process of change. Some of these social relationships and their associated improvisations have far more power to generate possible futures than others, and this is a fundamental source of inequality in urban development.

Material infrastructures such as asphalt roads have a reciprocal relationship with human infrastructures.[2] They are continually entangled. Specific networks of people—marked by age, gender, ethnicity, religion, and class—encounter lively materials such as asphalt that generate opportunities and limits for actualizing imagined futures. Struggles with road construction in Jimma emerged through encounters with irregular, place-specific conditions. As with many large-scale development interventions, road construction depends on using abstractions to overcome variation, specificity, and irregularity. When these conditions are not properly addressed, they may undermine the entire project. Road construction was successful in Hawassa precisely because government administrators improvised irregular culturally specific strategies to deal with local conditions. Such practices were also intertwined with the prophecies of Evangelical Christian preachers that predicted successful development for Hawassa. The improvised practices that supported road construction ultimately pushed out other improvised livelihoods, social networks, and settlements. These were the type of place-specific practices that are frequently at odds with modernist urban development (Scott 1998). Asphalt roads disrupted these practices, and the people who depended on them were often forced to move elsewhere. Such forced resettlement is a common result of urban development (Harms 2016; Rao 2013).

Throughout this book I examine the dialectic between the generalizing power of state regulations and the specifics of human practices. Asphalt road construction involves a particularly interesting relationship between the two. The specific techniques of government administrators enabled the successful construction of asphalt roads, which then imposed a regularized set of conditions on local residents. The regularities associated with asphalt roads disrupted established communities and their improvised livelihoods. In this sense, the encounter between improvisation and regulation produces construction and destruction. To the degree that the state is successful in building the city and generating economic growth, it also produces an excluded underclass.

Irregularities and Failed Road Construction in Jimma

When I visited Jimma for a month of research in 2009 it seemed that much of the city was under construction. Old roads were being scraped clean and prepared for the addition of new asphalt. Urban Ethiopians often assume that state-led development projects will fail. Although the road construction was clearly disrupting people's lives, I heard a surprising degree of enthusiasm for this construction, rather than the usual critiques of development.

In 2009 few roads had been completed, and for the most part the effects of construction were negative—roads torn up, clouds of dust, families relocated, and streets that had become piles of dirt or deep, muddy puddles (figure 2.1). Despite these challenges, discussions of roads were filled with faith in the possibility of modernization. Jimma residents believed that roads would bring "progress." They articulated an abstract vision of a modern Jimma. When I pointed out to a friend that the value of asphalt roads is questionable because most Jimma residents walk everywhere, he responded, "Yes, we don't travel by cars often, but without roads there will be no progress." Despite the lack of specifics, for many Jimma residents progress was certainly desirable and worthy of some discomfort in attaining it.

After three years away, I returned to Jimma in June 2012. I had heard from friends that the roads were still not finished, but I was surprised at how they had deteriorated. The problem with starting a road and not finishing it is that things get worse. In Jimma only a few major arteries were fit for heavy vehicles. Even after the asphalt was removed, trucks still needed to use these roads. Potholes developed, the rain came, traffic continued, and the potholes got worse. Soon the roads were almost impassable. When I lived in Jimma from 2003 to 2005, the asphalt road leaving town toward Addis Ababa was not in great shape, but it was certainly passable, with a couple of bumps here and there. In 2012 vehicles crawled along this road, swerving from side to side to avoid holes and ditches. Riding in a Bajaj on this road at night after heavy rain was quite frightening. It seemed that at any moment we would topple over in the reddish-brown mud.

Another asphalt road I knew well was under construction. It passed near the house I rented when I lived in Jimma from 2003 to 2005. During my 2012 stay it was near my hotel, and I traveled the road a few times every day. A narrow path, just wide enough for a single vehicle, wove around piles of gravel and sand. When it rained, which is nearly every day in June, a little stream formed on the road, flowing between the piles. The narrow road meant that walking was almost impossible and certainly not safe. I began paying one birr for a Bajaj taxi to take me up and down the road, something I had never done before. One birr is not a great expense for many Ethiopians, but many others need to save this money for food and other necessities. They walked, dodging traffic and hopping between piles of gravel.

FIGURE 2.1. Road construction at sunset in Jimma. Photo by Alise Osis.

When I visited Jimma briefly in February 2014 this particular road was finished, but many others were not. The main road connecting the Addis Ababa highway to the bus station was completely closed, and traffic was routed along smaller roads. The Regional Road Authority had taken over the construction from private companies and some progress was being made, but much of the city was still under construction. The general feeling among Jimma residents was one of great disappointment. They insisted that they would never again donate money for road construction.

Why did road construction in Jimma fail so miserably? Many Jimma residents explained the failure in terms of government mismanagement and corruption. They emphasized that because of corruption the government often runs out of funds before projects are finished, leading to a pattern of starting and stopping that leaves roads in worse shape than if construction had never begun. Others combined a critique of corruption with an analysis of ethnic federalism, explaining that the federal government insists on giving powerful positions to unqualified people who represent the ethnic and religious demographics of the rural communities that surround multiethnic cities. They argued that in Jimma Oromo Muslims were given jobs because of their ethnicity and religion rather than their qualifications for employment. Such critiques often say more about the speaker than actual political dynamics and demonstrate fears about shifting relations of power in the context of ethnic federalism (Mains 2004). Oromo Muslims also questioned the competence of government administrators but did not link their critique to ethnic and religious identity. Still others focused the blame less on the state and more on DMC, the construction company that the government contracted to build Jimma's roads. One young man, who perhaps not coincidentally was a low-level government administrator, claimed that the fault lay entirely with DMC. He argued that the owner of the company being arrested and many of the company's vehicles being impounded by the state demonstrated DMC's guilt. Ethiopian newspapers also reported that some of DMC's assets had been frozen (Sahle 2011).

In the past the Ethiopian Road Authority carried out most road construction projects, but beginning in the 1990s these projects were increasingly contracted out to private companies. DMC was one of Ethiopia's largest companies. It had contracts for construction projects at a number of different universities but was not involved in road construction until the early 2000s, when it received a contract to build asphalt roads in Hawassa. Eshetayehu and I met with DMC's public liaison at a café in Hawassa to discuss the company's experiences in Jimma and Hawassa. "Those stories about company leaders being arrested are completely false," he explained.

> They are just rumors. In Jimma the biggest problem was that the road we were building was right next to the old houses. We were clearing a road for new asphalt and there were toilets right where we were digging. We had to stop. It was very difficult. Jimma is an old city, built during the time of the Italians [1936–41], [and] it is not an easy place to work. The other problem is that the administrators in Jimma are not like [those in] Hawassa. They never paid us on time. After the Jimma government missed four or five payments, how could we pay our workers? We couldn't work.

Both problems caused delays and consequent setbacks in the construction process.

In a 2015 interview the head of urban planning in Jimma explained that when delays in construction occur, the price of materials increases. This is particularly true in a context of rapid inflation such as Ethiopia experienced from 2009 to 2015. DMC demanded that the municipal government provide additional funds to cover the increased cost of materials, but the government refused. The municipal government simply lacked the funds to handle major increases in construction budgets. The municipal urban planner explained that Jimma has problems with collecting local revenue. For example, at the time of our interview, the city's budget for the most recent year was based on anticipated revenue of 72 million birr. Infrastructural projects would absorb 53 million of the total budget. However, the city collected only 49 million in revenue, and much of the planned work would need to be postponed and left incomplete. When disputes over construction timelines and budgets could not be resolved, the state seized DMC's equipment. A court ruling ultimately forced the state to pay DMC for the losses it incurred by losing its equipment.

Jimma's head of urban planning also emphasized that the "black cotton" soil found in Jimma is a major barrier to all types of construction. Black cotton is an "expansive clay" that expands when exposed to moisture and contracts under dry conditions. Combined with distinct wet and dry seasons, such as those found in Jimma, black cotton soil produces extensive swelling that makes asphalt construction very difficult, and experts recommend avoiding building roads on expansive clay (Thagesen 2004, 174). In contrast, Hawassa has different soil conditions and receives around sixty centimeters less rain annually than Jimma. Although it is certainly possible to build roads on black cotton, it is another source of complications and delays, which then bring increased costs, erosion, and further setbacks. It also extends the duration of the construction process. During my visit with the head of planning, a resident came into the office to complain about the loss of water to his neighborhood as a result of the construction. Such complaints were common among my friends in Jimma as they endured year after year of construction.

The case of Jimma demonstrates that plans for the future often fail because of the numerous contingencies that are built into the construction process. Soil type, weather, corruption, mismanagement, revenue generation, ethnic politics, corporate greed, and prior urban development all undermine the strategies of engineers and urban planners. Each of these dynamics introduces irregularities into the construction process. These irregularities are not easily paved over. The nature of asphalt construction requires that it move forward. Plans cannot be adjusted on the fly to accommodate the particularities of a soil type, a budget shortfall, or a pit toilet. When construction is disrupted again and again, costs increase, conditions are degraded, the project ultimately fails, and people are forced to live in a work zone.

Successful Road Construction and Economic Growth in Hawassa

With its wide, palm-lined avenues, Hawassa is a clear contrast to Jimma (map 2.1). Asphalt road coverage in Hawassa approximately doubled between 2004 and 2014. In 2014 moving between neighborhoods on three-wheeled motorcycle taxis was easy and relatively inexpensive. Everyday discussions contained few laments about a lack of development. Some questioned the desirability of particular urban development projects, but almost no one denied that growth was occurring rapidly.

The difference between Jimma and Hawassa is partially due to roads. In the early 2000s, DMC was paid nearly 150 million birr to build twenty-two kilometers of new asphalt roads in Hawassa. DMC rapidly built high-quality roads in that city but failed to finish the job in Jimma. In Hawassa this new asphalt covered major arteries and significantly transformed possibilities for moving through the city. Roads connect different parts of the city, pushing and pulling people and things along different routes. The failed construction

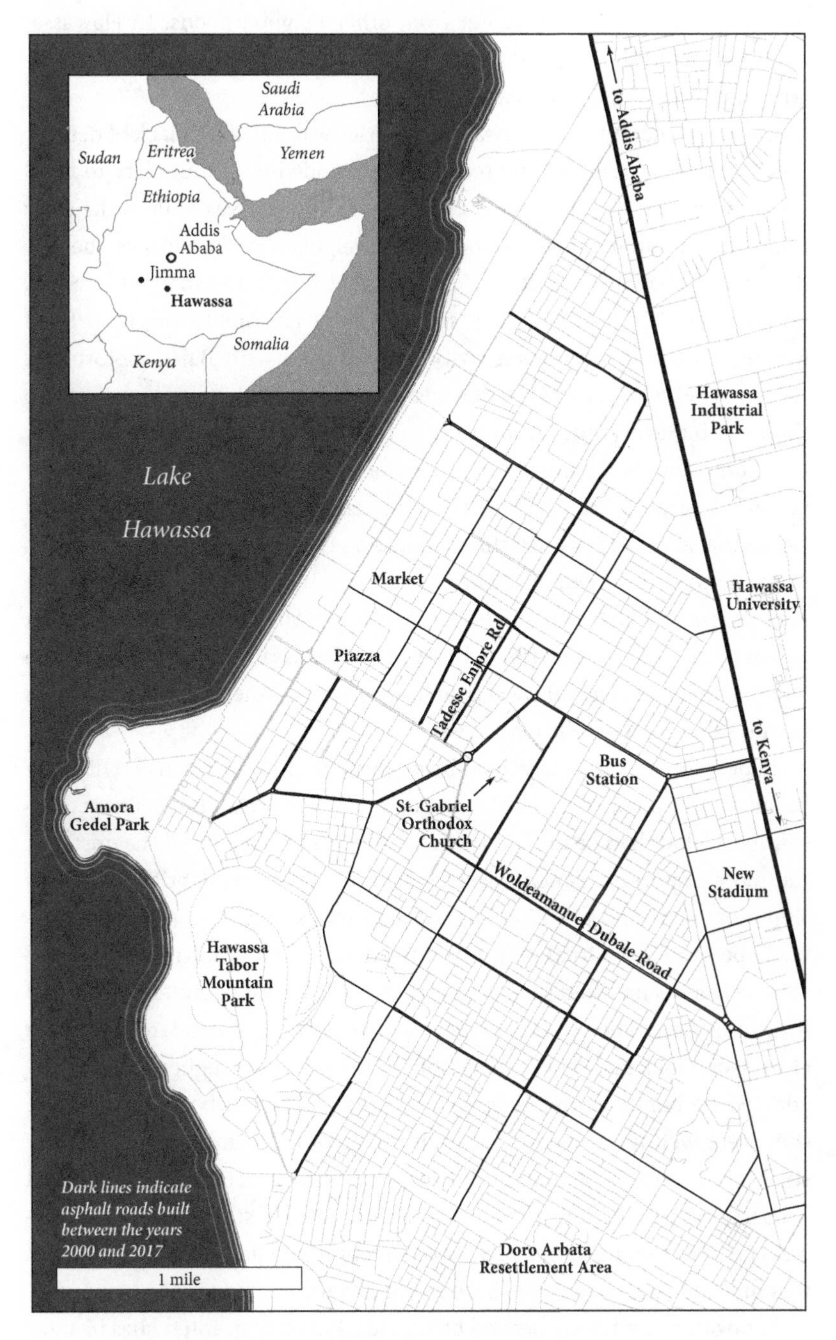

MAP 2.1. Map of Hawassa. Map prepared by Timothy Stallman.

in Jimma isolated the city center from other neighborhoods. In Hawassa, roads expanded the city and connected the periphery with the center, creating new points of centralization in the process.

The construction in Hawassa's peripheries was aided by a lack of densely populated settlements. Many roads were intended to pull the city to rural areas. When the Woldeamanuel Dubale (WED) Road[3] was built in the early 2000s it cut through sparsely populated neighborhoods south of the city (figure 2.2). Longtime residents claimed that before the road, "there was nothing here but corn." In 2013, six years after its completion, WED Road was teeming with business activity and crowded with Bajaj, motorbikes, and large vehicles. The sidewalks were thick with pedestrians attracted to shops selling everything from pizza to bicycle parts to imported clothing. Few homeowners remained on the section of WED Road closest to the city center. Most properties had been completely transformed for commercial use in the seven years since the road had been constructed. Plots set back from the road had been developed into coffee houses, restaurants, storage areas, or small courtyards surrounded by shops. All of the homeowners that Eshetayehu and I spoke with had moved to Hawassa from elsewhere in the country, and most had received land from the government in the early 1990s because they were public employees.

Rapid increases in land values, investment, and commercial activity only began after asphalt replaced the dirt road. For residents and business owners, the asphalt had beautified the neighborhood and reduced the dust, but the most important benefits were economic. Most residential properties were now worth 2–3 million birr. All had shops that were rented to business operators for a total of 3000–6000 birr per month. Most of the previous residents had sold their property or rented it for commercial use and lived elsewhere. The benefits to those who had been granted land here were clear. Good luck and their connection with the state brought them unprecedented economic gains. As government employees with steady incomes, they were well positioned to take advantage of the coming road and construct shop space to be rented. With minimal investment they transformed property granted to them by the government into substantial wealth. Owners increased rent for shops 200–300 percent immediately after the asphalt was finished, and those rents have continued to rise.

For example, a family headed by two teachers was granted land in 1991. Before the road construction in 2007 the neighborhood was entirely residential and horse carts were the primary form of transportation. In 2014 the

FIGURE 2.2. Woldeamanuel Dubale Road, Hawassa. Photo by the author.

family members used bicycles and Bajaj for transport. Indeed, WED Road residents consistently commented on the ease of access to motorized public transportation that came with the asphalt. After the road was complete the family, like their neighbors, built three small shops in front of their house. Initially they charged only 200–300 birr per month in rent, but in 2014 each shop operator paid 2,000 birr per month. The parents continued to work as teachers, but much of their income came from rent. They estimated that the property could be sold for 3–4 million birr. This family was unusual in that they chose to stay in the neighborhood. They explained that they liked the central location of their home and they were accustomed to the noise from the street.

Despite a rapid increase in rents, business operators claimed they had no plans to move elsewhere. For example, an older man who operated a small shop, crowded with tools and spare parts for bicycles, claimed that his rent had increased from 300 birr to 3,000 birr in the seven years since the road had been completed. Over the noise of traffic outside his open door he explained, "It is good to see progress. It gets things moving. Before it was all residential here, but now it is all business. It is nice to see the change from dust to asphalt. It makes you feel good to see this kind of change. Rents are high but I'm not going anywhere. This is where the business is, and this is where I will stay." Many of the business operators on WED Road had moved from Addis Ababa and other cities to take advantage of the excellent business climate in Hawassa.

This is asphalt-led growth. Asphalt increases property values and brings commerce. Development such as that on WED Road provided an important model that other Hawassa residents observed. Regardless of the location, others who lived near newly constructed roads planned to start businesses. However, the experience of WED Road residents is not so easily generalizable. The new asphalt road generated business opportunities in part because of the neighborhood's spatial and socioeconomic dynamics. The low population density meant that construction of the asphalt did not lead to displacement. Equally important, the residents commuted elsewhere for work and did not depend on the particular spatial dynamics of the neighborhood for their livelihoods. The residents, as government workers, had stable jobs and middle-class incomes. They owned their property and therefore could not be displaced by rising rents. Rather, they could afford to build shops and rent them for significant additional income. As an alternative, they could take advantage of rapidly rising land values by selling their home and using the profits to purchase homes elsewhere.[4] As I detail in later sections, however, new asphalt roads were far less desirable for those who relied on precarious improvised livelihoods and depended heavily on neighborhood-specific social relationships.

Improvising Road Construction in Hawassa

Why did road construction succeed in Hawassa but fail in Jimma? In Hawassa, ethnic and religious dynamics created powerful incentives for city administrators to address barriers to road construction. A former high-ranking member of the Hawassa municipal government explained that when he came to power after the 2005 election, he was saddled with the responsibility of repairing relations between the federal government and the Sidama people. He urgently needed to stop the "blood flow" resulting from conflicts between the Sidama and others over ownership of the city. He simultaneously faced the challenges of renewing urban residents' relationships with the ruling EPRDF party and building infrastructure. Road construction was a means of accomplishing both goals, and administrators used social networks and improvised techniques of governance to ensure that roads were built in a timely manner.

After coming to power in 1991, the EPRDF focused primarily on rural development. Attention to urban development began in 2002 and then increased rapidly after the 2005 parliamentary elections. In 2005, for the first time, opposition parties were given the chance to campaign freely. Opposition parties did very well in the elections, winning approximately one-third of Ethiopia's more than five hundred Parliament seats. Most of these victories took place in urban areas. The opposition appealed to voters who were unhappy with high urban unemployment rates and a lack of development in cities. The results of the 2005 election led the EPRDF to focus its attention on cities and urban development with the hope of winning back supporters.

Engineering is generally portrayed as an apolitical field, and yet in the Hawassa case, successful road construction depended as much on local ethnic politics as it did on calculations and measurements. For the EPRDF, in Hawassa the challenge of winning support from urban residents was coupled with renewing ties with the Sidama people, who have historically lived in what is now Hawassa. Soon after the EPRDF came to power in 1991, a Sidama regional state was created, but this was incorporated into the multiethnic SNNPR in 1994.[5] The SNNPR is the most diverse region in Ethiopia, containing fifty-six of the nation's approximately eighty ethnic groups (Barata 2012). According to the most recent national census in 2007, the Sidama are the largest ethnic group in the SNNPR, but with a population of around 3 million, at a national level they are still very much a minority in relation to larger groups such as the Oromo (more than 25 million) and Amhara (around 20 million) (Ethiopian Central Statistical Agency 2010). The shift from a Sidama region to a multiethnic one means that Amharic, rather than Sidama, is the language of governance and education in the area. It also means the loss of jobs and federal funds that come with regional status. The loss of their own regional state has been a major grievance for the Sidama people. In 2002, ten thousand to fifteen thousand Sidama marched on Hawassa. One of their key demands was that Sidama be granted regional status. The federal government responded to the protestors swiftly and violently. Police killed at least twenty-five protestors, and the protestors' demands were not met (Aalen 2011, 151; Human Rights Watch 2002).

The issue of regional status for the Sidama was raised again in the immediate aftermath of the 2005 election. Because of irregularities in the voting process, a revote was held for a selected number of Parliament seats.[6] EPRDF leaders in Hawassa promised Sidama elders that Sidama would be given regional status in exchange for supporting EPRDF party candidates (Aalen 2011, 151–52). In every case the EPRDF party candidates won the revote. However, the federal government did not follow through on its promise to create a Sidama region, and this renewed tensions between the Sidama and the EPRDF.

The prime minister at the time, Meles Zenawi, personally came to Hawassa to address tensions with the Sidama. A number of important symbolic changes were made. Hailemariam Desalegn, a Wolayta, resigned as president of the SNNPR and was replaced by a Sidama.[7] Many non-Sidama bureau heads in Hawassa were replaced by Sidama. Awassa was renamed as Hawassa, reflecting the Sidama rather than the Amharic spelling of the word. Debub (Amharic for "South") University was renamed Hawassa University, a move that both established a direct relationship between the university and Hawassa and eliminated an Amharic word from the university's name. Also at this time, various monuments to Sidama history were constructed in the city.

"Roads pull," a former high-ranking official in the Hawassa city administration explained. "We intentionally built roads in new neighborhoods on Hawassa's periphery to attract businesses and residents. First came gravel roads and electricity and then asphalt, and after the asphalt came the investments from the private sector." This administrator explained that after 2005 the municipal government gave Sidama preferential access to government jobs and land in order to make up for past injustices that had marginalized them from the city center. New plots of land on the edges of Hawassa were leased to Sidama people, and roads were built to connect these new neighborhoods with the city center.[8] Hawassa also dramatically expanded its administrative boundaries to encompass the surrounding rural area. At the time of the 2007 census approximately 100,000 of Hawassa's 250,000 residents were living outside the previous municipal boundaries. Almost all of these periurban dwellers were Sidama, meaning that with the expansion in administrative boundaries the Sidama were suddenly the most populous ethnic group in Hawassa. The success of opposition parties in the 2005 election was partially based on the readiness of Ethiopia's multiethnic urban population to reject the EPRDF's policies of ethnic federalism. In a few short years after the 2005 election Hawassa was transformed into a Sidama city that, in theory, was more likely to embrace the EPRDF and ethnic federalism (Mains and Kinfu 2016).

Roads connected these periurban Sidama residents to the city center, bringing them into the city and pulling the city to them. Expanding the city also had the potential to create conflicts with Sidama farmers. As the city expanded, land that was previously zoned for farming became zoned for residences and businesses. This meant that farmers working within the new city limits were forced to give up large amounts of their land. In Ethiopia, laws are complex regarding compensation for a loss of land. Land-for-land compensation depends on the availability of land and the purpose for which it will be used. A former administrator explained that Sidama farmers were removed from their land through multiple meetings with elder leaders of the Sidama community and officials at both the regional and city levels. In general, farmers were compensated with one square meter of land for every ten square meters they lost. This enabled Sidama farmers who were losing land to retain some land ownership and move toward the city. This process smoothed over some of the tensions between the Sidama people and the state. At the same time, the city granted land within the urban boundaries to some Sidama who had not lost any land. The city was able to grow and the Sidama were reconnected with the state simultaneously.

In other cases the Hawassa city administration worked around laws to ensure the timely completion of the road construction. City administrators had close relationships with members of the regional government. They obtained information about funds that had been earmarked for other projects but had not been used by the end of the fiscal year and would be returned to the federal government. A lack of flexibility in accessing funds was a key bureaucratic problem that delayed road construction in Jimma. When funds are not available and work is delayed, projects backslide and costs increase, leading to a cycle of delays and higher costs that has major implications for the completion of projects and the livability of the city. A former Hawassa administrator explained, "I would check with different offices on unused funds for their projects. I would convince people to allocate the unused funds to the road construction. I was working this way for three years. Good communication was very important for me. I would follow the progress of other projects[,] and if a project failed I knew some unused funds would be available. That's when I would do my work and get those funds." He went on to explain the importance of relationships and personality for this process: "Most of the time, my job involved diplomacy. I would go to different offices and talk to officials and convince them. . . . I could enter any office confidently. My work needed a lot of communication. In Ethiopia, there is not a lack of money rather a lack of work commitment."

In other words, government officials violated regulations to smooth out bureaucratic bumps in the construction process. Jimma residents argued that ethnic politics and corruption had led to the failure of roads, claiming that corruption wastes public funds and closes off opportunities for the future. In this case, however, corruption actually opened possibilities because it enabled the flexibility necessary to work around regulations. This is human infrastructure. Personal connections between administrators facilitated the movement of finances that ultimately supported successful construction. Human infrastructure is not homogenous. The particular characteristics of the people who formed this infrastructure were important. They were elder Sidama men with excellent social skills. Age, gender, power, ethnicity, and personality all shaped the successful movement of finances. This is not a democratic process, but for better or worse it supports construction. Personal relationships supported the particular improvisations that cut through government regulations and built roads. Improvisations were tailored to the challenges of specific places and times.

Administrators also used social networks and relationships to deal with informal settlements. One of the new roads crossed through areas that were occupied by informal settlements. Not only was it necessary to demolish homes to build the road, but the state also had to regularize these neighborhoods. Compensation paid to informal settlers for losing their land depends on the age of the settlement and the legality of the buildings. Road construction often results in significant losses of land without compensation for communities in informal settlements. Resistance from these communities can cause major delays in road construction. The Hawassa city administration addressed this problem by developing close relationships with elder men in the informal settlements. One man in particular had a valuable piece of land that would be affected by the road. City officials combined offers of land-for-land compensation with arguments that the road had value that outweighed the elder's personal loss. The elder then encouraged others to accept the road and the regularization that would come with it. City officials took pride in noting that the road was built without compensating most of those who had settled informally in the area. The municipal government was currently operating under severe budget constraints, making techniques such as these absolutely necessary.

Regularizing modernist urban planning relies on highly precarious improvised practices; this is not unique to Ethiopia. The construction of Brasília, for example, depended on massive illegal squatter camps for construction workers (Holston 1989). In the case at hand, the willingness of administrators to ignore state regulations enabled DMC to successfully complete its work. At the same time, the personalities of some administrators minimized conflict with Sidama community leaders in informal settlements. Residents in such settlements often dislike the coming of asphalt roads because they frequently lose land when it is regularized. In this case, government officials used personal relationships that were based on specific qualities such as ethnicity and personality to enable regularization and the enforcement of generalizable rules.

Urban Growth and Pentecostal Prophecies

Ethnic politics and power struggles after 2005 were not the only factors that motivated improvisational techniques of governance. Pentecostalism and associated religious prophecies created faith in not just the possibility but also the necessity of infrastructural development and economic growth. In 2017 Eshetayehu and I had coffee at Haile Resort with the head pastor of one of the largest Pentecostal churches in Hawassa. Haile Resort was an appropriate place for the discussion. When Ethiopians talk about Hawassa's growth they often cite Haile Resort, the sprawling luxury hotel on the edge of the city, built by the great long-distance runner Haile Gebrselassie. We sat in the shade of a huge sycamore tree overlooking the lake. Many of Hawassa's Pentecostals once gathered at this tree for baptisms in the lake.

"Hawassa has grown together with Christianity," explained the pastor. "The city is 90 percent Christian and 60 percent Protestant." He told the story of the Swedish missionary who was essential in founding the first Pentecostal church in Hawassa. The missionary had been working in Liberia when God told him to go to Ethiopia. Others discouraged him, telling him that Ethiopia was already a Christian country, but he came anyway. As he was walking to a meeting with government officials in Addis Ababa, God's spirit revealed itself to him and asked, "Did you come here to carry out my will or yours?" The missionary felt sad and responded, "God, I brought my children from a comfortable life and I left my country so that I can fulfill your will." At the meeting he spoke with Emperor Haile Selassie, who instructed him to go to Hawassa. When he arrived in Hawassa, a large rainbow stretched over the town, and he took this as a message from God that he was in the place that God had chosen. In explaining the significance of this story, the pastor noted that God chooses people to go to places where He wants His will to be carried out. "God is the one that picks places and people when he wants something accomplished. We see this in Abraham's story; he was chosen from among his family.[9] God also chose Jerusalem among all the places. God called Jerusalem the 'Pearl of the World.'" The pastor explained that God chose Hawassa as an "Ethiopian Jerusalem."

"Many in politics, business, and education are Christians," the pastor explained.

> Ninety-seven percent of city officials are Evangelicals. There is no other city government like Hawassa in Ethiopia. This tells us that the Gospel plays a big role in people's personal development. It increases their intelligence and opens their minds. The Gospel enlightens people's life and thinking. You can see big differences in development and lifestyle in the areas where the Gospel has been preached compared to where the Gospel was not preached. These areas have the same government system, but the difference is within the people. The Gospel is what enlightens these officials. The presence of God is what shapes these good officials. The initial reason for European and American civilization is the Gospel. During Luther's breakthrough, European people were enlightened. I believe the Gospel has positively shaped Hawassa the same way. When preachers come to the city and preach the gospel, it brings blessings to the city.

In the early 1990s, around the time that the EPRDF developed Ethiopia's new constitution, there were many important prophecies about Hawassa's development. The visit by the German evangelist Reinhard Bonnke was a major breakthrough for the city.[10] "Bonnke brought people to God and broke the power of Satan. Bonnke converted many people and after this Christians began to invest in the city." The pastor noted the Lewi Hotel chain as one example of Protestant Christian investment. "Factories and hotels were built by Christians who had a great respect for God. God has blessed these businesses." The Ethiopian pastor Tolosa Gudina also delivered a major prophecy at this time. He spoke of growth and spiritual transformation for Hawassa. Other pastors noted Tolosa's prophecy, explaining that it led to a spiritual awakening that brought further blessings from God. Tolosa inspired the congregants of one Pentecostal church to take to the streets and preach directly to the city. City administrators consistently cited Pastor Tolosa's prophecy in explaining Hawassa's success.

For religious leaders, however, Hawassa's growth presented certain spiritual dangers. "Hawassa will continue to grow and it is important that the church is strong. This city may be an Ethiopian Las Vegas or Jerusalem," explained the pastor. "Secularism is increasingly being practiced and getting into members of the church. People have also increasingly been attracted by globalization. For this reason they are not working on their spiritual growth; they are not reading their Bible and praying. Instead, they are focusing more on chasing money. Therefore, the church has to wake up and preach the gospel. I have been challenging every church to preach the gospel now more than ever. We will win the battle in Jesus's name!" In response to concerns about rising numbers of bars, clubs, and prostitutes, the pastors of all the major churches in Hawassa were meeting weekly to pray. "We are now planning our move strategically. We are working with priests and pastors to hold meetings and prayers. In addition, we are preaching, waking people up to practice discipleship and challenge the government. During our next meeting, we plan to call and challenge some key political leaders."[11]

A shared religion certainly enhances the relationships among administrators that are necessary for improvisation, but perhaps even more important is the sense of faith in a prophecy that motivates administrators to build the Ethiopian Jerusalem. Faith in a particular future does not necessarily make that future a reality, but in subtle ways it continually affects the work of city administrators. As one administrator explained in 2017, more than twenty years after Tolosa's prophecy, "There is freedom here. We can practice the religion of our choice. All of the major prayer conferences come to Hawassa. Bonnke and Tolosa Gudina came here and prophesized great things for Hawassa. They said that the value of land will rise." Faith in prophecy does not create reality, but it produces possibilities. It introduces ideas that may be actualized.

Furthermore, as Dena Freeman (2012) explains, Pentecostalism supports the belief that God wants his followers to experience material abundance. Similar to the Protestant spirit of capitalism described by Max Weber, success is a sign that one has been chosen. The pastor noted, "In general, I believe it is all due to God's blessings. . . . Even the fact that the industrial park is established here proves God's blessings for the city." God's blessings caused growth in Hawassa to be successful, and successful growth proves that Hawassa was in fact blessed. This claim echoes Meles Zenawi's teleological claims about the developmental state that I discussed in the previous chapter. As with Meles's beliefs about the developmental state, Pentecostals believe that God wishes to promote growth, and therefore growth is a sign that the will of God (or the developmental state, for Meles) has been successful. In contrast to a general skepticism regarding the developmental state, there are many Pentecostals in Hawassa who have faith in God. Their faith in Hawassa's status as an Ethiopian Jerusalem may necessitate action to prove that the prophecy was correct and the city is, in fact, chosen.[12]

The pastor's thoughts about the dichotomy between Las Vegas and Jerusalem demonstrate an awareness of contingency. In the context of rapid change and economic growth there is an increased awareness that life could be otherwise, and this is an incentive to take action to bring about a particular future. In the context of ethnic tensions and demands for development after 2005, there was already a heightened sense that roads must succeed, but religious prophecy adds a spiritual dimension to this process. Roads are not just necessary for the success of the developmental state; they are part of a spiritual war, the creation of a Jerusalem, the pearl of the world. In true Weberian fashion that war does not end. Similar to fears that Max Weber (1930 [2001], 118–19) described among Puritans, the prophesized economic growth creates new threats. Rather than accepting the inevitability of a secular consumer culture of sin (Las Vegas), the pastor demanded action. It is likely that this vision of a spiritual battle will push the culture of the city in unexpected directions, spurring new forms of construction and political struggle.

Engineering Asphalt Roads and Irregularities in the City Center

A new round of asphalt road construction began in Hawassa in May 2013. In this case the work was carried out by Yotek Construction. Yotek was paid 187.7 million birr[13] to construct approximately six kilometers of new asphalt roads. Of the roads currently under construction, I focused my research on the Taddesse Enjore Road, which extends from the Taddesse Enjore restaurant in the central Piazza neighborhood to the Moyale highway near Hawassa University. Yotek representatives explained that the road brings a number of benefits, including a reduction in vehicle accidents, faster transport, beautification of the city, and increased property values. Yotek engineers noted that of the four roads they were constructing, Taddesse Enjore was the most challenging and expensive, primarily because of its central location. The neighborhood behind the Taddesse Enjore restaurant is particularly dense and was not constructed according to city planning regulations. As a result many houses were leveled during the process of clearing the area for the new road. Like in Jimma, toilets built alongside the road created a particularly difficult "obstruction," and a bulldozer almost fell into a pit toilet. Poles supporting electric and telephone lines also had to be cleared.

In a 2014 interview, a Yotek engineer explained, "This neighborhood was built fifty years ago. There was no master plan here. We don't know where to begin working. Dealing with water is particularly difficult. We can't do anything until the Water and Sewage Ministry deals with the water issue. The water lines are all underground but we don't know exactly where they are. With the rainy season coming we can expect a lot of flooding as we are doing the excavation." Yotek representatives expected that the Taddesse Enjore Road would require additional funds and be completed after the other Hawassa projects.

The head engineer on the project lamented bulldozing a tree that a resident associated with his father. "I had to do it," he said, "but I felt very bad about it. There was no choice, and I must remember that even though some people will suffer, this road will have great benefits for everyone." Engineers were quite aware of the difficulties that road construction caused for neighborhood residents. To minimize the destruction of homes, the width of the road was reduced from the usual twenty-five meters to eighteen meters. A narrow road means a different and more expensive design that uses underground drainage pipes instead of the open ditches that are found in much of the city.

Because of complications such as this, Yotek engineers estimated that they were delayed by at least six months. In 2015 Yotek requested an additional three hundred days to complete the project, but the municipality granted only sixty days in order to finish before the 2015 election. As I discuss in more detail in the following chapter, there was a rush to complete major infrastructural projects before the May 2015 election. Money and time were also lost during an unusually long rainy season, when work stopped and rented construction equipment sat idle. Yotek engineers claimed that despite the difficulties, no additional funds were needed. Importantly, before completing the project, Yotek received contracts worth nearly 700 million birr to do additional work around Hawassa—more than four times the amount of the initial contract. Engineers noted that a desire to maintain a positive working relationship with the municipal government led them to accept the smaller extension and rush to complete the project on time. Again, specific relationships, both financial and personal, were key in smoothing over irregularities that could delay construction.

Living with Construction

If the dense, unplanned residences on Taddesse Enjore Road created problems for Yotek Construction, the construction also disturbed neighborhood residents. Living with road construction is always difficult, but delays of that construction compound and extend difficulties. I observed changes in the road over a period of six months. As other roads were being rapidly completed, progress on the Taddesse Enjore Road was slow (figure 2.3). In November 2013 the road was bulldozed. Widening the road peeled back a layer of fences and outer walls, revealing interior spaces where clothes were washed and meals prepared. Families quickly replaced fences with simple stick and tin barriers to create space between the road and their homes.

In December a shopkeeper told me that "leaving the road like this, unfinished, creates all kinds of problems. The air is full of dust. People have started to leave their trash here. There used to be houses but now there are just piles of dirt and trash. The engineers come every day, they look at the road, and then they get back in their cars and drive off." By February 2014, Yotek had pushed much of this dirt and trash into what residents jokingly called "mountains," which were large enough to block the road to vehicles larger than a Bajaj. Two weeks later the mountains of dirt were smoothed out and the road was passable. In March a big storm rolled through and knocked out power and water in the entire city. Along the road piles of gravel were head-high, and the rain created massive puddles that were hard to avoid. A week later a drainage ditch was dug and eliminated much of the standing water. The rains continued, however, and by April it became clear that the ditch was not adequate. My shopkeeper friend, who rarely had anything good to say about the construction, noted that "the big pools of water never dry up. Children and elders can't move through the neighborhood. There are no streetlights here, so it is especially dangerous at night. If you look over there, across the street, you can see where a couple of toilets were bulldozed when they widened the road. There is a terrible smell that comes from there on hot days."

FIGURE 2.3. Tadesse Enjore Road under construction. Photo by the author.

In early May major work began on the Taddesse Enjore Road. Ditches, approximately twelve feet deep, were excavated on one side of the road. Cement pipes, around three feet in diameter, were crowded in the center of the road, ready for placement in the ditches (figure 2.4). The pipes would be used for drainage and eventually covered with a sidewalk, but at the time there was only a thin dirt path (two feet wide) between compound fences and the ditch. The ditch was far too wide to jump across, and it could only be crossed by using two bridges made from single wooden planks. Eshetayehu and I spoke with an older woman who lived alongside the road. "The ditch is very frightening," she explained. "I can't leave my house. My grandchildren help me go to funerals and church, or else I do not leave."

Living with road construction is difficult, but the long-term impacts of the finished road weighed most heavily on the minds of community members. Residents certainly noted potential benefits from the road, including reduced dust and the possibility of opening new businesses. For example, an older woman explained that she expected to sell *tella* (home-brewed beer) from her house once the asphalt was finished. By May 2014, six months after the initial demolition, at least one new shop had opened in the area, and

FIGURE 2.4. Drainage pipes on Tadesse Enjore Road. Photo by the author.

others were under construction. Shop owners explained that the road motivated them to start businesses. More generally, however, the reaction to the road was decidedly negative. Many residents claimed that the changes would only benefit the wealthy. As one resident argued, "No one in this neighborhood has the resources to take advantage of the opportunities the road will bring." Even the woman who planned to open a tella house tempered her optimism, explaining that the road will bring high-rises and large hotels, and a great deal of money will be necessary to take advantage of these opportunities.

In the Taddesse Enjore neighborhood I often observed the sort of livelihoods that are possible in the city center—women preparing two kilograms of unprocessed cotton for sale at the market, a woman collecting plastic bags that would later be sold, shops selling vegetables in very small quantities, less than a quarter kilogram at a time. Many of the residents had been in the neighborhood for twenty to thirty years. Their livelihoods depended on the cultural and economic dynamics of the inner city. They made their living buying and selling small amounts of goods for a limited profit. Success depended on close relationships with their community that provided access to cheap goods and information. The proximity to the central market also meant that residents did not need to pay for transportation, and this protected their limited profit margin. Residents improvised livelihoods in the sense that they adapted their economic behavior to the specific conditions of the moment.

As the former administrator quoted above explained, “roads pull.” On Taddesse Enjore Road the new asphalt has already begun to attract significant investment, and it is unlikely that a tella house could be successful here. The asphalt will support redevelopment of the neighborhood in a way that leaves little financial or social space for residents. In May 2015 the Taddesse Enjore Road was complete—a smooth asphalt road with two lanes of traffic traveling in each direction (see figure 2.5). The economic implications of the road were already apparent, as many of the residents had opened small shops in front of their homes and built rooms to rent. Those living along the road expressed a range of reactions. Some expressed feelings of excitement and awe for the new asphalt. Others were more ambivalent. Eshetayehu and I spoke with a young woman whose family opened a small shop after the road had been completed. The shop rented video games and offered space where customers could pay a small fee to use a video game console. Despite the profits that her family earned, she explained, “This road is dangerous for us. We don’t know what will happen, but I expect we will be resettled. Many of my friends and neighbors have been moved. For a young person this is not so difficult, but for elders who have been here a long time it is very hard.” She acknowledged that the asphalt was very good for business, but like others in the neighborhood she assumed that her family would be pushed out when a large commercial developer was ready to invest. In 2017 the business was still operating and had expanded to sell athletic equipment. Another woman expressed similar stress about the unknown future that the road would bring. “I don’t know the future and this is stressful. My neighbors were forced to move and this will probably happen to me. I will go if necessary, but I would prefer to build a shop here. But, without money I can’t build anything. Even if I could build a shop I might be forced to leave it behind. The road is good for the city, but not for us. Even when life is hard, we live with our neighbors and this is good.” The woman’s statement highlights the importance of social relationships, particularly in times of distress and uncertainty, but it is precisely these relationships that the road threatened.

By December 2017 a three-story building containing a high-end barbershop, liquor store, and men’s suit shop was open for business. In the case of the suit shop, the owner was paying more than 6,000 birr per month for rent.[14] She had moved to Hawassa from Addis Ababa to open the shop and

FIGURE 2.5. Tadesse Enjore Road, new asphalt. Photo by the author.

noted that although Addis was probably better for business, she preferred the clean and quiet environment in Hawassa. More small coffee houses, bars, and restaurants were popping up along the street. For the first time, I spoke to residents who were eager to be resettled. These residents lived in government-owned (*kebelle*) houses and expressed little interest in opening a business. “I am ready to leave,” claimed a middle-aged woman who was born and raised in the same house where she currently lived. “The government will give me a new house and it will be very good.” Others who had access to more resources had built small shops in front of their residences and hoped to expand further. In one case a family rented out two small shops, each for 700 birr per month. They wanted to develop their business further but recognized that they may not be able to compete with large commercial investors.

After living through the construction, many Taddesse Enjore residents did not believe they could take advantage of the road. Without stable incomes and access to land it was difficult for them to establish the sort of business that could be competitive in central Hawassa. Their precarious strategies for surviving from one day to the next depended on the specific conditions of the Taddesse Enjore neighborhood. To remain in the neighborhood, new strategies would be necessary. Some were opening shops and businesses to take advantage of the road, but others had given up on the neighborhood and were waiting for resettlement.

Asphalt Roads Push Out Improvised Livelihoods

The lives of those who remained in the Taddesse Enjore neighborhood were transformed, but those whom the government resettled experienced even more significant changes. At least six families from the Taddesse Enjore neighborhood were resettled in the Doro Arbata area (others from Taddesse Enjore were resettled elsewhere). Doro Arbata takes its name from the poultry farm behind which it is located, on the southwest edge of the city near the base of Alla Mura Mountain. Families displaced by development projects around the city were resettled in Doro Arbata, and they found living conditions that were far below what they were accustomed to (figure 2.6). No water pipes were present, and water had to be purchased and delivered for 2 birr per jerry can. By 2017 a few families had paid more than 2,500 birr to install a faucet on their property, but most still relied on water delivery. The ever-growing population of resettled families created opportunities for boys with donkey carts to deliver jerry cans of water, and in 2017 the price had increased to 3 birr per jerry can. Initially there was no electricity, and when it finally arrived there was often not enough power to illuminate even a single light bulb for a household.

Eshetayehu and I interviewed the head of the Housing and Resettlement Office in his dusty office. Hawassa residents continually interrupted our meeting with demands for housing or some form of assistance. The official explained that "resettlement is necessary to attract investment and support development. We must put families in outlying areas such as Doro Arbata because there is no space available in the city center. I know life in Doro Arbata is not perfect, but we must make sacrifices for development." Families in Doro Arbata recognized the futility of appealing to government administrators and politicians for support. One woman explained, "The politicians won't even let their son into their bedrooms, while I sleep side-by-side with other families every night," referencing the fact that her family shared a house with other families.

There were other challenges in addition to the lack of water and electricity. The Taddesse Enjore neighborhood is in the city center, and residents rarely need to use public transportation. The cost of reaching the market from Doro Arbata by Bajaj was at least 10 birr, round trip—much more

FIGURE 2.6. Housing for those resettled in Doro Arbata. Photo by the author.

if large amounts of goods were being carried. Walking from Doro Arbata takes three hours for a round trip. The distance from the market and lack of population density in Doro Arbata made petty trade and the sale of goods such as homemade beer and bread impossible.

Most of the families resettled to Doro Arbata were headed by women. James Scott (1998) draws on Jane Jacobs's work to argue that women, particularly those in cities, are more often embedded in multiple overlapping tasks than men. This is certainly true in much of urban Ethiopia, where women are responsible for caring for children, earning an income, preparing food, shopping, and numerous other tasks. Men rarely do more than earn an income and socialize with other men. Ethiopian women are also far more likely than men to earn a living from petty trade and other small-scale entrepreneurial activities. Given their marginal status, not only are women more likely to be resettled than men, but resettlement will more likely have a significant negative impact on their lives.

When families arrived in Doro Arbata, many houses had unfinished walls and no doors or windows. Resettled families paid to finish their house from their own pocket. Houses also lacked proper toilets and space for cooking. The residents from Taddesse Enjore are better off than others who were resettled to Doro Arbata, however. In some cases, three families shared a single room house divided by sheets for privacy.

Struggles with a lack of infrastructure and proper housing conditions were compounded by the shift in cultural context from the Taddesse Enjore to the Doro Arbata neighborhood. Of the resettled residents Eshetayehu and I interviewed, all had lived in the city center for at least thirty years. Resettled residents used the image of hyenas to convey the contrast between the city center and Doro Arbata. "In the evening," one explained, "we can't leave our house. There are hyenas everywhere." Without electricity in the neighborhood, hyenas crowded on the edge of town every evening at sunset. The hyenas trapped people in their houses, and after darkness came they were unable to move between the city and their home. The resettled were denied not only the economic benefits of urban development but also the city and the modern future that it offered.

For these residents the loss of their neighborhood *idder* was a particularly stressful experience. An idder is a funeral association, and most urban Ethiopians are members of at least one. An older woman cried when she spoke about the lack of space for a funeral tent in the new Doro Arbata neighborhood. Resettled residents continually came back to this point, noting that there is no space to mourn properly. They initially maintained their membership in their old neighborhood idder and did not see leaving as an option. One woman asked, "If I leave what will happen if I die tomorrow? Who will mourn for me? Will there only be twenty people at my funeral?" Resettled residents continued to return to their old neighborhood to participate in idder meetings and attend funerals.[15]

Social relationships are an essential aspect of the human infrastructure that takes the place of the often failing material infrastructures in many African cities. In the Taddesse Enjore neighborhood, the new physical infrastructure radically destroyed the preexisting human infrastructure. Just as the new road connected some residents with people, things, and business opportunities, it disconnected others from the social relationships they depended on. Commercial development often produces displacement. Growth in the center pushes inner-city residents to the periphery. The dense, intersecting networks of relationships that Taddesse Enjore residents depended on were based in the specific spatial dynamics of the neighborhood. The issue of disconnection is particularly acute in older, inner-city neighborhoods, where residents have had the time to create a vast infrastructure of social relationships. Improvisation requires making decisions on the basis of conditions that are often temporary, but these improvisations are based on long-standing relationships. Laments about the loss of the idder represent a broader sense of loss of the relationships that are necessary for improvisation.

Preserving Regularity

The issue of resettlement has one additional layer, and that is the question of why those who are resettled do not simply rent houses in the city center. When I made a brief research visit to Doro Arbata in 2015, residents reported that few, if any, of those who had been resettled had left to find housing closer to the city center. I asked a group of those who were resettled from Taddesse Enjore about the possibility of renting a private house, and they responded that at 500 birr per month, it would be far too expensive. I pointed out that they face numerous expenses living so far from the city center—water, transport, and most important, a loss of work. Some of the families who were resettled in Doro Arbata have jobs that pay regular salaries, and they could easily afford the cost of house rent. They responded that renting a private house brings other stresses. House owners continually increase the rent and may force one to leave with very little notice. These are good reasons to stay in Doro Arbata, but the decision does not seem to be entirely economic. Although resettlement severs important relations with one's community, it does preserve at least one very significant relationship: one's connection with the state. Those who are resettled in Doro Arbata continue to live in state-provided housing. The housing is free, and this is important, but perhaps equally significant is that the housing is provided by the state. The resettled residents preserve the possibility that the state will provide better housing in a more desirable location at some point in the future. If those who are resettled choose to rent a private house, the state's obligation to provide housing is lost and they are exposed to an increasingly expensive rental market. The state does nothing for private renters who lose their homes because of urban redevelopment.

In some ways the decision to remain in Doro Arbata involves maintaining a degree of regulated formality in lives that are highly dependent on precarious improvisations. Connections with the state can be very valuable in the context of rapid urban development. Although Doro Arbata is very much on the periphery of Hawassa now, it is likely that this dynamic will change soon. Asphalt and regularization will quickly reach this neighborhood in what was the very edge of the city. When it does, the resettled residents living in state-owned housing will be able to make a claim to some level of state support. They may be pushed out once again, but at least they are in a position to make demands on the state, which is far better than simply being cast aside and left to fend for themselves amid a rapidly changing real estate market. Those who remained in Doro Arbata sought to construct and maintain multiple types of relationships. At least initially, they invested time and money in returning to their old neighborhoods for the funerals that are so important for social life. Over time they formed idders with their new neighbors, including both the resettled and rural residents who preceded the expansion of the city. They also maintained their contact with a state. Despite their complaints about the resettlement process, Doro Arbata residents recognize that the state is a valuable resource for the future, and they are not willing to walk away from these potential benefits.

Informal settlements in Hawassa also had a complex relationship with regularization. Hawassa's head urban planner noted that informal settlements often conformed to plans for future roads. Indeed, many of Hawassa's newer informal settlements, located near new asphalt roads, are organized in a regular grid pattern. The municipal urban planner suspected that someone within the city government was communicating with community leaders in informal settlements, advising them where to build houses so that they would not be destroyed when neighborhoods were eventually regularized. Personal relationships seemed to be used in order to conform to city plans in a way that facilitated the regularization of informality. Urban residents strategically manipulated the boundaries between regularization and informality to advance their own interests.[16]

Conclusion

Although the maps and plans of urban administrators are often far more flexible than they seem, the material qualities of asphalt roads are inseparable from the production of regularity. Land must be graded, houses must be cleared, and paths must be straightened and widened. Specific irregular conditions—in the form of politics, the urban landscape, and informal settlements—present a challenge for construction, sometimes entirely preventing the completion of roads. Administrators, planners, and engineers improvise to circumvent these irregularities. In Hawassa, government administrators violated laws to finance roads and deal with obstacles created by preexisting informal settlements. These extralegal practices supported the timely completion of asphalt roads and allowed Hawassa to move forward, as residents and government administrators actualized their visions for progress and a modern city. The same asphalt roads that were constructed through improvised practices transformed older inner-city neighborhoods where residents have long relied on precarious, improvised livelihoods.

Road construction in Hawassa demonstrates that not all forms of human infrastructure are created equally. The social networks that powerful male politicians used to smooth over bureaucratic barriers to building asphalt roads are quite different from the relationships among women heads of household in the Taddesse Enjore neighborhood, which were essential for engaging in petty trade. Humans function as infrastructures, but humans differ in terms of gender, class, and ethnicity, among other factors. The elite male social networks that moved massive amounts of money to build asphalt roads were at odds with the social relationships that reproduced life in inner-city Hawassa. Both relied on improvisations to negotiate changing and unstable conditions. However, one set of improvisations was far more precarious than the other. The construction of infrastructures such as asphalt roads relies on elite networks and social relationships.

Asphalt roads project an illusion of permanence that may be shattered by examining the construction process. Walking along the finished asphalt road in the Taddesse Enjore neighborhood in 2017, little evidence indicated the struggles that took place during the process of construction. It is during the process of construction that improvised human infrastructures are particularly important. Engineers and government administrators negotiate over cost and construction techniques, and the outcome of these negotiations may partially explain the differences between cities such as Jimma and Hawassa. Long-term relationships between neighbors, which are anything but temporary, also allow residents to improvise and deal with the social and environmental transformations associated with new asphalt roads.

Attention to the construction process is a reminder of contingency and an important caution against adopting simplified narratives of temporal change. Neither the failure of Jimma nor the relative success of Hawassa is inevitable. Both are contingent on the possibility of improvisation in response to irregular, shifting conditions.[17] In the time of construction, different human infrastructures compete with each other over the building of material infrastructures and the production of possible futures. It is through elite improvisations that the construction of roads simultaneously builds and destroys a city. The same roads that have attracted investments such as the new three-story shopping complex on Taddesse Enjore Road have also undermined the precarious improvised livelihoods of the inner-city poor. As I explore in the following chapter, this complex relationship between construction and destruction shaped urban residents' affective relationships with the state.

THREE. Feeling Change through Dirt and Water

The Affective Politics of Urban Development in Jimma, 2009–2015

In May 2015 I was back in Jimma for another visit, eating a breakfast of scrambled eggs and injera at a hotel near the bus station, just across the street from where I had stayed when I first visited the city in 2001. This hotel was not here then. None of the multistoried hotels were. The only large building in the area that I remember being under construction in 2001 was still not finished in 2015. It remained a concrete skeleton. As with most neighborhoods in Jimma, the area around the bus station had changed dramatically, and yet much was the same. For me the neighborhood still had a comfortable familiarity, even amid the nearly constant construction.

The national election for parliamentary seats, held once every five years, was just a few days away. The ruling party held around 99 percent of the seats in Parliament, and there was not a great deal of excitement about this election—at least among the residents of Jimma. The broadcasters on Ethiopian Television (ETV), however, were quite excited. Watching ETV as I ate my eggs, I had trouble differentiating between the news and advertisements for the ruling EPRDF party. Both consisted almost entirely of stories of successful development. When music played over a video montage of trains, roads, bridges, and power stations, I knew that I was watching an advertisement. During a historical overview of the positive relationships that the former prime minister Meles Zenawi had established with international leaders, however, the distinction was less clear.[1]

The prime minister, Hailemariam Desalegn, and the president of the Oromia region were in town, accompanied by soldiers and police riding in the open beds of trucks and standing around busy intersections. The government officials had come to inaugurate projects aimed at supporting infrastructural development and economic growth—in this case a new train line and an industrial park. These celebratory inaugurations would eventually be broadcast on television and radio. A friend joked that "these politicians are very smart; they inaugurate so many projects right before the election. They celebrate the project's beginning to make us think the project will fall apart if the EPRDF is not reelected."

For urban Ethiopians, the state's legitimacy is inseparable from infrastructural development. Legitimacy, however, is not necessarily based on a calculation of the costs and benefits of various infrastructural projects. Rather, it is better understood in terms of affective attachments to governments, infrastructural technologies, and temporalities. My conversations with cab drivers in Addis Ababa upon arriving in Ethiopia are always essential for orienting myself to the country's current political dynamics and the mood of the people. During one of my rides in 2015, the driver was highly critical of the ruling party, claiming that no one in his neighborhood supported the EPRDF. Then the conversation turned to infrastructure. "Most of the road construction in Addis Ababa is finished," he explained. "Five new roads were inaugurated just a few days ago. The light rail will start soon, and it is going to be much easier to get around the city. Huge hydroelectric dams are being finished. All of these are good things."

"Why," I asked, "if the government is doing so many positive things for Ethiopia's development do so many people continue to oppose the EPRDF?"

The cab driver's response was brief: "Even a bad person does good every once in a while." In other words, all of the investments the state was making in infrastructural technologies were having minimal impact on people's attitudes concerning the ruling party. The state was a bad person. What makes people perceive a state as good or bad? Why are people attracted to some political leaders and repulsed by others? The state's accomplishments are certainly part of any answer to this question, but one's feelings for an object, a person, or a state are always more complex than this. The state's legitimacy is an intimate relationship that is based in sensation, mood, emotion, feeling, and attachment. Affect provides a means of conceptualizing these intensities. Political messages are communicated through affect, but neither the sender nor the receiver of the message is necessarily immediately conscious of its content.[2]

An example of affective communication: During conversations, Ethiopians often interject a sharp inhalation of air as they listen. It sounds like a small gasp. The listener does not intentionally gasp. It just happens. The speaker hears and sees the gasp, but she is not necessarily conscious of what was communicated. The gasp is visceral and emotive. It involves the whole body. The gasp does not represent a specific word; rather it communicates a sense of affirmation and assent. When someone gasps as I am speaking I experience a subtle pleasure, a very low-level physical sensation. It is a powerful feeling but not necessarily one I recognize in the moment. Ideas and beliefs about the state are often formed through similar types of communication. In Ethiopia, affective politics occurs through infrastructures rather than through individual political personalities. The state deploys images of infrastructure in political posters, but affective communication is rarely this simple. A more intense form of affective political communication occurs through the process of building a city. When the city feels different, politics feel different as well. As urban Ethiopians carefully walk on muddy roads, they may not be consciously aware that political communication is taking place, but they are developing feelings for the state, and materials such as mud eventually find their way into political critiques. It is through construction that urban Ethiopians feel the state and grapple with its legitimacy.

In this chapter I explore three key dimensions of affective politics in urban Ethiopia: temporality, sensory experience, and the intimate politics of exchange.[3] The experience of rapid change in one's lived environment is the foundation for affective politics in urban Ethiopia. Despite the pre-election cynicism regarding state-led development, residents had few doubts that, for better or for worse, Jimma had changed dramatically during the past ten years. In 2005 I finished eighteen months of fieldwork in Jimma. I returned for short two- to six-week visits in 2008, 2009, 2012, and 2015.[4] During those visits my conversations always seemed to begin with the question, "What's new?" This line of conversation was in part how I caught up with old friends, but it was also a response to the boom in the construction of roads and buildings, particularly in the city center, where I had focused my long-term research. Jimma residents were interested not only in documenting changes in their city but in assessing the rate of change. They asked themselves, Is change occurring fast enough? Is the city moving in the right direction? What possible futures are within reach? And perhaps most important, Has there been progress? Has life improved?

Although questions of development and transformation were particularly salient at the time of the 2015 election, given the rapid transformation of Jimma between 2009 and 2015, these issues were never far from people's minds. At its heart, development is about change. Development assumes that life should change and that change should occur in a specific direction. Growth and its desirability are the basic assumptions of development. These temporal dynamics are intertwined with affective politics. What does development feel like? How does it feel to have one's home transformed completely? How do feelings about one's environment translate to feelings about the state? Answering these questions is essential for connecting affect with legitimacy.

Change is sensed (Parr 2010; Schwenkel 2015a). It is felt through the dust from road construction; it is heard in the sounds of heavy construction equipment; and it is experienced visually through ongoing power outages. Sensations of change and infrastructural development shape people's feelings for the state. This process is mediated by specific materials such as dirt, water, asphalt, and cobblestone. Through these materials, the city is built and people feel change. These materials are also incorporated into people's discursive practices as they assess the role of the state in promoting progress. An affective politics emerges from sensory experience and incorporates sensuous materials into political critique.

As with intimate relationships in much of Africa (Cole and Thomas 2009), affective citizen–state relationships in urban Ethiopia are shaped by exchanges—in this case, exchanges surrounding infrastructural development. Citizens provided both financial contributions and political allegiance, while the state was expected to provide infrastructure. When those intimate relations of exchange broke down, citizen–state relationships eroded as well, shifting from a sense of care to one of mutual distrust. To the extent that Jimma residents felt they had been personally rejected or forgotten, the state's legitimacy was undermined.

This chapter covers a roughly six-year period that was shaped by plans for development designed by the Ethiopian government in cooperation with the IMF and the World Bank. In my first book I examined how young men evaluated their lives in terms of linear narratives of progress. In this chapter I return to some of these men and explore their shifting engagement with the future and the passage of time. I begin in 2009, near the end of Ethiopia's five-year Plan for Accelerated and Sustained Development to End Poverty, when major road construction projects were just beginning in Jimma. At that time Jimma residents spoke about road construction projects with a mix of hope, uncertainty, and skepticism. Feelings for the state were caught up in discussions of progress and imagined futures as people grappled with a period of rapid change. By 2012 much of that hope had faded as road construction and other projects had stalled and in some cases actually went backward. In 2015, at the time of the national election, many roads had finally been finished, and it was clear that Jimma had been transformed. However, residents still claimed that this transformation was inadequate, and they desired a deeper, more abstract sense of change. The first half of this chapter describes a recent history of change and construction, and the second half examines the politics of affect that emerged from the construction process.

Progress, Displacement, and Hope

In the early 2000s two asphalt roads cut through Jimma's densely populated city center. Just off one of these roads was a one-room house where a young woman named Frehiwot lived with her parents. I first met Frehiwot in 2004. Her family's house was simple: a single room with well-swept dirt floors, two beds, and a few stools and benches. Frehiwot's mother was a compact woman with sharp eyes. She moved to Jimma from the surrounding countryside in the early 1970s and she sold locally distilled liquor out of her home to make a living. Frehiwot's father was a butcher, but by the time we met he no longer worked.

Anyone walking by could see into Frehiwot's house, and in this neighborhood, where everyone knew everyone, generally all were welcome. It was a house where people gathered to sit on stools, drink coffee, and tell stories. Frehiwot lived in a neighborhood where a person with limited means could make a living. With so many people and so much commerce, it was not difficult to sell liquor and beer out of one's home.

In 2008 Frehiwot told me that her family would be forced to move. With the renewal of roads in the neighborhood, a large building for coffee sellers would be constructed where her home was, and the state would give her family a house on the edge of town. The new neighborhood was in a low-lying area known to be full of mosquitoes. The friends and neighbors who had always been inseparable from Frehiwot's life would no longer be present. Few potential customers lived in the new neighborhood, and it was not clear how her mother could make a living.

When I walked by Frehiwot's house in 2009 it was shut off from the street by a corrugated metal fence. Construction had not begun on the new building. I asked some of the local youth what happened to Frehiwot. They said her family moved to the new house, and she was gone. Her brother had sent her to Dubai to work as a domestic servant.

The destruction of Frehiwot's house was part of a larger process of state-led urban renewal in Jimma, one related to the EPRDF's increased attention to urban development. The most visible element of the plan was the construction of roads. Roads throughout the city were scraped away, eventually to be replaced with fresh asphalt. The road near Frehiwot's house was like this. Dirt had been pushed into large piles at the end of each block, creating deep pools of water and making the roads very difficult to navigate, especially at night.

Frehiwot's was not the only family forced to make way for commercial development, and it is easy to imagine suspicion and controversy regarding road construction, similar to what I encountered concerning other projects. In this case, however, I heard few critiques of state-led development. At least in 2008 and 2009, among residents there was a general sense of enthusiasm about the construction of roads and Jimma's renewal.

Frehiwot's old house was just a few blocks from a house where friends of mine would often gather to chew khat (a leaf that releases a mild stimulant when chewed). In the hot and noisy city, Ahmed's house was a cool and quiet oasis. When I visited in the afternoon, Ahmed and his friends were usually lounging on floor mats chewing khat and talking. My closest friend who spent time at Ahmed's house was a teacher named Getachew. Unlike during most of my conversations and interviews, Getachew and I spoke primarily English. At one of these gatherings Getachew expressed a surprising degree of enthusiasm for the government's urban renewal projects. As a Turkish soap opera played quietly on the television, he explained that there is only one possibility for "Third World cities to develop": push people out of desirable areas.

> Unless and otherwise, development will never occur! People simply build houses without having permission from the government. These houses are crowded together and they don't conform to any plan. . . . The city has a master plan. The master plan designates certain areas for business, living, and recreation. To encourage the city to grow according to the plan, the government will give the residents two options. When the

government improves an area by building a new road, the residents can improve their homes and businesses to fit with the new standard or sell their property and move somewhere else.

At this point I was getting a little uncomfortable with Getachew's monologue. I interrupted: "Won't people be reluctant to move away from homes where they've lived their entire lives?"

"No! People are happy to give up their homes. When a new modern building appears next to their home they won't be comfortable there. They might be forced to move to a neighborhood on the edge of the city where they don't know anyone, but chances are that the new house will be larger than the old one. Most people will welcome this change."

Getachew explained that the government had promised to finish the road as soon as possible. A telethon fundraiser was scheduled at the Sheraton in Addis Ababa. Tewodros Teshome, a filmmaker who was born and raised in Frehiwot's neighborhood, would host the event, and people from all over the country would call in and donate money to support development in Jimma. All of the teachers had agreed to contribute one month of their salary to the road project. Getachew claimed that although teachers actually had little choice in the matter, they were relatively happy to support the road project because they recognized that the roads are something good and necessary for their community.[5] An unemployed young woman told me that she donated five birr and she would have given ten if she could afford it. With great enthusiasm she announced, "It makes me feel wonderful to be able to give even a small amount of money to help my country!"

Such sincere support for a state project was rare in Ethiopia, and yet I encountered many people who equated roads with progress. Specific interpretations of progress were not always clear, but it was certainly something worthy of sacrifice. Sometimes people offered more complicated explanations of the importance of roads. Roads promote the movement of goods, which increases commerce and economic growth. Better roads will most likely decrease the cost of Ethiopian goods sold both domestically and internationally. More commerce should bring more jobs, and with high urban youth unemployment, young Ethiopians were desperately in need of work.

Whether it was giving five birr or a month's salary, donations to road projects implied that a major investment was taking place, both financially and emotionally, and this provided a good feeling to those who donated. This dynamic is shaped by an Ethiopian context in which power relations have long been legitimized by the perception that those in power protect and support their subordinates (Hoben 1970, 1973; Poluha 2004). In his work on land tenure among rural Amhara in northern Ethiopia, Allan Hoben (1970, 1973) explained that relations of power were almost entirely vertical and were generally structured along the lines of a patron–client relationship. Put simply, lords provided a degree of protection for peasants and sometimes assisted them in litigating for land; in turn, peasants paid taxes in the form of grain and labor, and gave their lords social and political support. In this sense, the continued power of the lord was based in part on his ability to provide tangible benefits for his subjects. With urbanization, government employment took the place of nobility as a source of power and a means of distributing favors to others, and education replaced military activity as a means for accessing social mobility (Hoben 1970, 222).

Although the ideologies and structures of rule have clearly changed, Eva Poluha (2004) has argued—on the basis of research conducted among children in Addis Ababa—that the patron–client model represents a source of continuity in Ethiopian power relationships, extending from the prerevolutionary period, through the Derg, to the current EPRDF regime.[6] Under the revolutionary Derg, the state increasingly sought to legitimize itself through large-scale development, but the patron–client model has persisted as an important dynamic for structuring relations of power. Like the power relationships Hoben described, in contemporary urban Ethiopia subordinate individuals and groups accept and support the rule of others as long as they are provided with social, emotional, and economic safety (Poluha 2004, 95). In interviews I conducted in the early 2000s concerning unemployment, young men and women often said it is the government's responsibility to provide them with an education and a job, and they blamed the state for the problem of unemployment. Although young people had little faith that the government would solve their problems, on a personal level they sought to form relationships with government workers in order to receive increased access to opportunities for education, work, and housing.

The gift of financial support created a relationship between citizens, state, and roads. Those I spoke with assumed that this relationship would be reciprocal in a way that mirrored valued patron–client relations associated with the state. Citizens give money and the state gives back in the form of roads. Roads would bring benefits for all. The relationship between Jimma residents and the state was based on a mutual willingness to fulfill a need of the other.

Despite the displacement of families such as Frehiwot's, with road construction just beginning residents felt a sense of hope that the city would be transformed in a way that fit people's progressive ideals for the future. Established rhythms and social relationships were certainly being transformed and disrupted, but at this point in the process Jimma residents had a sense that these sacrifices might be a small price to pay for progress. When they described their enthusiasm and willingness to donate to road construction projects, they were expressing a positive relationship with the state. Citizen and state were collaborating on a shared vision of the future. People I spoke with did not articulate in detail the good feeling that came from supporting road construction, but in relation to the state there was, at least briefly, a sense of trust and togetherness that I have rarely encountered in urban Ethiopia. Whether it meant giving up a portion of one's salary or one's home, some Jimma residents were willing to endure hardship if it supported linear growth and development.

Hydropower, Seepage, and Suspicion

Relative to the hydropower projects I discussed in chapter 1, the Gibe I Dam, located near Jimma, was small, costing around $200 million and generating 180 megawatts of power. The Gibe I Dam came on line in 2004. A few years later, in 2009, the Ethiopian government began scheduling rolling twenty-four-hour power blackouts for the entire country. Half the country received power for twenty-four hours and then the other half received power. Without power, the ambient experience of life in Jimma was transformed. By 7:30 p.m. Jimma was almost completely dark, with just a few candles flickering in the windows of kiosks. Large hotels were marked by the rumble of a generator and dull light illuminating the windows. The lack of light did not stop Jimma residents from taking their usual evening stroll along the city's main avenues. The difference was that it was now very difficult to identify other walkers, making the exchange of greetings nearly impossible. Life during the day changed as well. Small businesses such as barbershops and coffee houses, which relied on electricity but could not afford a generator, were forced to close every other day. This did not stop some owners from showing up at their workplace, if only to hang out and chat with their neighbors.

In 2009 the dam, blackouts, and critiques of the state dominated my conversations, many of which took place at my friend Ahmed's house. Getachew and I often talked about the Gibe River Dam. Getachew, a lifelong

Jimma resident, explained that when he was born about fifty years ago there was no problem with electricity. Jimma initially received much of its power from a generator, and later from Finchaa Dam. Only when Gibe I became the primary source of power did the outages begin.

I told Getachew about a conversation I had with a friend who worked for the state electric power office. My friend's explanations were similar to those that had appeared in state-run media—the power cuts were due to supply and demand. Demand had increased for two reasons: first, there was more industry in Ethiopia than in the past, and second, the government had committed to providing electricity to at least 50 percent of the rural population. In terms of supply, Ethiopia relies entirely on hydroelectric power, and other power sources were needed to meet the additional demand created by bringing electricity to rural areas. When I mentioned the Gibe River Dam, my friend at the electric power office explained that the project was not finished. Furthermore, without more rain the dam could not supply adequate power.

These sounded like reasonable explanations, and yet according to Getachew they all were in some way flawed. "There is a lot of new industry near Addis Ababa," Getachew explained, "but almost none in the rest of the country. These new factories are not enough to be the cause of the blackouts. Supplying the countryside with power is difficult, this is true, but why would the government do this without adequate resources? If this is really the problem, then the government could easily reverse its decision and cut off electricity to the countryside." "What about the shortage of water?" I asked. "It's true, there is a shortage of water in Gil Gel Gibe," Getachew argued. "But it cannot be because of lack of rain. It has been raining. There is no denying that it has been raining. We have seen the rain."

Weather and water, in the form of rain, play significant roles in these competing explanations. On one hand, the state employee emphasized a lack of rain. In doing so he placed the failure of the dam outside the control of the state. The dam is failing because of weather and the government can do nothing about it. On the other hand, Getachew pointed to the obvious visibility of rain. The weather and the rain are apparent for all to see. They cannot be disputed. In this claim water was constructed as something tangible and easily understood—simple observation could determine its presence.

In the absence of an acceptable explanation, Getachew claimed that something else is happening, something secret: "seepage." The fact that no one could see where the water goes makes it all the more mysterious. It was a problem without a clear explanation, a secret that the government could not be expected to reveal. In contrast to his discussion of the visibility of rain, here Getachew pointed to the unseen properties of water. He knew that water may seep into the ground or evaporate into the air, but neither of these processes could be directly observed. The loss of water was suspected, perhaps even firmly believed, but Getachew and other Jimma residents lacked identifiable evidence to confirm their hunches.

The actual technology involved in hydropower is important, as it is both visible and hidden. From the road that connects Jimma to Addis Ababa one may see a large body of water that was not previously present, but all else remains hidden. Many Jimma residents do not even have a chance to get this small glimpse of the dam. Although water is often spoken of in terms of its clarity and transparency, in practice a large body of water may obscure more than it reveals. If water were seeping into the soil, how would anyone know? Seepage takes place entirely beneath the surface. The process of generating power is also murky. How can the generation of electricity be observed, and who knows where that electricity travels?

The state's plan to sell electricity to neighboring nations was well known, and many suspected that this was the cause of the power shortages. They believed that Ethiopia lacked electrical power because it was being sold to Sudan and Kenya, and that the Ethiopian government was keeping the profits. Similar rumors were common regarding negotiations over the Ethiopia–Sudan border. Urban residents often claimed that the Ethiopian state willingly made deals with Sudan that led to a loss of land and resources. The implication was that government officials were more likely to collaborate with other states in order to line their own pockets than to act in the interests of Ethiopian citizens.

Like a loss of water through seepage, urban Ethiopians could not access definitive evidence regarding the generation and sale of electrical power. Large-scale infrastructural projects are notorious for their lack of transparency and create numerous opportunities for money to seep away and disappear. Salini Impregilo was building all the Gibe projects and the GERD on the Nile River. The lack of transparency in awarding these contracts drew accusations of corruption from international observers (Fantini and Puddu 2016; Hathaway 2008). Getachew and others I spoke with shared narratives filled with confusion and suspicion. They had little faith in the explanations advanced through state-run media linking the power shortages to broader development projects. The visibility and invisibility of water created a fertile environment for rumors concerning the actions of the state and private corporations.

In practice, seepage and evaporation represent real issues for controlling a substance such as water. Water wants to move. The pull of gravity causes water to flow into any space that is available. This is part of the reason why hydropower is possible in the first place—water may be contained and corralled by impermeable materials and then released in a controlled flow that generates power. At the same time, the fluid nature of water represents a constant challenge. The instability and unpredictability of water and earth was perhaps most apparent at the second Gibe hydroelectric project, which consisted of a series of underground tunnels for channeling water and generating electricity. The project cost around $500 million and was expected to generate 420 megawatts of power. Shortly after the dam came on line in 2010, a portion of an underground tunnel collapsed, setting back power generation by one year. Critiques such as Getachew's recognize this instability and use it to question the state's ability to develop adequate urban infrastructure.

Jimma residents experienced a wide variety of affective responses to these early stages of construction and transformation. It is significant that Getachew—the same person who argued that, in the case of roads, displacement and disruption are necessary for progress—was highly suspicious of the dam project. Getachew expressed the somewhat contradictory feelings of hope and suspicion. Both are based in the connection between the material dimensions of development projects and perceptions of time. He was hopeful that road construction and urban renewal would support progress toward a different, more modern future. However, he used the qualities of water and the process of seepage to express suspicion regarding the state's ability to carry out this project. Faith in road construction was sustained by the perception of a positive and nurturing relationship between citizen and state. Suspicion regarding the efficacy of the Gibe I dam was connected to a sense of doubt that the state would act in the interests of citizens. In the following section I tell how hope and suspicion combine to form a general feeling of uncertainty. In 2009 Jimma residents had a feeling that things could go right and a relatively high degree of trust in the state, but in the context of rolling blackouts, such optimism was always heavily tempered with doubt.

Uncertainty and the Coming Transformation

In 2009 the air in Jimma was filled with dust from construction and the increasing number of motorized vehicles on the road. I particularly noticed it talking to my friend Tafiq at his workplace along the main road leading to the city center and market, where he sold socks and other small items. I first met Tafiq and some of the other petty traders in the area in 2002. Some of these young men participated in my research in 2003–5, and in the process I became particularly good friends with Tafiq. By 2009, Tafiq was in his mid-thirties. I always felt welcome to pull up a stool and sit and talk as Tafiq worked, but now spending time with him was not as pleasant as in years past. The noise of the traffic had grown, and I had to yell to be heard. The dust was thick. Parts of the road were under construction and every car that passed threw more dust into the air. I could feel it in my mouth, my throat, and my lungs—a layer of dust. I asked friends, "Which is better, dust or mud?" People enjoyed this line of conversation and consistently answered that mud is better. Mud you just wash off. Dust gets in your eyes and nose. It makes you sick.

When I first met Tafiq in the early 2000s he was living with his wife and daughter in a rented room near the city center. By 2008 he had two more daughters and had purchased a house on the outskirts of the city, in a rapidly growing neighborhood near Boye Swamp. A few years earlier this area had been an empty flood plain. With a house of his own, Tafiq began to invite me to his place for lunch whenever I visited Jimma, and between 2008 and 2015 I observed the gradual growth of his neighborhood. When Tafiq built his house there were only a few other residences, electricity had not yet reached the neighborhood, and the area was still swampy, especially during the rainy season. To get electricity the community had to pay for the power poles. The price was 800 birr per pole, and originally Tafiq was told that five poles would be required. By chance, one time when I was at Tafiq's house for lunch, a government representative showed up and insisted that eight poles were needed. Tafiq argued with him and refused to pay. Tafiq told me that he had a friend who works for the government electricity bureau and this other fellow who claimed that eight poles are necessary just wanted a bribe.

Tafiq's encounter with the worker from the state electricity bureau is just one glimpse of a growing pattern in which the government of Ethiopia has passed to residents the responsibility for accessing public services. Whereas in the past the state provided the infrastructure for transmitting electricity, now residents in newer neighborhoods were required to purchase the poles to support the electrical lines. As with replacing state-subsidized electricity with generators during the rolling blackouts, the costs for an expected service had been privatized. An opportunity for graft was also created. The government agent had the power to determine how much a community should pay to access electricity. Although Tafiq and his neighbors accepted the initial cost, they resisted when they were asked to purchase more poles than they thought necessary. This was not the same cost sharing as the small donations toward road building that created positive relations between citizen and state through reciprocal exchange. In demanding payment for additional poles, state representatives crossed a moral line. Residents such as Tafiq perceived the actions of those representatives as exploitative rather than enabling a mutually beneficial exchange, and an affective relationship between citizen and state was shifted to one of antagonism rather than cooperation.

As I spent time with Tafiq and his friends, discussions often turned to power outages. In speculating how the problem of powering a growing city could be solved, one of them mentioned that Jimma University had set aside land to build a biogas plant. I asked where this would be located. "In my neighborhood," Tafiq responded. "From the university to a plant near the swamp, waste will be moved downhill by pipe and then be used to generate power. If this brings power and we are finished with these blackouts, it will be good."

"What about the people living there now?" I asked, "Will they be pushed farther out? They are already on the edge of the city."

"Won't this make for an awful stench?" someone asked.

"What if there is an accident? Won't this poison the land and the soil? In Ethiopia there are always accidents," someone else interjected. "Why can't they build this plant somewhere else? Why are these things always near our homes?"

The conversation paused. No one knew the answers to any of these questions. The group felt a sense of confusion and frustration. On one hand, everyone agreed that something must be done to end the power outages. On the other hand, no one trusted the state to do the right thing in this case. Just as Tafiq encountered corruption and inefficiency in trying to bring electricity to his neighborhood, he believed it was likely that any project to generate power from biogas would create similar problems. When things went wrong, he did not trust the government to set them right; instead this responsibility would be passed on to individuals. The state could not provide basic services such as electricity, and Tafiq and his friends feared that attempts to address these gaps would create new and unexpected problems.

As when suspicion was directed at the Gibe I dam, there was a great deal of doubt among Tafiq and his friends. Tafiq took advantage of the opportunity to lease land in the newly opened area near Boye Swamp, and he acknowledged the potential for the biogas plant to solve some the city's problems with power. In response to my complaints about the dust, he remarked that eventually I would not notice it. One's body could become accustomed to the feeling of construction and transformation. Tafiq was grappling with change, and during these initial stages of urban growth and transformation he expressed a sense of openness that good things could come. However, struggles over accessing electricity and other forms of infrastructure soon led Tafiq to doubt the possibility of desirable change. For Tafiq, opportunity certainly existed, but the state was an obstacle rather than a source of help. He was highly uncertain regarding the potential for the state to act in his interests. The already tenuous affective relationship between citizen and state was eroding further.

Feeling Mud and Corruption

In her book *Sensing Changes*, environmental historian Joy Parr (2010) argues for more attention to the everyday sensory experience of transformations in the lived environment. Parr explains that "the sensuous ways of interacting with the world are best distinguished as phenomenological or corporeal embodiments. By their resistance to communication in words, the parts of technologies, environments, and everyday practices accessible through these senses are those most marginalized by the methodological turn to discourse analysis" (10). Although I appreciate Parr's attention to the sensory experience of environmental change, I believe it can be usefully combined with an analysis of discursive practices. The discursive construction of the state and urban development emerge from sensuous interactions with the world. Change is felt through sensations associated with particular materials (Limbert 2001, 2010; Thompson 2014). Just as people feel infrastructure through soil and water, in Jimma mud and dust were often used discursively to understand and critique state-led development and transformations of the urban environment. Such critiques represent a peculiar sort of intersection of nature and technology. Symbols of the natural world were invoked to critique particular technologies and forms of development.

I was away from Jimma between 2009 and 2012. As usual, when I returned, Tafiq invited me to his house for lunch. As in most Muslim households in Jimma, Tafiq's furniture consists of floor mats and firm pillows. We sat on the mats, sharing a large plate of injera covered with spicy red beef stew. This was followed by coffee and khat. As the stimulating effects of the coffee and khat woke us up from our food-induced stupor, Tafiq began to explain that the state had done almost nothing for his neighborhood. Convincing the municipal government to provide any sort of support was a continual struggle. Neighborhood residents were expected to pool their funds to cover the costs of electric lines, water pipes, drainage systems, and roads. As the neighborhood representative, Tafiq met with city administrators again and again but achieved no results. Tafiq's neighborhood amassed 6,000 birr (approximately $325 in 2012) from the community, but the government had not yet provided its half. He complained that often the government's offer to complete a project came at the beginning of the rainy season, when it is nearly impossible to work, and any unfinished projects deteriorate. In Tafiq's words, "One step forward, two steps backward." For Tafiq, the central problem was that the state had given to citizens land on which to build homes, but it had not provided the essential infrastructure necessary to maintain an expected standard of living. Rather, the state demanded that citizens pay for infrastructure, but such payments ended up in the pockets of corrupt officials instead of bringing electricity, water, and a functioning drainage system.

Tafiq extended his critique to road construction, including asphalt, cobblestone, and rural roads. He claimed that the government consistently starts projects but does not finish them because of corruption. Private contractors are also complicit in this process. Tafiq described a pattern in which local administrators accumulate funds from the community for the completion of projects. Under the EPRDF administrators are commonly shuffled from one position to another, and Tafiq noted the example of a recent Jimma mayor who was appointed to Parliament. Tafiq claimed that when administrators leave, they take the community's funds with them. The federal government steps in and makes some noise about corruption but actually does little. The new local administrators decry the corruption of their predecessors, claiming that they need to begin the process of building from scratch, and the cycle begins again. Meanwhile, as I detailed in the previous chapter, with work stopping and starting, the actual condition of the infrastructure is often worse than before the project began. The uncertainty and vague sense of hope combined with cynicism that I encountered in 2009 had been replaced with a sense of certainty. By 2012 Tafiq and many others had no doubt about the nature of development: progress would not occur and an imagined future would not be actualized. Government administrators and private contractors would enrich themselves, and people such as Tafiq would be left with mud and dust. Whatever trust had previously existed between citizen and state had vanished, replaced by feelings of betrayal.

Even more common than the critiques of government corruption and mismanagement were discussions of the sensory experience of failed infrastructure. Tafiq's descriptions of corruption and struggles with city administrators are marked by references to the fact that his neighborhood is built on a swamp. When I visited Tafiq's house in 2012, a horse-drawn cart pulled us through the muddy roads until we reached a point that could be passed only by foot. Drainage was a major problem. We leaped over a few unfinished drainage ditches that formed miniature canals of stagnant water. At his house Tafiq took me into his backyard to show me his small outhouse. The pit latrine had only about six inches of space above the water. When it rained, the latrine overflowed. Committing to deal with these drainage issues was another promise that the government had made but did not keep. Tafiq discursively connected overflowing pit toilets, flooded roads, and mosquitos to his battle with the city government.

For Tafiq and his neighbors, the politics of infrastructure were shaped by the soggy ground of the swamp. Poor residents of Jimma were given land that had been assumed to be worthless because it was saturated with water. Although residences could be built and established, water was everywhere, and it made movement and disposal of waste particularly difficult. It also provided an ideal breeding ground for diseases such as malaria. The particular mix of water and earth made this neighborhood attractive for certain types of development, but it also posed numerous barriers to the area's transformation. With its proximity to the swamp, Tafiq's neighborhood was not suitable for commercial development or farming, meaning that the state had little to lose and much to gain in leasing plots of land for residential development. The flowing nature of water also supported attempts at development, as government officials may have believed that the swamp could be easily drained. Of course, water is not so easily manipulated, and it was not simple for the state to construct roads that could be easily traversed and sewage and drainage systems that functioned.

The slow movement through the mud-filled streets of Tafiq's neighborhood was mirrored in his experience of slogging through endless government bureaucracy. Tafiq was caught in the mud of corruption and inefficiency. As with power cuts and hydropower, the physical properties of water acted as a metaphor for struggles with infrastructure and power. The mixing of water and earth created a sticking, sucking mud that prevented movement. The state was also sticky and opaque. It was unclear who within the sprawling bureaucracy of the municipality was responsible for providing infrastructure in Tafiq's neighborhood. His attempts at contacting state administrators were met with long waits and cancelled meetings. When funds were collected and given to the state, it was unclear how they were used; any results from the use of these funds were not visible. Tafiq and his neighbors were mired in a swampy state.

Struggles with roads and movement through central Jimma were also experienced in terms of a mixing of water and earth. Walking is the most common method of transportation in urban Ethiopia. My recent visits to Jimma have all been during June, the beginning of Ethiopia's rainy season. When the rains begin, the mud comes. Roads in residential areas are generally unpaved. Mud is created when dirt encounters water and traffic. The rain usually comes at night and in the early morning. As more and more people and animals walk the roads, the texture of the mud changes. It becomes a thick, red sludge—both sticky and slick, with the potential to cause a slip or pull off a shoe (figure 3.1). As annoying as the mud was, people learned to live with it. They walked slower and used various techniques for keeping their clothes clean—spreading their feet far apart, tucking pants into socks, and hopping from one dry spot to another. Bodies adapted to mud, learning to unconsciously negotiate muddy streets. Business boomed for shoeshine boys, who waited where the dirt roads met asphalt, cleaning and polishing the shoes of those on their way to work or meetings.

If the mixing of earth and water that results in mud and dirt was key to the day-to-day experience of road construction, it was equally relevant for the actual construction of roads. Road construction typically stopped during the heavy rains that come to Jimma between June and September. The combination of vehicles and wet, unpaved roads created even more mud than usual. During the 2012 rainy season, trips between Jimma and Mizan,

FIGURE 3.1. Muddy road in Jimma. Photo by the author.

a town approximately two hundred kilometers southwest of Jimma, took close to eight hours, rather than the usual four. A Korean company had been widening and paving this road, and they stopped work for the rainy season. I spoke briefly with a few of the Korean engineers and managers, and they explained that all they could do during the rainy season was try to keep the roads relatively passable and safe by smoothing and packing down the mud. Rain softens the earth and heavy vehicles tear up the roads, creating potholes that undo much of the construction that has been completed. In most cases the construction was eventually finished, but the rain prolonged the amount of time that people must live with mud, dust, and nearly impassable roads.

In conversations with Jimma residents I often heard direct critiques of state-led development. However, even more common was the simple statement, "In Jimma we don't have roads, we have mud." This claim is about more than the condition of roads in Jimma. To argue that Jimma has mud instead of roads is to discursively use the qualities of water and soil to carve out a particular position within a localized politics of infrastructure. "The government treats Jimma like a stepchild. Without roads there is no city," a friend explained in 2012. This same friend, who owns a large business, had contributed significant amounts of money to road construction in Jimma in 2009, only to see these efforts fail. Now she felt that the federal government had turned its back on Jimma, allowing the city to collapse to the point that it was almost impossible to drive from one side of town to the other. In Amharic, the term for stepchild is *ye'injera lij* (injera child). Injera is the staple food in urban Ethiopia, and the implication is that a stepchild is given food but not emotional sustenance. If Jimma is a stepchild, then any affective relationship between the Ethiopian state and the people of Jimma has been severed. Any support that the state provided was offered out of a sense of obligation rather than a true feeling of concern or care for the people of Jimma.

The second part of the statement—that there is no city without roads—denied the ability of the state to provide access to a desirable future. Other Jimma residents joked that the city had become a farm. Roads signify movement, progress, and commerce. The farm, however, represents a rural past in which one toils in the earth with ox-drawn ploughs and hand tools. In 2009, when the road construction was just beginning, Jimma residents felt a surprising degree of excitement for the project. People consistently spoke of roads in relation to progress and claimed that they were happy to donate their money to it. Roads enabled figurative and literal movement toward a desirable future. With the apparent failure of this project, a muddy farm was worse than being stuck in the present. It did not simply represent backwardness; rather, mud or a farm signified a breakdown in linear temporal movement. The present was somehow worse than both the remembered past and the previously imagined future. Mud provided no foundation for future construction, growth, and progress. One step forward, two steps backward. With each step through the mud, Jimma residents felt corruption and temporal breakdown.

In 2009, by donating portions of their incomes to road construction, Jimma residents were affirming a commitment to a citizen–state relationship in which the citizen provides support for the state in exchange for leadership and direction in moving toward a desirable future (Mains 2012a). The claims I encountered in 2012—that Jimma's infrastructure has been transformed to a muddy farm—imply that the state has failed to hold up its end of the bargain. Residents were insisting that the state is unable to move them toward a desirable future and that a change in leadership is necessary. In 2009 there was a sense of uncertainty among Jimma residents. A powerful cynicism and distrust of state-led development was certainly present, but residents could also clearly see that their city was in the midst of a process of construction and rapid change. Although construction continued in 2012, the possibility of movement had been replaced by discussions of sticky mud. Change was occurring, but at least for the moment Jimma residents seemed to be confident that their lives were mired in mud and corruption.

Elections, Infrastructure, and Legitimizing Power

Three years later, in 2015, Jimma had transformed further. Tafiq's neighborhood no longer felt like a cluster of houses on the outskirts of town. It was not necessary to take a horse cart to reach his house. Minibuses ran on newly constructed roads, some asphalt and some dirt, that directly connected Tafiq's neighborhood to the city center. Other houses, organized in a grid, now surrounded Tafiq's. Water and electricity were present, but they had not come cheap. Each of the neighborhood households had paid 300 birr to bring a water line to the neighborhood; Tafiq had then paid an additional 2,000 birr to install a faucet in his compound. His wife used to bring water to the house in a jerry can. Electricity ended up costing the neighborhood 5,000 birr, and Tafiq claimed that this was paid as a bribe to a government representative. The neighborhood still experienced problems with drainage. When I visited it had not rained for a few days, but many of the drainage ditches were full of standing water. Tafiq told me that the community members had dug these ditches themselves. It was clear that Tafiq and his neighbors had invested a great deal of their own resources in bringing infrastructure to their homes. Despite this expense, it should be noted that they had also profited from increases in land values. Tafiq had leased the land from the government less than ten years ago for 30,000 birr, and in 2015 he estimated that he could sell the lease to his property for 200,000 birr. Even with the birr worth less than half of what it was at the time of the initial sale, this was still a significant increase.

Tafiq had never been a supporter of the EPRDF, but over the years his critique had shifted. It had moved from a sense of cynicism and uncertainty regarding change, to the disappointment of being stuck in the mire of mud and corruption, to an acknowledgment that certain things had improved but that this change did not come close meeting his needs. Particularly in the days leading up to the 2015 national election, the role of the EPRDF in securing development and improving quality of life was a frequent topic of discussion. The Jimma municipal government made a great show of improving roads. As I departed Tafiq's house we observed a dump truck dropping loads of dirt along the side of the road. Tafiq was not impressed. "This road has been under construction for five years," he explained. "As soon as the election is over the workers will be gone." As I returned to the city center by minibus, bumping along the dusty road from Tafiq's house, a grader came from the other direction, smoothing out the road. The woman sitting next to me remarked to the driver, "What does that accomplish? It's a dirt road; either there will be dust or [there will be] mud. It is all politics." Dust and mud, different combinations of dirt and water, contrast with the urban transformation that many Jimma residents desired. The work of dump trucks and graders was assumed to be a sort performance, a means of demonstrating the commitment of the ruling party to development in advance of the election. Tafiq and many others did not accept this narrative. Instead, they continually contrasted the reality of mud and dust with what they felt was an illusion of development. In Jimma, cynicism about the state made the successful performance of development nearly impossible.

There was an interesting contradiction in these critiques of state-led development in advance of the election. Although Jimma residents consistently claimed that development projects were intended to win votes, many of them also believed the election was a sham. They lacked faith in the electoral process for good reason. In 2015 there was very little organized opposition to the EPRDF, and the election allowed the EPRDF to expand its control to 100 percent of the parliamentary membership. People I spoke with were convinced that the EPRDF would easily win the election regardless of the fact that no one they knew actually supported the party. For example, a Jimma University professor told me a joke about the elections: A man votes for the opposition and tells his friends this. His friends tell him all the wonderful things the EPRDF is doing and the man decides to change his vote. When he returns to change his vote the people running the polling station tell him not to worry, they have already changed it for him.[7] It was not clear why a government that provided so little space for the opposition to operate was concerned about attracting votes. If the results of the election were predetermined, then why go through the effort of simulating development?

Even if the EPRDF did actually need to attract voters, the development projects that were completed successfully did little to convince urban residents of the value of EPRDF rule. As I explained in the previous chapter, projects such as the Taddesse Enjore Road in Hawassa were rushed to completion before the election. However, successful development did little to legitimize the power of the ruling party. I sometimes asked why it mattered that development projects were motivated by a desire to win elections, as long as development was occurring. Although I received various responses to this question, it was clear that development alone was not enough. It had to be accompanied by a particular quality of citizen–state relations. Legitimacy depended on an affective relationship between citizen and state that is based in reciprocal care.

As my friend's comment about Jimma as stepchild indicates, urban Ethiopians wanted a state that cared about them and was not simply interested in winning elections. Relations between true kin, in contrast to relations with a stepchild, should not be based in interest in personal gain. However, the time and money invested in development projects before the election indicate that the state's primary concern was winning votes. The EPRDF wanted the support of the people, but if this could not be accomplished, it took no chances with the possibility of losing even a single parliamentary seat. Ironically, it seems that many people in Jimma, at least, had reached a point at which even successful development would not change their perceptions of the EPRDF. The fundamental dynamics of citizen–state relations had already been established during the long period of construction. The experience of construction was inextricable from an intimate emotional relationship with the state. Nothing the EPRDF offered up could be fully embraced. The roads under construction in Tafiq's neighborhood were somehow tainted. This is not to say that there were not EPRDF supporters in Jimma. However, the vast majority of people denied that the state operates in their interests. Urban growth was not enough; a deeper sense of concern and affective attachment was necessary to legitimize the state in the eyes of Jimma residents.

Growth without Progress in a Changing Urban Landscape

Discussions of development and transformation in Jimma in 2015 did not always reference politics. Particularly for many of the young men whom I had known for more than a decade, changes in their lived environment were interpreted in relation to shifts in their own lives. In Jimma, the major urban asphalt road construction projects that began in 2009 did not go smoothly, but by the end of 2014, many of the roads had been finished. New roads were accompanied by new high-rise buildings and additional resettlement of families, particularly in the central Mercado neighborhood.

In 2015, I ran into Centayo, one of the young men who had been involved in my previous research. I had not seen him since 2005. In the early 2000s he had had an unusual haircut and a certain energetic charisma that caused him to stand out from his peers. In 2015 he had the usual short hair worn by Ethiopian men and had developed a prominent belly, but his smile and cynical sense of humor were unchanged. He had traveled to the Gambella region, near the Ethiopia/South Sudan border, to work on a rice plantation and had only recently returned to Jimma. Back in Jimma, Centayo was working as a construction foreman on one of the new buildings going up in the Mercado, the neighborhood where his parents had lived for more than forty years before they were forced to leave to make room for new commercial development. Centayo's father worked as a tailor, a common profession in the city center. His parents had been resettled in the same outlying area as Frehiwot's family. "We had no choice," Centayo explained. "The government claims this is development and we have to do it." The new location lacked regular transportation and Centayo's parents ended up living with one of his sisters in a more central location.

We sat in a rooftop café sipping macchiatos and looking out at all of the new buildings that had gone up in the neighborhood. Where once there had been simple shops made from corrugated tin, there were now four- and five-storied cement buildings, filled with shops and cafés. "This is only progress for the rich," Centayo claimed. "It does nothing for the poor." Pointing across the street at one of the other new high-rises he noted, "These building are empty." He clarified that he was referring not only to some of the empty spaces for rent, but to the fact that so many of the shops offered the same goods and services. Cafes, mobile phone shops, internet access—many of the shops sold the opportunity to connect with others. In contrast, Centayo claimed that there was no reliable access to water, electricity, or phone networks. This was a comment that I heard frequently from Jimma residents: "What good are new buildings and roads when there is no water and no electricity?" From this perspective, growth was empty. There were certainly new physical structures to be seen, but these were contrasted with a more abstract sense of change, a change that would not only transform the landscape, but would transform people's lives (figure 3.2).

In speaking about his own life, Centayo complained that there was no progress and every day was the same: "I go to work, chew khat in the afternoon, drink in the evening, go to sleep and do it all over again the next day." I asked him what progress meant for him, and he described building a house, marrying, and having children. In many ways Centayo had experienced progress. When we first met he was working along a busy road making sandals from used tires. Working first for a large company in Gambella and now as a foreman certainly brought him more income and prestige. As with the "empty" buildings going up around him, however, this did not bring satisfaction. In another conversation Centayo critiqued the architectural design of the new buildings, complaining that they were all similar and unattractive. Centayo, and many others, could not deny that Jimma had been transformed, but these changes did not match up with their idealized conceptions of progress. Something was absent, both in their lives and in the growing city.

Also in 2015, shortly after the election, I spent a morning wandering through a residential neighborhood with Temesgen, another young man who had participated in my earlier research. When we met in 2004 he had finished tenth grade but did not qualify for higher education and was unemployed, occasionally helping his mother with various entrepreneurial ventures such as selling coffee beans at the bus station. Now, as we walked along the new cobblestone roads, he commented on how much the neighborhood had changed. At some point we turned off the cobblestone on to a dirt road to make our way to Temesgen's home, where he continued to live

FIGURE 3.2. Construction boom in central Jimma. Photo by the author.

with his mother and siblings. As soon as we left the cobblestone the road turned into the thick, slippery mud that I associated with the rainy season in Jimma. Suddenly the conversation shifted. Now he was telling me that there had been no change, everything was the same. Our walking pace slowed when we encountered the mud. We picked our way along the muddy path until we reached his family's small, two-room house. Like many other unemployed young men, Temesgen had found a way to return to school, and he was taking evening courses for a bachelor's degree in civil engineering at Jimma University. He showed me the yearbook and photos from when he completed his diploma at a technical college a couple years earlier. Temesgen had reentered the narrative of progress associated with education: step-by-step, linear movement from one level to the next. He was quite proud of this, and he had immediately announced his educational status when we first ran into each other. However, once we moved away from the asphalt and the cobblestone, into the interior neighborhoods where the majority of Jimma's population resided, the experience of the city changed. It became a world of stasis, rather than one of change—a world without progress.

Young men such as Temesgen do not complain about boredom as they once did (Mains 2012b). Many of them are working and attending school, increasingly confident that they are experiencing linear change in their lives. However, living in a context of rapid technological change and urban growth seems to have introduced new doubts about the nature of progress. Growth has occurred but access to basic necessities such as water and electricity has become increasingly unreliable. There is a new asphalt road and a five-story hotel just minutes from Temesgen's home, but what does that do for him? Temesgen was initially excited about the novelty of these developments, but the reality of the muddy path leading to his home was left unchanged. Across the street from the hotel where visiting dignitaries stayed lived another friend of mine, who could still be found every afternoon chewing khat and lounging on an old mattress in the dirt-floored room he had built in his family compound. Growth was occurring in Jimma, but many people were still waiting for something else.

Jimma residents struggled with a reality that did not conform to their expectations for the passage of time. They are waiting for state investments in infrastructure to touch their lives. For many people, a deeper sense of change will only occur when they are able to personally experience the benefits of new technology. Perhaps even more importantly, for development to be meaningful it must be accompanied by a positive affective relationship with the state. Reactions to the roads and buildings that are associated with the state's developmentalist policies demonstrate how dissatisfaction with the passage of time may emerge in different ways. Particularly in places such as urban Ethiopia, where growth is rapid and residents are continually bombarded by state propaganda concerning development, evaluating the passage of time is a common activity. Temesgen and Centayo experienced an emotional letdown in relation to the changing urban environment. Although they did not always articulate exactly what was missing, it was clear that they expected something more. Like the city itself, these young men were no longer mired in a period of waiting, stuck in the social category of youth. Centayo was working in a relatively desirable position and Temesgen was moving forward with his education. After years of being unfinished, many of the asphalt roads had been completed and new hotels such as the high-rise in Temesgen's neighborhood dominated the landscape. However, so much of this growth was superficial, impressive to the visitor such as myself who returns after time away but not meaningful for the residents who live in the same house they always have or who have even been pushed out of the city center. As Centayo indicated, the buildings are empty; the transformation is hollow. When a state's legitimacy hangs on promises of development and renaissance, a hollow transformation dooms the construction of a positive affective relationship with citizens.

Conclusion

I have a tendency to indulge in nostalgia. I have fond memories of a Jimma from the early 2000s—one that was a bit quieter, a bit easier to navigate without the constant construction, and a bit friendlier without so many of my acquaintances displaced from the city center. For the most part, however, Jimma residents have embraced change and the temporary discomfort that comes with the construction process. I did not encounter laments about the city of the past that had been lost. If the city felt different, this in itself was not a problem for most people. Instead, it was the city of the future that people missed. Charles Piot's (2010) notion of "nostalgia for the future" is quite fitting here. The imagined future that had been embraced when construction was beginning in 2008 and 2009 had slipped away. With it was lost whatever faith people once held that state-led development could be successful. It was not just that many projects had failed. There was also a sense that the state's promises had been broken and that any potential for a positive affective relationship between citizen and state had been shattered. The experiences of people such as Tafiq draw a sharp contrast to narratives of Africa rising. Despite clear signs of growth in terms of GDP and in Jimma's built environment, I repeatedly encountered denials that life was improving. After years of waiting, the change that finally arrived did not satisfy.

The Ethiopian state continually sought to assert its legitimacy through the performance of development, but by 2015 people's skepticism was very difficult to overcome. Legitimacy is not simply based in a calculated assessment of the state's success in supporting development. Rather, it is more a matter of people's feelings for the state. In Jimma, an affective relationship between citizen and state depended on a sense of movement toward a desirable imagined future. To what extent does the construction of roads, buildings, and hydroelectric dams inspire hope, excitement, and optimism? For these feelings to be present, the city must do more than grow. It must meet people's desires for a more abstract sense of change and progress that is deeply felt. This experience is partially tactile. The feeling of dust in one's eyes or mud beneath one's feet is a reminder that desired change has not occurred. Feelings of development go beyond such sensory experiences and encompass emotional relationships with the state. Comments about the "hollow" nature of new buildings indicate a sense that growth is superficial. Jimma residents were left feeling like stepchildren, neglected and abandoned by a callous parent that cares for little other than winning elections. The state's legitimacy depended on successful development, but when an affective citizen/state relationship was thoroughly broken, not even new roads and urban growth could bring that sense of legitimacy back.[8]

It is through the affective politics of legitimacy that construction may lead to destruction. In the process of constructing infrastructure, urban residents encounter the state in ways that are far more tangible than the propaganda that is continually deployed on television. Neat narratives of development, progress, and renaissance quickly break down when people encounter the day-to-day challenges of construction. The joy that comes with sharing one's money to help build a road is replaced with frustration and resentment. Infrastructures are forms of affective communication, but many urban Ethiopians feel these messages in ways that are directly opposed to the state's interest in legitimacy. When Tafiq saw roads under construction at the time of the 2015 election, he did not feel hope for progress; rather, he felt a deep anger. The road pulls up feelings of injustice, reminding Tafiq of his personal struggles with infrastructure during the past five years. The case of Jimma is quite different than the successes of Hawassa. Jimma is a reminder of the inherent instability of construction. When construction fails, it is not only the city that suffers. Affective attachments to the state erode as well.

FOUR. Governing the Bajaj

States, Markets, and Multiple Materialisms

In March 2015, drivers of three-wheeled motorcycle taxis in Hawassa refused to work, and the city came to a standstill. In Hawassa, a city of 250,000 people and only four state-owned buses, most residents relied on the three-wheelers, known by their brand name, Bajaj, to move through the city. As one passenger noted, "If the Bajaj is lost, then everything is lost. Without the Bajaj we cannot move and there is no city." In other words, a city without Bajaj transportation is not a city because people are not free to move, socialize, or engage in commerce. Although Bajaj were owned and operated for profit by private individuals, they were tightly regulated by the Ethiopian state. The Bajaj driver strike was the culmination of long-standing anger among Bajaj drivers and owners regarding state regulation of the Bajaj system. As one of the leaders of an association for Bajaj owners told me, "Government administrators know nothing about how transportation works in this city! Passenger fares, Bajaj routes—all of this should be left to the market."

In contrast, Hawassa city administrators responsible for roads and transportation consistently expressed dissatisfaction with the Bajaj. In his spacious third-floor office, the head of transportation for the region summarized what administrators saw as the root of the problem: "Bajaj drivers work for injera;[1] they are not working for the people, and this creates a problem." He went on to explain that because drivers are motivated by profits, they will not work in less densely populated neighborhoods that are still in need of transportation.

To some extent, both sides perceived the conflict in terms of a clash between the logics of the governing state and the market. Bajaj owners generally lease the vehicles to drivers, who earn profits by attracting large numbers of passengers. At the same time, these vehicles perform a public service for the vast majority of the population that does not own private vehicles. They allow people to move through the city in a way that supports commerce and facilitates urban livelihoods. There is a central point of tension here. On one hand, in Ethiopia, Bajaj drivers receive no support from the state,[2] but the state requires them to follow certain guidelines to meet public demand for transportation. From the state's perspective, these regulations ensure that everyone has access to transportation. On the other hand, Bajaj drivers argue that state regulations prevent them from a livelihood and keep passengers from effectively moving through the city.

Conflicts such as these are increasingly common in a world where states struggle to meet the day-to-day needs of urban populations for goods such as water, transportation, and electricity, and people and their social networks are essential for provisioning infrastructure (Simone 2004).[3] In this chapter I bring together vital materialism and historical materialism to understand the tense encounter between state regulation, market forces, and the people who provision infrastructure. Conflicts such as the Bajaj driver strike are based less on the opposition between states and markets than in struggles over labor and the specific characteristics of infrastructural technologies.[4]

Historical Materialism, Vital Things, and Urban Transport

Matteo Rizzo's (2011, 2017) work demonstrates many of the strengths and flaws of applying a class-based analysis to the transportation sector in African cities. In his study of bus public transport in Dar es Salaam, Rizzo emphasizes the importance of ownership of capital for understanding class relations. Like those in Hawassa, the vast majority of drivers in Dar es Salaam lease their vehicles from owners. Rizzo argues that bus drivers and operators cannot be categorized as self-employed entrepreneurs because they lack control over capital (2017, 78–79). For Rizzo, the relationship between the owner of capital and the worker is the fundamental source of tension in the urban transport sector. Rizzo is absolutely correct that relationships between owners and operators of transport vehicles deserve greater analytical attention. The supply of vehicle operators greatly outnumbers the vehicles available, and this gives owners the power to demand expensive leases, which threaten the drivers' livelihoods. In the Tanzanian case that Rizzo examines, drivers speed and violate traffic regulations in order to carry more passengers and earn a profit beyond what they pay to lease vehicles from owners.

Vehicle operators, however, are not wage employees—they lease capital and use it to generate incomes. In assuming that ownership of capital drives conflict, Rizzo overlooks some of the peculiarities of public transport in African cities. First, exploitation of labor cannot be reduced to ownership of capital. To understand exploitation one must examine the specific relations of production that are at play. The fact that drivers lease vehicles from owners means that relations of production are different from those typically associated with wage labor. Second, this approach ignores the relationship between the state and the people who provision infrastructure. The state depends on vehicle operators for a functional city, and it shapes their livelihoods by determining where they can work and what they can charge passengers.[5] Third—and this critique is true of many Marxist approaches, although not of Marx himself—for the most part Rizzo ignores technology. Important differences between operating a bus and operating a three-wheeler affect labor relations. For example, only one person is necessary to operate a three-wheeler, and their small engines mean that it is difficult for drivers to use excessive speed to increase profits.

To be clear, I do not wish to minimize the importance of the owner/operator relationship, but ownership of capital is not the only source of tension in the urban transport sector. In understanding conflicts over urban infrastructure through the lens of historical materialism, I draw primarily from Donald Donham's classic work, *History, Power, Ideology: Central Issues in Marxism and Anthropology*.[6] Donham's (1999a) interpretation of historical materialism is particularly useful not only because it is based on ethnographic research in southern Ethiopia, but also because Donham sought to apply Marx's ideas outside of the context of industrial capitalism. In the case of the Bajaj, conflicts cannot be understood only in terms of ownership of the means of production. The state does not own the means of production (the Bajaj), nor does it consistently support the interests of Bajaj owners, yet the state is in direct conflict with Bajaj drivers. The Bajaj case is also complicated by the fact that capital does not hire labor; rather, drivers lease vehicles from owners—a dynamic that is common to many cases of paratransit. Following Donham, attention to productive inequalities is essential for understanding these complexities and the conflicts surrounding the Bajaj system. Productive inequalities are differences in power over the total social product that allow some people to live off of the labor of others; that is, they are inequalities in control over the products of labor. The specific nature of productive inequalities differs with level of technology and mode of production, but they are always at the center of social conflict because they deprive people of control over the products of their own labor. Donham explains that Marx's conception of productive inequalities was rooted in his view of human nature. "What is distinctive about humans, according to Marx, is not simply that we depend on symbols but that we, in a sense, create ourselves through symbolically formed action in the world—'labor'" (Donham 1999a, 56). I have no interest in advancing a universal definition of human nature, but Marx's notion of creating oneself through labor resonates with one of the central themes in this book—construction. Humans have a tendency to use their labor to construct themselves in relation to others. When people lack the power to control the product of their labor during this process of self-construction, productive inequalities generate conflict.

In capitalism, ownership of the means of production determines productive inequalities—owners exploit the labor of workers during the process of generating surplus value. The relationship between owners and drivers is certainly important for understanding the Bajaj system, but drivers were far more concerned with their relationship with the state. The state does not live off of the labor of the Bajaj driver in the same manner as Bajaj owners—no person within the government directly profits at the expense of the driver. The state does, however, exert significant control over the product of the driver's labor, and this allows the state to reproduce itself. In the case of the Bajaj, two central productive inequalities shape conflicts between drivers and the state. The first productive inequality concerns control over the fares that drivers collect while transporting passengers. As I detail below, the state determines a Bajaj driver's access to the product of his (nearly all drivers in Hawassa were men) labor through regulations on passenger fares and when and where a driver may work. In Hawassa, state regulations undermined drivers' abilities to use the income from their labor to construct themselves through engagement in relations of reciprocity with others. The second productive inequality is related to control over the city that is made through the labor of Bajaj drivers. As the Bajaj passenger quoted in the chapter's introduction noted, without the Bajaj, there is no city. The product of a driver's labor is not only an income; it is the city that is created by moving people from one neighborhood to another. This is one of the peculiarities of infrastructural labor—it often constructs things that are shared by the public. The Ethiopian state's legitimacy rests in part on the successful development of urban infrastructure, but the state depends on people such as Bajaj drivers and their improvised social networks to provide infrastructure. The state needs functional urban transportation, but it provides only four busses for a city of more than 250,000 people. In Hawassa, like elsewhere in the global south, the people who function as infrastructure fill this gap. These two productive inequalities are related in the sense that the same state regulations that threaten drivers' livelihoods are necessary to achieve the state's vision for the city. Therefore, construction of an ideal city threatens drivers' constructions of themselves.[7]

With this second productive inequality I have clearly drifted from Donham's more literal approach to assessing the total social product. The production and control of the image of the city cannot be quantified, and yet they are clearly very important. Marx assumed that productive powers develop and new technologies are introduced in order to increase production, but new technologies are adopted for a variety of reasons, including creating jobs, disciplining citizens, and taking advantage of the technology's symbolic dimensions. It is here that the value of a synthesis with a vital materialism becomes apparent. Although Donham (1999a, 70–71) avoids a "vulgar Marxism" in which changes in technology directly determine productive inequalities, he ultimately analyzes technology largely in terms of its implications for production. Vital materialism reminds us not only that the purpose of a given technology is highly variable but that objects have agency in the sense that they push humans in unexpected directions and create new limits and opportunities for human action. Pipes (Anand 2017), water meters (von Schnitzler 2016), toilets (Chalfin 2014), and three-wheeled motorcycles each distinctly shape conflicts between states and the networks of people who provision infrastructures. Both of the key productive inequalities that are associated with the Bajaj system are inseparable from the specific qualities of the Bajaj technology.

On the basis of this synthesis between historical and vital materialisms, I advance two primary arguments. First, when people and their social networks function as infrastructures, conflicts are created that are best conceptualized not in terms of a state/market binary, but in relation to productive inequalities. Historical materialism and attention to productive inequalities offers a method of analysis that is particularly well suited for understanding the complex relationships between states and markets that are associated with the construction of infrastructure. Second, lively technologies and materials shape productive inequalities. The Bajaj actively participates in the conflict between drivers and city administrators. Like other motorized vehicles (Bürge 2011; Lamont 2013; Lee 2012; Rollason 2013; Truitt 2008), the Bajaj brings issues of speed, safety, traffic, and mobility to struggles over labor and income, but it also does more than this. The particular characteristics of the Bajaj—an inexpensive, flexible, and labor-dependent transportation technology—shape conflicts between administrators and drivers.

The bulk of this chapter examines struggles between city administrators and Bajaj drivers as they grappled with the limits and possibilities of Bajaj technology. Administrative attempts to govern the Bajaj were based in a struggle to force the vehicle to conform to specific conceptions of movement within a modern city. Administrators also advanced a discourse in which the Bajaj was associated with criminality. The city that administrators wished to create by regulating the Bajaj depended on increasingly denying Bajaj drivers' income from their labor. In contrast, drivers discursively constructed the Bajaj as a key element in supporting valued networks of reciprocity. In the latter half of the chapter I examine conflicts over changing prices of fuel and passenger fares that eventually resulted in the brief Bajaj driver strike. Drivers perceived their work in terms of accessing incomes that would support relationships with others. They demanded that the state regulate the Bajaj system in a way that facilitated the maintenance of their livelihoods and their participation in networks of reciprocity.

Movement and Economics of the Bajaj in Hawassa

I have worked and conducted research intermittently in Ethiopia since 1998, but the ten months I spent in Hawassa, from 2013 to 2014, was the first time that the Bajaj was my primary mode of transportation. In 2005, fifty-seven Bajaj were operating in Hawassa (Kebede and Alemayehu 2007). According to city administrators, more than 2,400 Bajaj were registered in 2013. My ten months in Hawassa were enough time for me to become a serious Bajaj enthusiast. On one occasion during my field research I met a scholar from the University of Wisconsin who was interested in promoting bicycle use in Hawassa. He expressed concern that the Bajaj had replaced the bicycle and that this was having a negative impact on people's health. I love cycling and I cycle to work in the US, but I also knew that this scholar was new to Ethiopia and had little firsthand experience with the Bajaj. I made sure that he took a few rides with me so he could experience the pleasures of the Bajaj system and to demonstrate that using the Bajaj requires a significant amount of walking. I appreciate the feeling of hopping into a vehicle and immediately moving. The breeze flowing through the open sides is an ideal way to cool down on a hot afternoon. In contrast to other modes of public transportation, the small size of the Bajaj facilitates conversations between passengers and the driver. I mention my relationship with the Bajaj not only to situate myself in relation to my object of study, but to demonstrate that we all have affective relations with technologies—perhaps particularly with transportation technologies. I argue below that state regulations of the Bajaj were based in part on a dislike for the aesthetics of the Bajaj. But first, more about the Bajaj system in Hawassa.

Before the introduction of the Bajaj in the early 2000s, Hawassa had little in the way of public transportation. Most Hawassa residents walked, rode bicycles, or hired horse carts to move through the city, primarily on dirt roads. The early 2000s brought significant state investment in urban areas throughout Ethiopia. The population of Hawassa quickly grew from around 150,000 to 250,000, making it one of the largest cities in Ethiopia. The city grew physically as well, expanding to about fifty square kilometers. As I detailed in chapter 2, asphalt coverage also expanded significantly during this time. The expanding city and the new asphalt roads created an ideal environment for the Bajaj to replace the horse cart. The size of the city meant that commuting to work on foot could take well over an hour, and the extensive asphalt eased the way for motorized vehicles. In 2013 and 2014, upper-level state administrators and wealthy businessmen generally owned motorbikes, but for the most part, the use of private vehicles was rare in Hawassa. Most people relied on the Bajaj to navigate the growing city.

Three-wheeled motorcycle taxis are referred to with different names in different places: *tuk-tuk* in Thailand, auto-rickshaw in India, and tricycle in the Philippines. The term *Bajaj* comes from the name of an Indian company, one of the major manufacturers of three-wheeled motorcycles.[8] Although Indian-made TVS brand three-wheelers are also common in Ethiopia, all three-wheelers are simply referred to as Bajaj, and I have adopted this usage. The Bajaj uses a fuel-efficient but highly polluting two-stroke engine. The vehicle is open on both sides, allowing for the free flow of air. A bench behind the driver allows room for three passengers to sit, although occasionally more are crammed in if some of the passengers are children or if the group is traveling only a short distance.

In Ethiopia, the Bajaj created possibilities for inexpensive and flexible movement through the city that did not previously exist. The Bajaj fills quickly and leaves quickly. In contrast, shared minibuses usually hold around twelve passengers, meaning that at their point of origin, five to ten minutes may be spent waiting for the often hot vehicle to fill. With only three passengers, the Bajaj also makes few stops for people to get on and off.

Its low fuel consumption meant that in 2013–14 a Bajaj could be hired for 10–20 birr ($0.50–1.00) to pick up and drop off wherever one wished. Such door-to-door trips are referred to as "contracts." Although contracts were considered expensive, many people in the expanding urban middle-class could afford them. Door-to-door trips such as this are especially useful when traveling with small children and to and from the city's main market with loads of goods. Particularly for women, who are often verbally harassed if they are walking alone at night—or even during the day in some neighborhoods—the Bajaj created opportunities for moving independently.

It was far more common to travel in a Bajaj shared with other customers along specific routes determined by the municipal government. Bajaj routes in Hawassa were generally two to four kilometers long, and each passenger paid between 1 and 2 birr to travel the entire route (1 birr was around 6 cents at the time of my research). For day laborers earning less than 40 birr per day, this was a significant expense, but many urban residents could afford frequent Bajaj trips.

Although some Bajaj drivers own their vehicles, the Bajaj owners' associations estimated that approximately 75 percent of Bajaj are operated by non-owners. Individuals rarely owned more than two or three vehicles, meaning that no one had a monopoly on Bajaj ownership. The most common arrangement at the time of my research was for the driver to pay the owner 100 birr per day (a little more than $5). Before changes in the cost of fuel and passenger fares, discussed below, drivers estimated that they usually brought in 300 birr per day; 100 birr would go to the owner, 100 would be spent on fuel, and 100 would remain for the driver. The vehicle owner was responsible for all maintenance and upkeep. Drivers noted that there were far more qualified drivers than vehicles, and the driver had little choice but to accept the owner's terms. I never heard drivers questioning the fairness of this arrangement.

Given the choice, drivers would generally stick to the most profitable routes, leaving people in less densely populated outlying areas without transportation. Beginning in 2012 the municipal government determined routes for Bajaj. All Bajaj owners were organized into five associations. The leaders of these associations were charged with communicating government regulations to the Bajaj owners and assigning each Bajaj to a route. Bajaj drivers were not permitted to leave their assigned route unless they had a letter documenting and approving a regular contract with a customer. A Bajaj driver could, for example, take a customer to work every day or deliver someone's children to school. In these cases a driver needed a letter, signed and stamped by the customer's employer or a representative from the child's school. If a driver left his route without this letter, the police could stop him and impose a 500-birr fine. A driver's route changed every two weeks so that no one was stuck too long on an undesirable route. The requirement to stay on one's route was waived after 6:00 p.m. and on weekends and holidays, and no Bajaj were permitted to operate after 10:00 p.m.

In practice, drivers often went off route and fines were not common, but the threat of a fine was still significant. Certain drivers chose to operate outside large hotels and worked, illegally, entirely on contracts. These drivers told me that they were generally fined once every three months, but they could often talk down the price of the fine to around 300 birr. One experienced driver claimed that the police enforced regulations regarding assigned routes only every two or three months. During these periods of intense enforcement it was necessary to avoid deviating from one's assigned route, but at other times one could move freely through the city.

Bajaj association leaders and drivers often complained about these regulations, but even more controversial were state attempts to limit the number of Bajaj on the street. Near the end of 2013, the municipal government in Hawassa stopped giving permits to operate a Bajaj. At the same time, administrators began to formulate plans that would limit the Bajaj to what they called "secondary" streets. Under this plan, Bajaj would primarily operate on cobblestone roads and would not be permitted to drive on Hawassa's main arteries, the smooth asphalt roads that provided the infrastructure for the Bajaj to emerge as the city's primary mode of transportation. Instead, minibuses would provide transportation on the main routes.[9]

Regarding control over the product of their labor, drivers faced a number of constraints. Bajaj owners collected 100 birr daily from drivers in exchange for access to the vehicle. Clearly, this represents a major productive inequality, but in contrast to their relationship with the state, drivers never expressed any resentment toward vehicle owners.[10] Owners claimed that they sympathized with the struggles of drivers and sometimes accepted lower payments when fuel prices were high. Perhaps this paternalistic relationship between owners and drivers explains the lack of tension between the two parties. In the case of the Bajaj, the fact that labor hired capital rather than the reverse is also important. It limited the Bajaj owner's control over the driver's labor: beyond leasing the vehicle, the driver had no obligation to share his income with the owner. Although I do not want to minimize the importance of the class relationship between drivers and owners, I focus my analysis in this chapter on the state/driver relationship because this is where tensions were centered. In terms of productive inequalities, by controlling passenger fares the state determined the amount drivers could earn from their labor. Regulations on routes and contracts also shaped drivers' abilities to earn an income. Finally, isolating Bajaj to secondary roads would drastically limit driver incomes. I return to these productive inequalities in the second half of this chapter, but first I examine how policies governing the Bajaj were based in a particular modern aesthetic of the city.

Regulating the Bajaj: Performing a Modern City

Eshetayehu and I conducted interviews with all city and regional administrators responsible for roads and public transportation in Hawassa. During this process we got to know particularly well Mr. Hayyamo, a city administrator responsible for urban transportation. As with most meetings with government officials in Ethiopia, arranging a meeting with Mr. Hayyamo took time: first we needed to wait in his office simply to schedule a meeting; once a meeting was scheduled it would often be cancelled; and meetings were nearly always delayed. Once we were in a room with Mr. Hayyamo, however, he patiently answered all of our questions, despite interruptions from others who poked their heads into his office seeking his attention. We met with him multiple times in 2013 and 2014, and once more during a brief period of follow-up research in June 2015. In general, all upper-level administrators are members of the ruling EPRDF party, and Mr. Hayyamo's responses to our questions partially reflected the party's position on particular issues. In Ethiopia, where the EPRDF controlled more than 99 percent of all parliamentary seats at the time of our research, there is often very little distinction between party, state, and government workers. That said, many of the claims that Mr. Hayyamo made were not necessarily rooted in specific party ideology; instead, they reflected a particular vision of Hawassa's future that was shared by other local administrators.

After making sure Eshetayehu and I were comfortable and offering us coffee and bottled water, Mr. Hayyamo explained that "Hawassa is a modern city. The Bajaj is not good for Hawassa. It is better to follow the example of Addis Ababa and rely on buses and minibuses. This is why we need to separate the Bajaj from other types of transportation—so that Hawassa can continue becoming a modern city." He went on to note that one of the city government's successes was replacing bicycles with a more modern mode of transportation—motorcycles. Like other administrators, Mr. Hayyamo emphasized the importance of the city's image, noting that guests from other cities complain that Hawassa's streets are crowded with Bajaj and that "to preserve the image of the city we must confine the Bajaj to secondary roads. We need to make a beautiful and green city." Another administrator offered similar ideas, claiming that Hawassa's streets are "closed." He explained that "the streets are so crowded with Bajaj that private car owners, government officials, and business owners can't move as they wish. The streets must be opened for cars."

As Mr. Hayyamo indicated, a key point of tension between city administrators and Bajaj drivers was based in the contrast between conceptions of a modern city and the flexibility of Bajaj transport. The vision of modernity advanced by Hawassa city administrators conflicted with the particular way that three-wheeled vehicles such as the Bajaj move. When administrators complain that Hawassa's streets are "closed," it is because the Bajaj, with a maximum speed of sixty to seventy kilometers per hour, moves more slowly than four-wheeled vehicles, and it carries fewer passengers. Interestingly, in more than fifty interviews with Hawassa residents regarding their Bajaj use, lack of speed was never one of their complaints. In fact, most noted that Bajaj are quite useful in moving quickly through the city. However, the pace of the Bajaj is certainly slower than that of a four-wheeled vehicle. The small Bajaj can easily weave in and out of traffic, passing other vehicles at will, but larger four-wheeled vehicles cannot do this without endangering pedestrians and other vehicles.

The image of the city is important for administrator critiques. Like the 1974 Ethiopian revolution (Donham 1999b), conceptions of what it means to be modern are very significant here, and in this case they specifically apply to technology. To allow the city to appropriately perform modernity, administrators sought to push the Bajaj to secondary roads, out of sight of visitors to Hawassa. Importantly, many of the minibuses that were being imported to replace the Bajaj were manufactured in India, the same location where the three-wheeled motorcycles were produced. It is not, therefore, the location of production that determines the modernity of vehicles in this case. Although city administrators did not provide much explanation for their claims that the Bajaj is not modern, they did note the way in which Bajaj move in the street. City administrators seem to be expressing a version of the "high modernism" critiqued by James Scott (1998) in the sense that they connected a functional city with a particular aesthetic sensibility.

Administrators at this level have completed some type of postsecondary degree, but one not necessarily in their field of work. For example, Mr. Hayyamo had an educational background in business. Administrators usually do not develop policy on the basis of academic research and theories of urban transportation. Instead, they often cited their personal experience with moving through the city in government cars. Bajaj "close" the street because they swerve through traffic and at times move in small clusters. Ideally, four-wheeled vehicles are organized into neat lines, confined to specific lanes unless passing another vehicle. At least, this was the image presented in models of Hawassa's future, as displayed on posters in some city planning offices. Administrators noted that an alternative to banning the Bajaj from major streets was to confine it to specific traffic lanes. However, the Bajaj is not easily confined. A three-wheeled vehicle is much narrower and has a tighter turning radius than a four-wheeler. Its light weight and slow speed also enable the Bajaj to stop quickly, meaning that it need not maintain a great deal of distance from the vehicle in front of it. It seems that the car has set a standard for how a modern vehicle moves through the city, and it is difficult or undesirable for the Bajaj to conform to this standard. In this case the interests of the small elite population of car owners and the orderly aesthetics of high modernism overlap.

Interviews with city administrators indicate that the problem with the Bajaj is not simply that drivers "work for injera." After all, nearly all transportation workers in Ethiopia work for profits. The politics of transportation are shaped by the particular intersection between Bajaj technology and administrators' visions of modernity, as administrators struggle to control and contain the peculiar agency and vitality of the Bajaj. This is based in part in an affective relation to the technology. Affective attachments to transportation technologies are common (Lutz 2014; Truitt 2008), and in this case state administrators' desires for a modern city drive their approach to regulating transportation. As in conflicts over the regulation of motorbikes in Southeast Asia (Sopranzetti 2014; Truitt 2008), Hawassa's regulators have difficulty managing the mobility of the Bajaj. State actors in Hawassa, however, have interests that are not simply regulatory, and they use transportation policy to impose a particular aesthetic associated with modernity.

The Bajaj does not fit administrators' standards of modernity, and therefore it is not appropriate for the future city they seek to create. Regulations are intended to achieve a particular aesthetic sensibility that transforms the visual and temporal experiences of moving through the city. It is no accident that state administrators stressed visitors' impressions of Hawassa. Like attempts to regulate motorbike taxis in Kigali, Rwanda, where the state's highest priority is constructing an idealized image of development (Rollason 2013), attempts to regulate the Bajaj in Hawassa are intended to help the city perform a particular vision of modernity. The Ethiopian state is certainly regulating the market, but these regulations are largely based in the aesthetics of modern mobility, rather than a concern with the ability of markets to properly distribute transportation.

In terms of productive inequalities, the state's vision of an orderly city comes at the expense of Bajaj drivers' livelihoods. Only by strictly controlling where Bajaj drivers may operate are state administrators able to advance their vision of Hawassa as a modern city. The proposed policy changes would sacrifice driver incomes to achieve a particular aesthetic sensibility. This productive inequality is inseparable from the vitality of the Bajaj. It is the specific way that a Bajaj moves and operates in an urban context that brings it into conflict with state visions for the city.[11] As I explain in the following section, government administrators also connected the Bajaj system with immoral behavior. In their critiques, the particular qualities of the Bajaj once again formed a foundation for an opposition between driver livelihoods and state visions of the city. Administrators argued that the regulations that limited driver incomes were necessary to prevent Bajaj drivers and passengers from engaging in criminal and immoral behavior.

The Morality of Mobility

Mr. Hayyamo explained that a key problem with the Bajaj is the drivers themselves. "Bajaj drivers have no respect for customers. They overcharge tourists and they ignore pedestrians." In his typically friendly but firm manner he argued that there is never a need to take a contract taxi that deviates from its assigned route unless it has been properly authorized. In the case of a medical issue an ambulance should be called (in fact, there were very few ambulances in Hawassa). As he explained, "If we let drivers deviate from their routes, they will be all over the place. Allowing people to travel by contract, especially at night, encourages crime. Drug dealers, prostitutes, and thieves all use [illegal] contract Bajaj."

State critiques of driver morality were based in the inexpensive nature of Bajaj transport. There is nothing intrinsically criminal about Bajaj drivers[12] and their passengers, but administrators believed that the Bajaj allows them to move through the city in a way that is unexpected and potentially dangerous. As the city has expanded, movement between neighborhoods that are increasingly stratified in terms of class has become more difficult. The horse carts that were once common in Hawassa are not functional for moving from one side of the sprawling city to the other. The morality of the driver, and to some extent of the passengers, is an issue because the inexpensive and fuel-efficient nature of the Bajaj provides very flexible transportation. The size of a minibus means that it is far too expensive to hire on a contract basis for point-to-point trips. Minibus travel requires that passengers ride on specific routes and then walk to their destination from the main road and back. Traditional four-wheeled taxicabs are rare in Hawassa, and they charge four to five times the amount a Bajaj driver would charge for a point-to-point trip. The Bajaj offers relatively inexpensive contracts and therefore gives Hawassa residents increased access to the newly expanded city.

For Mr. Hayyamo, the Bajaj is a technology that must be limited because it provides a mobility that allows people to engage in immoral behavior. By associating Bajaj use with crime and immorality, Mr. Hayyamo undermines the transportation needs of the poor and particularly women, for whom contract Bajaj provide a relatively safe means of moving through the city at night. I do not believe city administrators intended to impoverish citizens, but they did so by using associations with crime and immorality to justify limiting access to inexpensive, flexible transportation.

City administrators' attitudes toward two-wheeled motorcycles were also shaped by the intersection between class and perceptions of morality. The number of two-wheeled motorcycles on the streets of Hawassa has increased dramatically since the early 2000s. In contrast to Southeast Asia, however, where motorcycles are often associated with the working class (Truitt 2008), in Hawassa they were owned almost exclusively by upper-middle-class men. Indeed, all city administrators I spoke to were men, and most traveled by motorcycle. Although motorcycles provide the same sort of freedom of movement as a Bajaj, they were only available to a small, wealthy, male portion of the urban population. Administrators interpreted the rise in motorcycle ownership as a step toward a modern city rather than the reverse, and they did not assume that motorcycle ownership promotes criminality. A technology that enables flexible movement was only dangerous and potentially criminal when it was accessible to nonelite passengers. Like the discussion of modernity above, attention to Bajaj technology demonstrates that state regulation is not aimed entirely at taming an unruly market. In this case, assumptions that increased mobility will support criminal behavior justified denying specific segments of the urban population access to certain types of transportation technology. Similar to the way that administrators' visions of a modern city affected transportation policy, their perceptions of how Bajaj technology would undermine a safe and moral city supported regulations that limited drivers' incomes and their ability to engage in valued relations of reciprocity.

Competing Transportation Technologies

Proposed changes in Hawassa's public transportation policies were intended not only to reduce reliance on the Bajaj but to introduce a new type of minibus. Toyota minibuses have long been the dominant form of transportation in urban Ethiopia. Called "blue donkeys" because of their distinctive blue and white paint, these minibuses have provided much of the public transportation both within and between Ethiopian cities. However, smaller, cheaper, and more fuel-efficient vehicles have recently begun to appear on Ethiopian streets. In 2014 two new types of minibuses were being sold in Hawassa—the Damas produced by General Motors Korea, and the Indian-made Magic, produced by Tata. Although an increasing number of Damas were seen on the streets of Hawassa, I was unable to locate a company that was responsible for their sale. A single company, however, Red Star International, handled the import and sale of Tata minibuses.

Mr. Hayyamo introduced Eshetayehu and me to the owners of Red Star International after we told him that we were interested in talking with companies that are importing minibuses. Mr. Hayyamo hopped on his motorcycle, leading the way to the Red Star International showroom; Eshetayehu and I followed behind on Eshetayehu's motorcycle. Red Star International sells TVS brand three-wheeled motorcycles (the employees at Red Star are some of the few people in Hawassa who do not refer to them as Bajaj), and a few shiny new vehicles were on display in their showroom. Despite the moratorium on permits for operating a Bajaj taxi, vehicles could still be purchased for personal use. Also in the showroom, a woman in a traditional Ethiopian white cotton dress prepared coffee in a *jebena*, a handmade Ethiopian coffee pot. She served us coffee and snacks as we lounged on large, comfortable couches and watched satellite television.

Upon our first visit to Red Star International, the owner was on a business trip to India, and we met instead with the sales manager; we eventually learned she is married to the company owner. She explained that Red Star International has exclusive rights to sell ten-seat Tata minibuses. The minibuses will eventually sell for around 180,000 birr—about twice the price of a Bajaj. The sales manager noted that more than seven hundred people are on a waiting list to purchase the Tata minibus, and it will be available after they complete research on the vehicle's fuel usage, potential routes, and appropriate price.

We discussed the Hawassa municipal government's plans to replace the Bajaj with the minibus. The sales manager offered arguments that were remarkably similar to those we heard from state representatives. "Bajaj are problematic because they crowd the road. They expose the passenger to wind and rain. There are too many Bajaj in Hawassa. For a country to grow better things are needed, and Hawassa must change to grow. The drivers are also problematic. It is too easy to get a license and there are too many drivers. We have done research on the quality of Bajaj drivers and we found that they are very poor drivers." Around three months later, we returned to the showroom and interviewed the assistant general manager. He was more guarded about his opinions of Hawassa transportation policy. He claimed that transportation policy should be left to city administrators, and he did not have a strong opinion about transportation in Hawassa. If there is no market for Tata minibuses in the city, he was confident that they would be used in more rural areas.

The assistant general manager invited us to the home of the company owner to see the new Tata Magic minibus. Parked behind the company owner's Infiniti sport utility vehicle were a few Tata minibuses. These are nine-seat minibuses that are covered with canvas and have plastic windows on the sides that can be zipped down and left open. The owner explained that the canvas would be replaced with metal and glass in order to better fit the desires and expectations of Ethiopian passengers.[13] We asked whether the Tata Magic could stand up to the rough road conditions in Ethiopia; he responded, "Have you been to India? It is almost exactly like Ethiopia—the same climate, same terrain, same road quality, same road width, and same culture. Tata vehicles are well suited for Ethiopia. However, Chinese-made vehicles won't work here. The climate is very different than Ethiopia. The Tata Magic is perfect for Ethiopia." The owner might have also added that Ethiopia's low standards for vehicle safety and emissions make for a good fit with certain types of vehicles. For example, GM Korea recently resumed manufacturing Damas minibuses after the Seoul government chose to waive occupant safety and emissions rules for these models (Joon-seung 2014). Similar to city administrators, the assistant general manager conceptualized transportation policy primarily in terms of appropriate technology. The minibus is preferred to the Bajaj because of its technical qualities. The value of the Tata model is also established by comparing the Indian and Ethiopian contexts, and by arguing that what works in India will work in Ethiopia. As the sales manager noted, growth depends on having the best things, and change that supports growth is needed. In other words, one form of technology better supports modernization than the other.

Although government administrators and Tata representatives sought to justify their position regarding transportation policy with appeals to the aesthetics of technology, for drivers and Bajaj owners' association leaders, the policy was about wealth and inequality. Bajaj drivers and owners claimed that public and private interests were cooperating to consolidate control over the transportation market. They argued that the real beneficiaries of replacing the Bajaj with minibuses are the *bal habt*, the owners of wealth. Specifically, they noted that companies that import and sell minibuses would profit significantly if the municipal government makes the minibus the primary mode of urban transportation, and that government administrators had a financial interest in facilitating this shift.

To be clear, I have no evidence that this occurred. However, the possibility of collusion between government officials and minibus importers demonstrates the value of an analysis that is based in historical and vital materialisms. What if state officials were seeking to change transportation policy in order to prioritize the interests of minibus importers over Bajaj owners? If so, it would seem to be a clear case of accumulation by dispossession, in which the state intervenes to transfer the means of production from one group to another. Bajaj ownership was spread among a large group of people. Replacing the Bajaj with the minibus would have provided government administrators with opportunities to exert control over who owns the vehicles that allow the city to move. Officials could demand payoffs from the minibus importers in exchange for removing their main source of competition—the Bajaj. If this were to occur it would be a case of elites colluding to advance their economic interests at the expense of the small-business owners and laborers who own and drive Bajaj.

This type of historical materialist analysis has great value in clarifying the winners and losers in transportation policy. However, it also assumes that government administrators' claims about aesthetics, modernity, criminality, and the particular qualities of minibus and Bajaj technologies are simply a mask for advancing economic interests. Vital materialism reminds us that affective attachments to things are real and important. Administrators prefer the minibus to the Bajaj at least in part because they believe it is essential for reducing crime and actualizing their vision of a modern city. Technology is not simply a tool for advancing one set of economic interests over another. Different technologies are valued for a variety of reasons that are not necessarily directly connected with productive inequalities. It is for this reason that we must synthesize historical and vital materialisms. Infrastructural technologies have qualities that cannot be reduced to issues of exploitation.

The Bajaj System and Redistribution of Wealth

In contrast to government administrators, Bajaj drivers expressed a passionate critique of transportation policy that was based in a very different understanding of the relationship between morality, livelihoods, and Bajaj technology. For drivers, the implications of Bajaj technology for morality were directly related to productive inequalities. Many of my conversations with Bajaj drivers took place in the small coffee houses where drivers gathered for their midmorning and midafternoon breaks. Houses typically seat less than twenty customers, creating an intimate atmosphere in which group conversation is possible. These houses serve small cups of strong coffee brewed in a jebena. In the early 2000s I began to see a marked increase in the number of jebena coffee shops in Ethiopian cities. In Hawassa at least a dozen jebena coffee shops were within a five-minute walk from my home. Many Bajaj drivers patronized one particular shop, which also happened to have very good coffee. I often spent time there, for both the coffee and the conversation. In my experience jebena coffee shops are always run by women, and they sometimes develop business relationships with the Bajaj drivers who patronize their shops. For example, at the shop I frequented, the owner participated in a voluntary savings organization (*ikub*) with many of the Bajaj drivers.

During one of my visits I asked about the impacts of the government's decision to stop giving out new licenses to operate a Bajaj taxi. Setting down his coffee, a driver responded angrily, "It is not only the driver who works; one Bajaj creates at least four incomes. In addition to me, there is the owner, the mechanic, the guy who washes the Bajaj. All of us have families, and if we don't have work our entire family will suffer. If the government does not let us work, what can we do? We have to eat. We will be forced to steal." From this perspective, the Bajaj is a "pro-social" (Ferguson 2006) technology that supports a range of different jobs that prevent people from resorting to crime. In contrast to the city administrators, the driver made no mention of traffic problems or issues of creating a modern city. For the driver, the Bajaj was important in part because of the low passenger-to-vehicle ratio. This necessitated more vehicles on the street and therefore created more work.[14] Hundreds if not thousands of drivers worked every day to move the people of Hawassa through the city. The driver may "work for injera," but this injera was shared with his community.

A similar perspective was advanced by leaders of Bajaj owners' associations. Eshetayehu and I met with leaders from two Bajaj owners' associations in one of their offices—a desk and a few chairs in the back of a spare parts shop located near a busy intersection. The association leaders were adamant in their critique of state regulation. They claimed that a single Bajaj vehicle supports seven families, and that the jobs created are especially important for young people. Over the noise of traffic from outside the open door, an association leader passionately argued that "these new government regulations come because our drivers have a bad name, but the administrators don't know the truth about our drivers. They don't know how much we give to charity." Throughout the interview, leaders continually returned to this issue, telling stories of how drivers are harassed by police for deviating from their assigned routes, even if they are just returning home to eat. The association leaders were not denying that drivers do in fact violate state regulations. However, they insisted that this does not compromise the drivers' morality. Instead, they faulted the state for creating regulations that do not fit with the way the Bajaj enables drivers and their passengers to move through the city. Their concern was less that the state constrains a free market and more that state regulations prevented the redistribution of wealth that occurs as Bajaj drivers and owners support their dependents. In other words, policies that separate the driver from the product of his labor are immoral not simply because they affect the driver but because they prevent his engagement in relations of reciprocity.

Drivers also made a counterattack on the morality of government officials. In multiple conversations drivers explained that although Bajaj permits are not officially being issued, they can still be accessed through informal channels. They claimed that government officials give out permits on the basis of ethnicity or personal relationships. By closing off the regular means of obtaining a permit, administrators empower themselves, placing themselves in a position to dole out favors and build networks of dependents. Permits are not always given out on the basis of relationships. In some cases bribes are accepted. Drivers explained that a permit to operate a Bajaj previously cost 200–300 birr, but people were now paying 3,000 birr. In arguing that the state should not determine the availability of Bajaj permits, drivers were not necessarily calling for free access to permits, with the assumption that new permits will not be sought if the market is saturated. Rather, drivers contrasted the sharing and creation of work that the Bajaj system supports with the opportunities for graft and exploitation that are created when access to the Bajaj is limited. Drivers were positioning themselves as key actors in networks of redistribution and demanding a state that supports, rather than interferes in, their activities.

The conflicting perspectives on the moral dimensions of Bajaj technology offered by administrators and drivers were rooted in a system in which people functioned as infrastructure. The Ethiopian state sought to advance an agenda based in a very particular conception of a modern city in which people's movements are regulated and conform to established patterns and guidelines. Without the capacity to fund public transportation, however, the state has limited means of enacting this agenda. Instead, the state must require private transportation providers to conform to its plans for the city. In relying on private transportation providers, the Bajaj system supports personal mobility that is difficult for the state to control, but it also creates numerous jobs and opportunities for sharing one's income. In the absence of state-funded public transportation, drivers claimed that the Bajaj system generated income that is then redistributed through social networks. The struggle for states to provision infrastructure is common, but the particular conflicts generated by this dilemma were specific to the Bajaj technology. It is the flexible mobility of the Bajaj that led to administrators' claims that the vehicle supports criminality and opposes modernity. It is also the dependence of the Bajaj system on massive social networks of labor that led drivers to moralize the Bajaj as the foundation for desired relations of reciprocity.

The Risks and Rewards of Resisting Regulations

In practice, the movements of Bajaj drivers were shaped less by the driver's morals and more by the peculiar intersection of Bajaj technology, driver decision-making, state regulations, and market-based rewards. Bajaj drivers faced constant decisions that required balancing risks and rewards. They frequently deviated from their routes to make extra money, but this always carried the risk of a fine. Violating government transportation regulations was a means of resisting productive inequalities in the sense that drivers circumvented the laws that separated them from the product of their labor. An example: An empty Bajaj picks me up, and when I tell the driver that I am headed for the bus station, he responds that he is on the Market route and can only take me to the next Bajaj hub. Then he sees someone else waiting for a ride and picks her up. When he learns she is also going to the bus station, the driver agrees to make the trip. He gets a third passenger and continues dropping off and picking up, keeping his Bajaj full along the way. By the time we reach the bus station the driver has probably made 8 or 9 birr out of the trip. If he had stayed on his assigned Market route, he probably would have also picked up passengers, but in this case he was guaranteed two passengers taking the relatively long trip to the bus station. He definitely profited from his decision to defy city regulations. The degree of risk he faced here is unclear, but he certainly did hesitate to go off route. On a different occasion a driver picked me up at the same location. All three passengers needed to go to the bus station, but the driver refused to deviate from his route, choosing to avoid risk despite the opportunity to make a few extra birr.

Some drivers were certainly more cautious than others. A driver that my family frequently used for contracts was very careful about deviating from his route. He would deliver my family and me to our destinations—we represented a lucrative contract—but he often would take circuitous back streets to avoid traffic police. Typically, we would hire a different driver to return us home, and the driver would express no concern with fines.

Why did some drivers take risks in order to increase their profits whereas others refused to do so? I never found a satisfactory answer to this question. Drivers' backgrounds varied as much as their decisions. The driver who my family often called had worked for a number of years for an Evangelical Christian NGO in a nearby town. He was originally from Hosanna, and he claimed that people of Hadiya ethnicity, like himself, were discriminated against by the Sidama and Wolayta majorities in Hawassa. His girlfriend was working as a domestic servant in Lebanon, and he hoped to save enough money before her return to start a small business. More than once, when drivers dropped me near the university they asked about opportunities for pursuing a master's degree. Many had finished their bachelor's degrees and felt that a master's would allow them to find more desirable work. Many drivers came to Hawassa from elsewhere because a family member or friend owned a Bajaj and offered them work driving. I once met a Bajaj driver from the Amhara region, in northern Ethiopia, who had been working as an assistant on a heavy truck. When the truck broke down in Hawassa, he scrambled around and found work as a Bajaj driver. He had been in Hawassa for three years when we met.

If any connection exists between driver background and economic decision-making, it was too complex to be observed with the research methods I used. Perhaps more important than understanding sources of variation among drivers is simply acknowledging that the variation existed. Drivers have different personalities, backgrounds, and experiences, and these led them to make different decisions when they calculated rewards and risks. This variation introduced additional contingency in the struggle over city regulations. The municipal government is not only regulating a technology, it is regulating people, and people behave in very different ways, sometimes interpreting and responding to economic incentives in nearly opposite manners. Part of the state's vision of a modern city depends on the ability to organize traffic, separating different vehicles onto different routes and into different traffic lanes. Human behavior never makes its way into these models. Passengers want to get to their destination as quickly as possible, and they do not mind if drivers violate regulations. Drivers vary in terms of how they react to these incentives: some are happy to violate regulations for a few extra birr, whereas others refuse.

This human dimension interacts with the technology of the Bajaj and the market-based Bajaj system. In a larger vehicle with more passengers, it would not be possible for the driver to respond to the needs of a few and change his route. With a maximum of three passengers, the Bajaj is designed for flexibility. The Bajaj provides inexpensive flexibility that can be tailored to the needs of individuals. Without a market-based system, the incentive to deviate from one's route would also be absent. If drivers were simply paid a salary, either by the state or by vehicle owners, they would have little reason to violate state regulations. As I explain in the following section, changes in fuel prices and passenger fares introduced additional variables that shaped the willingness of drivers to follow state regulations. As productive inequalities increased to the point that drivers were able to earn very little from their labor, they were pushed beyond a breaking point, and the vast majority of drivers chose to reject state regulations.

The Fuel Crisis, the Bajaj Driver Strike, and Demands for Governance

Tensions that erupted during the March 2015 Bajaj driver strike had been brewing for some time. In early 2014 it was common to see lines of thirty to forty Bajaj waiting at the only station in Hawassa that had the blended benzene fuel used by Bajaj and other motorcycles. Drivers often waited three or four hours for fuel, and other times fuel was simply not available. For approximately two months only very small amounts of fuel were available, and stations were not permitted to sell more than three liters to a single customer. The absence of cheap, easily available fuel began to strain the Bajaj system to the point that drivers could no longer earn a livelihood. This was experienced not simply in terms of a loss of employment, but as an erosion of social networks that were based in reciprocity.

In the absence of fuel at state-regulated stations, drivers often bought fuel illegally on the black market. The state price for fuel was 22 birr per liter, and it typically cost around 25 birr per liter on the black market. During the fuel shortage, however, drivers were paying at least 40 birr per liter and occasionally as much as 70 birr. City administrators refused to increase the fare for passengers, and Bajaj drivers were put in a bind. In addition to the daily payment to the vehicle owner, drivers were expected to pay for their own fuel. Many drivers found that they were actually losing money or were working all day for 10 or 20 birr in profits. Drivers who owned their own vehicle could still make a profit, but those who worked for an owner often elected to stay home. Others chose to continue working, just as a way of keeping busy, even if their incomes barely covered their fuel expenses.

The fuel crisis interacted with expectations for a livelihood that were shaped in part by drivers' gender and age. Although Bajaj drivers came from a wide range of backgrounds and had varying levels of education and family support, they were almost exclusively young men, roughly between the ages of eighteen and thirty-five. For most of them, driving a Bajaj was a step toward something else. It was a means of saving money, helping one's family, and eventually taking on the normative responsibilities of an adult. Young men conceived of social maturation largely in terms of shifting their position within relations of reciprocity—moving from a position of dependence, to one of independence, to one in which they could support others (Mains 2012b). In a context of high urban unemployment, working as a driver provided an opportunity for young people who felt they were stuck in the social category of youth to mature. For a young driver, power over the product of his labor was essential for constructing himself as an adult man.

One driver explained that he had been a soldier and used his savings of 2,000 birr (around $125 at that time) to obtain a Bajaj driver's license. He claimed that even a determined day laborer could save that amount. Then he used personal connections to find an owner in need of a driver. Relationships are also important for maintaining one's livelihood as a driver. As another driver explained, "The most important thing for a driver is that people have your phone number. This is how we get paid, through contracts." On a 1.5-birr route, a driver would need to make more than four trips with a full load of passengers to equal the value of a 20-birr contract. Typically, driving routes involves the use of more fuel, which also cuts into profits. Access to regular contracts depended on one's social network. Hawassa residents often saved the phone numbers of a handful of Bajaj drivers. In this sense, working as a Bajaj driver is intertwined with a process of maturation in which one repositions oneself within relations of reciprocity. Social networks are utilized to access work and increase profits. As noted above, ideally that income is then redistributed to family members and others who assist with Bajaj maintenance. The experience of the fuel crisis was so painful in part because it decreased drivers' control over the product of their labor, ruptured relations of reciprocity, and inhibited self-construction.

Although city administrators did not authorize an increase in the amount charged to passengers, many drivers chose to illegally increase passenger fares. Typically, they charged around twice the usual fee and informed passengers of the price as they were boarding. For two months, Bajaj passengers and drivers talked of little other than fuel price and the state. Passengers expressed very little resentment regarding the increased fares; instead, most sympathized with the drivers and argued that if the state would increase passenger fares, at least prices would be consistent and known in advance.

On one ride the driver increased the price by 25 percent, stating, "The government won't raise the fare, so I have to."

Conversations were particularly heated at the coffee shop where I spent time. One of the drivers commented, "We need a benzene government." When asked what he meant by this, he explained that the city needs a government that will fix the fuel shortage. "The owners of power and wealth are working together to make money. The law and the poor never meet. If the price of benzene goes up, the government always promises to raise passenger fares, but it never does. If the price of benzene goes down, the government lowers fares immediately." The driver's claim that "the law and the poor never meet" was not entirely accurate. In refusing to raise passenger fares the state was protecting the interests of the working poor who rely on Bajaj for transportation. However, the state's governance of fuel also constrained drivers' ability to earn an income.

In the absence of state intervention, drivers relied on each other. On one midmorning visit to the coffee shop, the place was full of drivers. The conversation was lively and animated, focused almost entirely on benzene. Which fuel stations have it? Who is selling it on the black market and for what price? Drivers telephoned friends to get updates from around the city. Merchants were bringing in fuel from other cities and selling it on the black market. The police tried to combat this by forbidding fuel stations to fill jerry cans—only vehicles could be filled. One driver pestered another to sell him a couple liters of fuel, but the other driver refused, explaining that even if he had extra fuel he would not sell it. Friends exchanged information, but the support that could be accessed through relationships was limited at the time of a crisis. Such reliance on informal, relationship-based networks is often valorized as a solution to the inability of states to provide basic services (Elyachar 2012). However, drivers were very clear that they expected state intervention.

As the situation progressed, frustrations among drivers increased. At the coffee shop, around a month after the shortage began, a driver responded with annoyance to my question of why nothing has been done about the shortage. "Who will take care of it?" he responded. "There is no government." A different driver responded to a similar question by simply saying, "The government is unable to do anything."[15] The implication was that the state is weak and incapable of providing the basic governance needed for regular transportation. The same state that drivers often complained was too oppressive, and unnecessarily regulated their movement through the city, was now absent. For drivers, a government that could not solve their problems was no government at all. Drivers were calling for a particular type of governance in which the state facilitates their use of technology to maintain a livelihood. This is not an absent state, but one that provides the resources the people need to do their work. It is a state that recognizes the human dimensions of transportation and allows people to use technology to provide a public service.

Just as the Bajaj system allowed young men to earn incomes, support their families, and create work for others, a shift in that system undermined these relations of reciprocity. If the Bajaj has agency, then its ability to act is shaped by other materials. In this case, fuel was the most important. The explanations I encountered for the fuel shortage were connected to other technologies and regional politics. For example, I was told that all fuel trucks were required to be fitted with GPS trackers. After one year the regulation was finally being enforced, and many fuel trucks were unable to operate until they were outfitted with the trackers. Others claimed that war and instability in South Sudan and Sudan were disrupting supply chains. Still others claimed that petrol station owners had inside information that state-regulated prices would soon rise, and station owners were holding back fuel until the price went up. These rumors make it clear that tensions over the regulation of the Bajaj were embedded in deeper layers of technopolitical relationships.[16] It is no accident that drivers demanded a "benzene government." The Ethiopian state could support drivers and their livelihoods only if it could properly govern a material such as benzene and the complex supply chains through which it arrives at fuel stations in Hawassa.

On March 26, 2015, Bajaj drivers collectively refused to work. The strike did not last long. The municipal government ordered minibuses that usually provide intercity transport to cover Bajaj routes within Hawassa. Some of the leaders of Bajaj owners' associations were arrested and jailed until the drivers went back to work. Administrators also threatened to revoke the taxi permits for any vehicles that did not return to work. By the afternoon of March 27 the strike was finished and nearly all drivers were working.[17]

At the time of the initial fuel shortage, I had asked drivers why they did not strike to force the government to increase passenger fares. Drivers found the suggestion almost incomprehensible. At that time a strike was not given even minimal consideration. The strike of March 2015 was precipitated by a significant drop in the state-mandated passenger fare. The municipal government reduced fares to the point that for drivers, challenges in the day-to-day struggle to get by became nearly insurmountable.

In August 2014 the municipal government actually increased fares. Drivers claimed that the new fare finally allowed them to earn a steady income. They could eat three meals a day and still take home 30–40 birr ($1.50–$2.00) in profits. In early 2015, the global price of oil dropped, and in Ethiopia the state-regulated price of fuel was reduced by around 3 birr per liter. Soon after, the municipal government reduced fares for Bajaj passengers. The new fares were even lower than the rates before the August 2014 fare increase. Drivers complained that before the change there had been no discussion between state administrators and drivers, passengers, or association leaders. The rates were simply announced. They argued that these new low rates were a way of making residents happy in advance of the national election in May.

The new rates made it very difficult for drivers to earn an income. "We are working to improve our lives; work is meaningless if there is no profit," a driver noted before detailing all of his daily expenses, including meals and coffee. "When the government reduced the passenger fares, there was simply not enough money. I could work all day and not be able to eat. How can I support my family? We had to strike." Other drivers offered similar sentiments and framed the decrease in passenger fares in terms of food, claiming that they were forced to skip meals.

When Eshetayehu and I met with Mr. Hayyamo to discuss the strike, we anticipated that he might argue that reducing passenger fares is a pro-poor policy designed to ensure that everyone can access transportation. Instead, he repeatedly emphasized the role of research in determining passenger fares. The August 2014 fare increase was based on "estimates" and was not thoroughly "researched." In contrast, the decision to decrease fares was based on two months of research conducted at the regional level in different cities. Researchers assessed the price of fuel, average Bajaj fuel consumption, and the price of spare parts and vehicle repairs. We obtained a copy of the research report. The document is a detailed assessment of expenses and income, but entirely from the perspective of the Bajaj owner. The driver, and his need for an income, is almost absent. Based on the research report, the new reduced passenger fare would provide vehicle owners with an annual profit of around 40 percent on their investment. However, there was no calculation of how this fare would affect the people, predominantly young men, who drive the Bajaj. The document demonstrates a close examination of the details of Bajaj technology and the expenses required to keep a Bajaj on the road, but the human/technology relationship is entirely absent. Government research did not acknowledge that the Bajaj system depends not just on a single driver, but on hundreds of drivers to move people through the city.

The characteristics of a Bajaj that make it so functional as a form of urban transport depend on a large pool of low-cost urban labor. The relatively low income demanded by drivers supports urban transportation in cities such as Hawassa, but low income is not the same as no income. Drivers desired a state that provides minimal interference as they move people through the city, yet recognizes their need to maintain a stable livelihood. In the process of reducing passenger fares, the state refused to recognize the labor of drivers as a public good that allows the city to function. This is one of the peculiar dilemmas of paratransit—the state cannot afford to even subsidize driver salaries, and yet the state depends on their labor in order to maintain a livable city.

From the perspective of drivers, a functioning state is essential to maintaining a Bajaj system that is based in social relationships and reciprocity. The state is expected to intervene in order to ensure that drivers are properly compensated for their work. As the Bajaj passenger quoted at the outset of this chapter noted, there is no city without the Bajaj. Many drivers would have taken this statement a step further and clarified that there is no Bajaj without a driver, and there is no driver without an income. The Bajaj strike was an explicit demand for recognition of the role that Bajaj drivers play in maintaining a functional city and their reciprocal relationship with state administrators. It was a statement that the city depends on the labor of drivers, and therefore drivers deserve greater control over the products of their labor.

Conclusion

The dynamics at play in governing the Bajaj in Hawassa are increasingly common in relation to struggles over urban infrastructure. Particularly in a world where states struggle to provide basic public services, people and their social networks often function as urban infrastructures. In discussions of contemporary Africa, a narrative has emerged in which young urban entrepreneurs use new, inexpensive technologies to fill gaps in services that states cannot or do not provide (Olopade 2014). In many ways the Bajaj is just such a technology. Because it is cheap and fuel efficient, the Bajaj enables urban residents to move through the city and carry out the business necessary to sustain livelihoods. Through the Bajaj system, vehicle owners and drivers earn profits while providing a service that is far beyond the means of financially strapped municipal governments. This dynamic is certainly not unique to developing countries. In cities in the United States, companies such as Uber and Lyft take advantage of widespread ownership of smartphones and private vehicles to supplement a largely dysfunctional public transportation system. Although paratransit systems such as ride sharing or the Bajaj exist in part because of the failures of the state, they should not be conceived of as independent from, or opposed to, the state. The Bajaj case demonstrates that the transportation market is thoroughly interwoven with the work of governance. States depend on paratransit for cities to function, and the people who drive and maintain vehicles need state regulations to maintain viable livelihoods.

The interaction between state regulation and market incentives need not be conceptualized in terms of a reified state/market binary. The synthesis between historical materialism and vital materialism offers an analytical lens through which we can see that tensions between states and the people who provision infrastructure are shaped by productive inequalities and the particular characteristics of infrastructural technologies. The Bajaj is an unusually flexible and inexpensive motorized vehicle. It moves people through the city in a particular way that potentially generates incomes for drivers and others, but also crowds city streets and allows passengers to access the city in ways that were not previously possible. Government administrators connect the types of movement enabled by the Bajaj with issues of modernity and criminality, and in regulating public transportation they seek to enact a particular vision of the future city that is only actualized by increasingly separating drivers from the products of their labor. State regulations create a city in which Bajaj drivers work and provide transportation but receive little in the way of income. The cases of the fuel crisis and the drivers' strike demonstrate that, rather than an idealized free market, drivers demand a particular form of governance. The Bajaj system depends on an extensive network of drivers, mechanics, and other service providers that is maintained through relations of reciprocity. Drivers demand a state that supports their participation in redistributive networks and compensates them for their work in maintaining a functional city.

Construction is not always about the physical process of building. Transportation is essential for the construction of a city, both in terms of the city's image and the movement of people and things. It is through Bajaj transport that Hawassa was made and remade daily. It is also in constructing a city through public transportation that the city may be unmade. Administrators in Hawassa sought to manipulate transportation policy to build a modern city. In doing so they placed such pressure on the drivers that the drivers refused to work and the city came to a standstill. In constructing the city, Bajaj technology, labor, and state plans all collided. Although this encounter was generally functional in the sense that movement was maintained, it was always tense and potential for major disruption lurked just below the surface. The synthesis of vital and historical materialisms that I have outlined in this chapter offers a lens for understanding this complex and shifting encounter.

A different sort of construction is also at work here. Bajaj drivers construct the city, but they also construct their own lives. Ideally, the labor of driving a Bajaj allowed drivers to experience social maturation by shifting their position within relations of reciprocity. In the following chapter on cobblestone roads, I further explore this intersection between the labor of building cities and one's life. Like the case of the Bajaj, with cobblestone roads the particular materials are essential to the process of constructing lives and cities. It is through technologies such as the Bajaj and cobblestone that young people interact with the state and transform their lives through labor.

FIVE. What Can a Stone Do?

Cobblestone Roads, Governance, and Labor

What can a stone do? According to the German Development Cooperation Office (GIZ), quite a lot. The GIZ document, "Making Good Governance Tangible: The Cobblestone Sector in Ethiopia," contains a figure explaining "how a simple piece of stone makes a difference" (2012, 2). The figure displays lines radiating from a cobblestone connecting with good governance and various other impacts: environment, health, social, employment, and economic. GIZ argues that it is the particular material and technical qualities of cobblestone that create these impacts.[1] In contrast to the nineteenth century, when the German government was one of the world's biggest builders of dams intended to support a "conquest of nature" (Blackbourn 2006), cobblestone is valued for its use of local materials and minimal environmental impact. Beginning in 2007, first with the help of GIZ and then with assistance from the World Bank, Ethiopia has employed well over 100,000 people to build more than one thousand kilometers of cobblestone roads, primarily in urban areas. This chapter explores the complex intersections between the multiple things that cobblestones build—roads, states, lives, and relationships. These processes of building simultaneously support and undermine each other.

Cobblestone roads are interesting in part because they are a clear deviation from how most roads are constructed in the twenty-first century.[2] Given the Ethiopian state's intense focus on modernization, it might seem odd to invest significant resources in cobblestone road construction. In much of the world cobblestone roads are associated with the past. For someone such as myself, raised on the west coast of the United States—a world of asphalt and concrete—cobblestone feels quaint, a comforting association with European cities and an idealized past. In Ethiopia, however, cobblestone is something new that replaces dirt roads. Cobblestone roads support faster movement and increased commerce. They are not, however, associated with technical modernity in the same way as hydroelectric dams and asphalt roads. The process of chiseling and setting cobblestones is visible to urban residents, and it is a variation on forms of masonry that Ethiopians have long been acquainted with. The pace of development associated with cobblestone is also distinctive. Cobblestone roads represent change, but it is a slow change, not the dramatic transformation of a new asphalt road or a megadam.

Cobblestone's agency—the manner in which it builds roads, lives, and states—is shaped by its specific temporality of development. In Ethiopia, both the government employees who administrate cobblestone construction and the young people who build the roads have particular goals to accomplish. In the case of the Bajaj that I examined in chapter 4, the particular qualities of Bajaj technology interacted with productive inequalities to create tensions between the state and the people, primarily young men, who provided public transportation. Cobblestone also mediates the encounter between the state and the people who provision infrastructure. In this case, however, the particular temporal qualities of cobblestone actually work to alleviate tensions between the state and the young people who build roads.[3]

In contrast to cases in which people function as infrastructure and fill gaps resulting from the state's failure to provide basic services, in the case of cobblestone the state builds infrastructure to create work. Cobblestone is a development strategy that has much in common with the public works projects of the New Deal in the United States in the 1930s in the sense that cobblestone roads are quite valuable for Ethiopian cities, but the jobs created through the process of construction are even more important. During the 1990s and early 2000s, rates of youth unemployment in Ethiopian cities hovered around 50 percent, and the duration of unemployment averaged three to four years (Serneels 2007). Idle young men had a particularly visible presence on the streets of urban Ethiopia (Mains 2012b). The chiseling and setting of stones has created jobs for some of them, allowing them to experience normative social maturation. The physically demanding nature of cobblestone work is not for everyone. My father was a self-employed stonemason, and after working with him for a summer when I was sixteen, I can definitely sympathize with Ethiopians who want no part of cobblestone work. For young people who are willing to engage in the slow physical work, however, cobblestone constructs them into adult men and women.[4]

For the Ethiopian state, cobblestone is an appropriate technology because it does more than create jobs. Cobblestone builds a relationship between the state and urban youth. The numerous urban development programs that the Ethiopian government initiated after the contentious 2005 elections were intended to reward members of the ruling party and increase dependence on the state for survival and employment (Di Nunzio 2014a, 2015). To the extent that cobblestone has created steady work for young people and allowed them to participate in progressive narratives of becoming, it has eased tensions between youth and the state. As I examine below, this process is in no way simple. Young workers and government administrators are not the only relevant parties in cobblestone road construction. International organizations such as GIZ have goals of their own for cobblestone, and at times their efforts to use cobblestone to support good governance undermine the Ethiopian state's attempts to engage with urban youth. The success of cobblestone as a development strategy ultimately hinges on the contrasting agendas of youth, government administrators, international funders, and the peculiar qualities of stones. Like the case of the Bajaj, cobblestone must be analyzed in terms of historical and vital materialisms—the encounter between struggles over the product of the labor of young cobblestone workers and the particular characteristics of cobblestone. In contrast to the other forms of construction I have examined, the young people who build cobblestone roads are organized into cooperatives that share the profits from their work, and this reshapes the inequalities associated with building roads.

I close this book with the case of cobblestone because it is a way of thinking about alternatives. What if the materials used in construction were selected with the intent of creating work? What if builders shared in the profits from their labor? How is construction different under these conditions? Like all development interventions, cobblestone has its advantages and disadvantages. My interest lies in using the cobblestone case to explore the possibilities that emerge when infrastructures create livelihoods.

Promoting Good Governance through Cobblestone

The story of cobblestone roads in Ethiopia is one of traveling technologies (von Schnitzler 2013). Cobblestone is a technology specifically borrowed from one context and placed in another. The mayor of Ethiopia's second-largest city, Dire Dawa, was impressed by cobblestone roads he saw during a visit to Europe in 2005. He tried to implement cobblestone road construction when he returned to Dire Dawa, but he did not have the institutional support necessary to sustain the project. In 2007 the Ethiopian Ministry of Education coordinated with GIZ to construct cobblestone paving for thirteen new universities that were under construction. Eight German craftsmen were hired to lead a training program in cobblestone paving. This soon led to training programs and cobblestone road construction in various Ethiopian cities. The encounter between German cobblestone trainers and Ethiopians was not a smooth one. I interviewed a GIZ administrator who described the trainers as "big guys from southern Germany" who "didn't speak English and sometimes used their fists" as teaching tools. If Ethiopian trainees did not complete a square of cobblestone correctly, the trainers would tear it out and make the trainee start again. Trainees were paid only for work done correctly. Despite these frictions, the program expanded. Ethiopian trainees were tested and evaluated. The best were hired to train others, and the program soon spread throughout the country.

The Ethiopian government used World Bank funds to finance the construction, and GIZ provided technical assistance relating to both the construction and administration of the cobblestone roads. In the first three years of the project approximately 350 kilometers of roads were constructed in Ethiopian cities. Two years later, with assistance from a $300 million grant from the World Bank's International Development Association, cobblestone coverage had almost doubled to 670 kilometers. In 2014 the World Bank announced that it would be providing Ethiopia with $380 million in loans to support urban local governments, with much of these funds devoted to cobblestone projects.

For GIZ, the particular nature of cobblestone construction is essential to the production of good governance. Although the cobblestone technology is borrowed, the purpose that GIZ intended it to serve in Ethiopia was quite specific to the challenges of a twenty-first-century developmental state. Urban infrastructural development projects typically are managed at the level of the regional state and carried out by large companies based in Addis Ababa. The small number of construction companies means that competition is low, bids are high, and most of the money funding construction flows into the pockets of wealthy business owners. In the case of cobblestone, some workers organized into associations and were awarded contracts to carry out specific construction projects. The relatively small size of cobblestone projects meant that they could be managed at the city level and carried out by the small associations of young people who were in great need of employment (German Development Cooperation Office 2012, 8). Initially, the municipal government granted all cobblestone association contracts without competition. As more associations formed and competition increased, associations were required to submit bids for contracts. As prices have decreased through competitive bidding, the private sector has gradually become more interested in investing in cobblestone, but as of 2017, most cobblestone associations continued to rely on government contracts for employment.

GIZ argues that the process of managing and awarding competitive bids for contracts has provided local administrators with valuable experience in overseeing the process of infrastructural development. Each cobblestone road construction project is no more than a few kilometers long. This means that inexperienced administrators can refine their management skills through these projects. Decentralization occurs as local governments develop the capacity to manage their own projects rather than rely on the federal government to do so. In contrast to the multibillion-dollar dam contracts that I discussed in chapter 1, these contracts, which are generally less than $20,000, are low risk, and a failed project does not doom the entire national or even a city budget. Furthermore, the various competing cobblestone associations generally know each other and often work together. As they share information about the process of procuring a contract, they create a level of transparency.

The tangible, visible nature of cobblestone is also important. Cobblestone roads are constructed in urban residential neighborhoods where citizens can directly observe every step of the construction process. Workers usually bring rocks from quarries located close to the cities where they will be used. The rocks are then chiseled into the appropriate size for paving. Walking through Jimma, one would frequently encounter large piles of chiseled stones waiting to be purchased by cooperatives for building roads. This can be contrasted with the remote locations of megadams, where no direct observation of construction is possible. Citizens can identify and critique the inefficiencies and instances of corruption that are often associated with state-managed projects, thus creating a degree of accountability that does not exist for larger projects that are not so easily observed from start to finish. For example, the photo in figure 5.1 was taken in 2012. In 2017 this road was a massive series of ruts and potholes as the stones had been pressed

FIGURE 5.1. Cobblestone road construction in Jimma. Photo by the author.

down into the soil and were barely visible. Jimma residents were quick to blame the municipal government for this problem, demanding to know why the surface had not been properly prepared before the cobblestone was set. Compared to asphalt, cobblestone roads are relatively simple to maintain, and crews of one or two people carried out this maintenance. The same work would have been far more costly and time consuming in the case of asphalt, as repairing large potholes often requires completely resurfacing the road. That said, in cases of severe deterioration such as that on this road, the road would need to be totally remade.

In many cases municipal governments established offices to handle urban infrastructural development, with cobblestone roads as their primary focus. GIZ argues that the tangible nature of cobblestone creates a cycle that improves governance and infrastructure. As citizens see and experience the rapid construction of cobblestone roads, they become more involved in participatory processes. They begin to demand infrastructural development and hold local administrators responsible when it does not occur in a timely manner. GIZ is correct that urban residents have access to city administrators. My meetings with city administrators were consistently interrupted by residents, often appointed by their communities, poking their heads into the office to demand that a grievance be addressed. Cobblestone seems to give citizens faith that urban infrastructural development can occur. The easily observable benefits of cobblestone also support financial contributions from those who live near new roads. In some cases, the municipal government asked those living along cobblestone roads to contribute funds. Community contributions generate a sense of investment and further increase demands for accountability.

GIZ discourse concerning cobblestone is based in an interesting interpretation of material agency. For GIZ, the stone and the broader system for the construction of cobblestone roads shape the state and its strategies for governance. In this sense both individuals and the state are assumed to be quite malleable. Individual goals, state ideologies, and broader patterns of behavior are all limited by the material dimensions of the stone. Undesirable techniques of governance can be transformed by implementing materials that support particular relationships and systems of infrastructural construction. GIZ is certainly correct to acknowledge the power of cobblestone to shape governance. However, the Ethiopian state and cobblestone workers do not simply react to the stones and let the cobblestone system shape them. They have their own goals, and they seek to incorporate cobblestone into their particular agendas. In the following sections I explore how the state and cobblestone workers use the material dimensions of stones to advance their interests.

Building Cobblestone Cities

In Jimma and Hawassa I spoke to government administrators who were responsible for overseeing cobblestone road construction. These administrators consistently described the value of cobblestone in building cities. Cobblestone roads increase the city's beauty, and this aesthetic shift has economic consequences as well. The cobblestone increases the value of urban real estate, attracts investment, and encourages the creation of small businesses. This in turn generates tax revenues for the city, which can then be reinvested in urban infrastructure. In this sense cobblestone provides the foundation for long-term, sustained economic growth and improvements in quality of life.

For the most part, my research in Hawassa supports these claims. My family and I lived for nearly one year along a cobblestone road that had been finished around two years before our arrival. The road was perhaps slightly less than a kilometer long, connecting two asphalt boulevards. It was not a primary transportation corridor; it was used mainly by local traffic. Before the cobblestone it was simply a dirt road and almost no shops existed there. In contrast to asphalt, cobblestone does not usually require that roads be widened, and few households lost significant amounts of property. By the time we arrived the road was lined with shops, and more businesses opened during our stay. Businesses included a wide range of shops and cafes. Jebena coffee shops and small general stores are often in the first wave of shops that open after cobblestone arrives, and these are followed by larger enterprises. A large restaurant featuring a shaded outdoor dining area opened shortly before we left the city. Restaurants such as this have the potential to become destinations that attract diners from other neighborhoods. Businesses on the street were gradually shifting from small enterprises catering to the needs of the local residents to larger businesses attracting customers from around the city.

Together with Eshetayehu, I conducted interviews with residents and business owners throughout Hawassa in neighborhoods where cobblestone roads had been constructed, such as the one pictured in figure 5.2. Business owners described an increase in profits and residents, higher rents and property values. Business owners often claimed that they specifically selected their location because of the cobblestone. The owner of a small restaurant in central Hawassa explained that "before there was nothing here, just dust and simple shops made of tin. Now, with the cobblestone, there is no dust and everything is beautiful. Things are moving, there is activity here. The Bajaj replaced the horse cart and now we have cobblestone. This is movement." Both literally and metaphorically, the roads get things moving. The cobblestone directly supports the movement of people and vehicles. At the same time, this movement refers to a more general sense that money is changing hands and a market is growing. Cobblestone brought a sense of opportunity.

The movement associated with cobblestone is different from that associated with asphalt. Relative to travel over dirt roads, moving over cobblestone is certainly faster and thus promotes more vehicle traffic, but vehicles move far slower than on asphalt. Cobblestone paving developed in Europe at a time when horse-powered transportation was common. The spaces between the stones provided traction for horses' hooves, and in some cases cobblestones were intentionally spaced to fit with horseshoes. In Hawassa the dominant vehicle is the Bajaj, not the horse cart. Cobblestone roads are

FIGURE 5.2. Cobblestone road in central Hawassa. Photo by the author.

not designed for horses and spacing between stones is minimized, but compared to asphalt, it still makes for a bumpy ride. Because cobblestone slows vehicles, the ambiance of a cobblestone road is different from that of asphalt. Cobblestone roads are quieter and invite more street-side activity, but they are not necessarily easier for walking, and their surfaces are particularly challenging for women in high-heeled shoes.

Building Relationships with Disenfranchised Youth

Cobblestone has brought significant changes to neighborhoods, and to some extent these changes represent a more gradual process of the pushing and pulling of residents that I described in relation to asphalt roads in chapter 2. Cobblestone roads do not directly displace residents, but the associated rise in real estate values and rents gradually attracts some while forcing out others. However, all city administrators that I spoke with were quite clear that the most important consequence of cobblestone roads is job creation. Like the GIZ analysis of cobblestone and governance, administrators' claims about job creation are linked to the specific material qualities of the stones.

Stones must be quarried, transported, chiseled, and set. Much of this work is done by hand. In urban Ethiopia, where rates of unemployment are high, city administrators appreciate labor-intensive methods of construction. In some other parts of the world, such labor-intensive methods would be prohibitively expensive, but in Ethiopia, where labor is cheap and plentiful, relying on local materials, simple technology, and manual labor is a means for governments to conserve funds.

It is important to note that the target population for much of this work was urban young men, roughly between the ages of eighteen and thirty. Although the role of women in road construction was valorized by the World Bank, only around one in three cobblestone workers were women, and in my experience many women were relegated to piecework such as chiseling stones. The state viewed unemployed men as a threat to stability and the reign of the ruling EPRDF party. Ethiopia's 2005 election brought to a head tensions between the state and urban young men. The election marked the first and last time (as of this writing) that opposition parties had the space to compete in a national election. The opposition had a great deal of support in urban areas, particularly among young people. The opposition won the majority of Parliament seats in urban areas, and when the EPRDF questioned the election results, protests broke out. Young men were the physical force behind many of the protests and riots in Addis Ababa after the national election, and as a result, thousands were imprisoned in detention camps.

Even outside the context of the election, young men who were unemployed or working in the informal sector habitually engaged in a number of activities that brought them into contact with the police—staying out late into the night, drinking, carousing, and sometimes fighting with each other. In response to the perceived social problems associated with unemployed youth, the federal government issued a "Vagrancy Control Proclamation" in 2004.[5] Although the proclamation is vague, it seems to give police the right to arrest anyone spending time on the streets without a visible means of subsistence (Ayele 2004). Joining a youth association and receiving a government-issued Youth Identity Card was one means of avoiding arrest for this offense. In addition to vagrancy, fighting, illegally operating businesses, and petty theft were common reasons for arrest, and many of the young men I worked with during my research in the early 2000s had spent at least a few nights in jail at some point in their lives.

Before the election, both youth and authorities acknowledged the possibility of young *duriye* (hooligans) creating disruptions. Another common term for a young man was *fendata*, which loosely translates as "explosive." The term *fendata* does not have the criminal connotations of *duriye* or *bozene* (idle youth; lumpenproletariat) and referred more to the nature of young men, who were seen as being full of emotions that they could not control. The use of *fendata* implied that young men are a time bomb that could very easily explode in the intense environment of an election. In 2005 many urban Ethiopians believed that almost all disenfranchised youth were supporters of the main opposition party, the CUD. "CUD is the party of *duriye*," one young man claimed shortly before the 2005 election. The reasons for this were not completely clear, but rumors of CUD representatives distributing petty cash or *khat* to youth were sometimes cited. According to youth, arrests of duriye were intended not only to eliminate a potential source of chaos, but to reduce the number of opposition voters.

Encounters between police and youth were particularly common during the postelection period, when protests sparked riots and violence throughout Addis Ababa in early June and early November of 2005. Government forces killed approximately two hundred people in the June and November uprisings, and thousands of young men were moved to detention camps outside of the city, where they were held without charge (Abbink 2006a). Police violence and the detentions were justified by arguments about the potential for unemployed young men to riot and spread violence in urban areas (Toggia 2008). For example, in an interview after the June 2005 violence, the state minister of information, Bereket Simon, said, "We are not happy that people have died. We are not happy that Ethiopians are being detained—some of those for reasons they don't stand genuinely for—but this is a country which needs to move forward, which needs to guard itself from anarchy taking over. If you allow violence and anarchy to reign in this country the result—that we have managed to avert—will take place and that, I assure you, would be very, very disastrous" (quoted in Henshaw 2005).

Although detaining thousands of young people certainly had a major impact on the urban youth population, it was clearly an inadequate solution to the problems of youth. As I discuss in more detail below, young men were frustrated with their inability to move forward through time and take on the normative social responsibilities of adults. Cobblestone work not only provided youth with an income and a path toward adulthood, it also directly connected them with the state. It shifted young people's engagement with the state from direct violence and oppression to something resembling cooperation.

Ethiopia is certainly not the first place where cobblestones and rebellious youth have encountered each other. From 1830 until 1968, cobblestones in Paris were associated with barricades and rebellion (Harsin 2002; Traugott 2010). Cobblestones were the tools that the working class could use to combat the state.[6] In nineteenth-century Paris, cobblestones were tools for building barricades or were stones to be thrown. At the beginning of the twenty-first century in urban Ethiopia, cobblestone was a means of getting the stone-throwing youth off the street and putting them to work constructing roads. If the Parisians of 1968 were searching for the beach beneath the cobblestone, in Ethiopia cobblestone was a means of building toward a very different future.

Cobblestone is intertwined with a progressive temporal process that fits quite well with the aspirations of young people. Administrators did not explicitly discuss the political implications of this process, but as I explain below, cobblestone directly addressed the frustrations of the disaffected young men whom the state viewed as threats to social stability. In this sense, cobblestone offered a very different means of state-building through infrastructure from dams or asphalt roads. In contrast to more monumental forms of infrastructure, images of cobblestone did not frequently appear in government propaganda. Instead, cobblestone was the foundation for building an urban youth population that was engaged with the state, and its success depended on supporting young people as they built their own lives and moved toward adulthood. Through the construction of cobblestone roads, the Ethiopian state sought to reengage with urban youth in hopes of establishing a degree of legitimacy.

Youth, Unemployment, and Expectations of Progress

Young men's engagement with cobblestone road construction and the state was conditioned by their experiences of time and unemployment. I have argued elsewhere that formal education created expectations that their lives would be progressive in the sense that they would experience linear improvement with the passage of time (Mains 2012b). Under the military dictatorship that ruled Ethiopia from 1974 to 1991, completing secondary education guaranteed access to government employment. At that time, and continuing until the early 2000s, government work was one of the most desirable forms of employment available in urban Ethiopia, both in terms of income and prestige. Education is also a progressive process in that it involves gradual linear improvements. One advances from grade to grade, and it is assumed that this movement creates a change within oneself. The educated individual expects to be transformed so that his future will be better than his present. Contrasts between unemployment and life as a student are revealing. For unemployed young men, school was the last structured activity they were involved in. One way school differs from unemployment is that it simply makes a person very busy, thereby eliminating the problem of how to pass excessive amounts of time. As one young man who had been unemployed for two years after completing grade 12 put it, "When I was a student I had no thoughts. I learned, I studied, and I didn't worry about the future. Now I always think about the future. I don't know how long this condition will last. Maybe it will be the same year after year." In contrast to student life, unemployment is the absence of change. Days pass, but one's material and social positions remain the same. Long-term unemployment prevented youth from imagining a desirable future and from placing their day-to-day lives within a narrative of progress. The social category of youth, as it exists for urban young men, emerges not just through an extended period of uncertainty regarding one's future but with the development of expectations of progress (Mains 2012b).

Young men's narratives of aspiration typically began with education, followed by work, and then helping younger siblings before moving out of their parents' home to marry and start families. Finally, young men believed that one should support his parents and create, if possible, a project or business that would benefit the community. Most urban youth were able to attain the first step in this narrative and pursue their education to the secondary level, but they were unable to find employment. This created a dead end in their pursuit of other aspirations.

Many young men believed that nearly insurmountable financial barriers prevented them from dating, marrying, and having children. They claimed that they would not marry before the age of thirty or thirty-five, and then only if they became wealthy. Children were seen as a natural and desirable result of marriage—the next step in youth narratives of aspiration—and the financial burden of raising children was an additional factor preventing young men from achieving their aspirations. To simply raise children did not involve any great costs, but most young men desired for their children a future that would be better than their own.

The underlying problem in achieving such progress was that the smooth transition between education and government employment had been ruptured. Many young men could have found work in low-status professions, but this would not have allowed them to develop the social relationships associated with their particularly urban Ethiopian notions of success, or to access an adequate income for raising children in the manner the young men desired. They sought both to preserve the quality of their social relationships with others by avoiding low-status work and to raise a family in which their children would lead modern progressive lives that involve more than "eating and sleeping," as they put it. As achieving this goal was thought to be impossible, many young men chose to remain unemployed. They could not access the economic resources necessary to become an adult in a normative sense, and therefore they could not move through time in the manner they desired. Young men were in the ambiguous position of continuing to aspire to become adults and reposition themselves within social relations, but lacking any faith that this process could be accomplished.

Young men often specifically blamed the state for their failure to take on the responsibilities of adults. In part because of the common expectation that they would eventually find government jobs, young men often argued that it was the state's responsibility to create employment opportunities. When urban young men took to the streets to protest the results of the 2005 election, they were implicitly connecting governance with opportunities for social maturation. They were demanding a state that supported their movement toward adulthood. For some young men, the introduction of cobblestone construction in 2008 provided a means of reengaging in narratives of social maturation, and of building their lives.

Cobblestone, Progress, and Becoming an Adult

Holyfield was one of the young men I could always find on a corner near the house I rented when I lived in Jimma between 2003 and 2005. He is very well built, with a broad, muscular back, and he takes his nickname from the American boxer his friends think he resembles. Although he was unemployed and his family was certainly not wealthy, he always managed to dress in fashionable soccer jerseys and jeans, and others occasionally teased him about the efforts he took to keep himself clean. He was one of the young men who participated in my research on unemployed youth, and he was nineteen when I first interviewed him in 2004. He had finished eighth grade a few years earlier and never pursued his education beyond that. He had been doing occasional construction work but considered himself to be unemployed. Like many unemployed young men, Holyfield spent much of his time hanging out in the shade from various trees near busy intersections, where he could keep an eye on the day-to-day happenings in his neighborhood. He complained that he was occasionally harassed by the police. It was nothing serious—they would just ask him to move on— but he assured me that this would never be a problem if well-paid work was available.

Like many young people, he had joined a youth association, and in 2004 he had been attending weekly meetings. He noted that initially many young people attended these meetings, but eventually the number dwindled to around ten. Through the youth association he was issued an ID card that he could show to police if they questioned him about vagrancy. During my first interview with Holyfield, he mentioned the possibility of using his contact with the youth association to organize with other youth to form a small company and receive loans and support from the city government, but this did not become a reality for many years. Before the contentious 2005 elections, youth associations were only informally connected with the state and had few funds to distribute to young people. In fact, at that time the office that managed the youth association in Jimma contacted me to request assistance in raising funds. It was not until the time of the 2005 election that the youth association became formally connected with the state and began to distribute small grants and loans to young people so that they could start small businesses (Di Nunzio 2014a).

I could always count on Holyfield for a bit of small talk as I made my rounds through Jimma in the early 2000s. During our conversations he often encouraged me to help him with some type of income-generating project. Eventually he convinced me to buy him simple woodworking tools so that he could start a business with a friend. The tools kept him busy for around a month, but he soon discovered that there was a limited market for the sort of curios he was carving. Both of us learned that starting a small business in urban Ethiopia is not easy and that sustained support is necessary.

When I returned to Jimma in 2008, Holyfield was not around. After a few years of unemployment he had left Jimma to find work with Salini on the second phase of the Gibe River hydroelectric project (Gibe II). Work on the project eventually slowed and Holyfield returned to Jimma, hoping to find work with a Korean road construction project. When this failed, he began doing cobblestone work. Many of the unemployed young men I had known in Jimma had left, at least temporarily, to work on various infrastructure construction projects throughout the country. As I will explain below, however, cobblestone work was distinct in its potential to create long-term change in the lives of young men.

When Holyfield and I met again in 2009 he was wearing a brilliant yellow tracksuit with "Brazil" printed across the front and dark wraparound sunglasses that took on a rainbow sheen when they reflected the sun. He took great pride in telling me about his involvement in cobblestone work, and he encouraged me to visit the work site. He was paid 1.5 birr for every stone he set. He could easily make at least 45 birr per day (around $4 at the time), and he often earned more than this. At that time, day laborers earned little more than $1 per day, so this was a significant source of income. For the first time in his life, Holyfield was able to set aside money, and he told me that he was saving for marriage.

Perhaps the most important shift in Holyfield's life since I had last seen him in 2005 was his relationship with family and community. He explained:

> I used to spend all of my time standing around on the corner, but now I am either working or indoors. People would insult me, call me a duriye or a thief. Now people give me respect. My family is very happy and proud. My parents tell me how to save money. All of this has greatly improved my mental health. This is the most important thing. Before, when I was not working, it was very stressful, constantly thinking about the future. Now I am so busy with work that I have no time for thinking. I work, shower, eat, and then sleep. My mind is free and it feels good.

When I returned to Jimma in 2012 and caught up with Holyfield, his life had changed further. He was still involved with cobblestone, but he had received a month of government-sponsored training. This helped him transition from working on a per-piece basis to operating a small construction association with five other young men, mostly friends from his neighborhood. Like other cobblestone associations, they submitted bids for projects that are organized by the municipal government. The members of Holyfield's association rotated different jobs among themselves, but one person was always responsible for accounting. Each member was paid a base salary of 500 birr per month, and then profits from completed jobs were shared among them, with some money set aside to invest in their company. Before forming a cobblestone association, Holyfield was working as a paver, being paid by the square meter. He was still doing paving, but he estimated that he now earned three to four times that amount when his association successfully won a contract. The organization of cobblestone workers into profit-sharing associations had profound impacts on the productive inequalities based in cobblestone construction.

Holyfield's association was just completing their first contract, and they were still saving money to purchase equipment. In the meantime they borrowed much of their equipment from the municipal cobblestone office. Holyfield claimed that running a cobblestone association was very educational, and it was possible to "learn with age and experience, not only from schooling." Like other associations, they hired others to assist with the labor, and these laborers generally came from associations that did not successfully win contracts.

Holyfield's financial independence had expanded significantly. He had opened a savings account at a bank and was saving money to obtain a driver's license. He had built a separate room for himself off of his parents' house and furnished the room with his own purchases. Holyfield continued to espouse a narrative in which work was associated with respect. "A person who does not work is not respected. This sort of person is a duriye. He has dirty clothes and bad hair. If youth from the neighborhood ask me for money, I tell them to come to our construction site and I will teach them how to work."

Holyfield's experiences were typical of young men who were involved in cobblestone construction. In 2013 and 2014 I interviewed young men in Hawassa who had been working with a cobblestone association for around three years. They spoke of beginning their work as pavers and then eventually becoming foremen. One used his earnings to invest in his family's rural land, planting trees such as eucalyptus that could be cut and sold in the future. Another supported his wife as she finished secondary school and entered a management program at Hawassa University. Others built rooms for themselves in their family's compounds and enrolled in evening classes at the university or the technical school.

Holyfield's was very optimistic about the future. He talked of starting a small business to create work for his sisters. His company planned to eventually take on larger and more capital-intensive construction projects. "Before, my thoughts were always negative," he explained, "but now I have hope for the future. Cobblestone roads mean progress for the community and the workers." Progress in this context means two things. First, for the community, cobblestone eases movement between neighborhoods and supports economic growth. More importantly, for Holyfield, cobblestone supports a very particular form of progress in which young men are able to reposition themselves within relations of reciprocity. Fitting with local conceptions of masculinity, young men use incomes from cobblestone work to move from a position of dependence, to one of independence, and eventually to a situation where they can provide support for others.

When I saw Holyfield in 2015 he was thirty, he had taken on many of the normative responsibilities associated with being an adult man. Shortly after I phoned Holyfield to let him know I was back in Jimma, he arrived at my hotel driving a Bajaj. In contrast to Hawassa, in Jimma owners are permitted to decorate their Bajaj, and Holyfield's featured a colorful painting themed after the British Arsenal soccer club. He had purchased the Bajaj with savings from his cobblestone work. He was a member of an *ikub*, a voluntary savings organization, in which each of the forty members contributed 100 birr per day, and one of the members received the accumulated savings every two weeks. When it was Holyfield's turn he invested in the Bajaj. He drove me to a café near Jimma University, an area of the city where I had never known him to spend time in the past, and he bought me a macchiato. He explained that he usually leased his Bajaj, creating work for a friend and an additional source of income for himself. Like many young men in Ethiopia, Holyfield's livelihood was based in multiple intersecting forms of infrastructure. He had worked for Salini on a large-scale hydropower project, was involved in cobblestone road construction, and had just purchased a Bajaj. Holyfield depended on Ethiopia's infrastructural development for an income, and the growth of infrastructure depended on his labor. He literally built some of the roads that made it possible to operate a Bajaj taxi in much of Jimma.

As we sipped our drinks, Holyfield explained, "When I look back on my life when we first met, I laugh. I was just standing around on the street all day. I would exercise in the morning, come home to eat, and then just hang out. I don't know what changed. Maybe it is just part of getting older, and realizing that I want to help my family. The cost of life is also more expensive now; you won't see youth just standing around on the street such as you used to. I am not a youth [*wettat*] anymore, I am a young man [*golmassa*]." Holyfield was maturing. He was working to build roads, and the roadwork was allowing him to build a family.

From the café we drove to the compound that Holyfield continued to share with his family. He introduced me to his wife, who was pregnant. Two of Holyfield's sisters were present. When I commented on the amount of new furniture and appliances in Holyfield's mother's house, they explained that most of them had been purchased with earnings from another sister who was working in the Middle East as a domestic servant. Holyfield's cobblestone work was important, but he would not have been able to save and invest in a Bajaj without help from his sisters and wife, who all earned incomes or provided unpaid domestic labor that supported the household.

A couple days later Holyfield gave me a tour of a recently completed project, a road near his home that required a total of 3,500 square meters of cobblestone. The rainy season was coming and it would be impossible to do more cobblestone work for the next few months. He explained that during the rainy season he often traveled to the nearby Dawro Zone to purchase sheep from farmers and then sell them at a profit in Jimma. Holyfield noted that opportunities such as this required a significant amount of starting capital, but once one had money there were many ways to make more. He identified this as a major difference between his present situation and his life in the past. Although he was investing in other income-generating opportunities, Holyfield planned to continue with his cobblestone work. It provided a steady source of income that could be combined with other opportunities. GIZ administrators also emphasized that cobblestone did more than create jobs. It "empowered" young people to "think about investment."

I have focused on the particular case of Holyfield because over the years I have gotten to know him well, but many of the young men who were involved in cobblestone work experienced a similar process of maturation. The slow, labor-intensive nature of cobblestone road construction creates jobs, but it is not only the materials that are important here; the method of construction and support from the state are highly significant. By supporting the organization of cobblestone associations, the state provided the opportunity for young men such as Holyfield to win contracts and reap significant profits that then supported other income-generating projects.

Cobblestone clearly is associated with progress, but a progress that is very different from that of hydroelectric dams. There is no Grand Ethiopian Renaissance Cobblestone, but all the same, cobblestone is associated with movement through time. It is movement in the lives of people and cities, rather than the transformation of a nation. It is also movement that is controlled by those who build the roads—the workers and city administrators. Holyfield had only an eighth-grade education, and he did not come from a particularly well-connected family, but his cobblestone work positioned him to make important decisions that would affect the possibility for progress in his own life. City administrators were also positioned to control the construction of roads and distribution of jobs within their communities. In contrast, large dams centralize resources and power in the hands of a few. High-level ministers in the federal government determine the distribution of electricity and profits from the dams. The construction of dams creates jobs, but large international companies such as Salini control the bulk of profits. Holyfield worked for Salini and was able to save a small amount of money. In contrast to cobblestone, this work, over the long term, had little impact on his ability to build his own life and reposition himself within relations of reciprocity because it did not provide him with the sort of control of capital he needed to generate further opportunities for accessing income.

In terms of productive inequalities, cobblestone differs from typical construction projects in two important ways. First, the members of the cobblestone association—such as Holyfield and his friends—are both owners and laborers. A cobblestone association functions as a kind of cooperative in which profits are shared. For example, in the case of one Hawassa-based cobblestone association, twenty-six pavers shared 70 percent of the profits between them. Holyfield's association had fewer members, and thus he received a greater share of the profits. These profits are in addition to a piecework payment that is well above market rates for manual labor. Second, the Ethiopian state has utilized grants and loans from the World Bank and GIZ to essentially guarantee at least occasional work for cobblestone associations. Not only are associations paid relatively well, but the state provides administrative assistance and help with accessing equipment. Not everything is equal within the cobblestone construction process, however. Managers and foremen take home a much larger share of the profits. Laborers working in earlier stages of the process, such as those who bring rocks from quarries, are not association members and do not share the profits. In general, however, the laborers in cobblestone construction are able to exert much more control over the product of their labor than other workers in the construction industry. It is worth asking how the construction of asphalt roads and dams would differ if the laborers who built these infrastructures shared among themselves the profits from million- and billion-dollar contracts. Cobblestone demonstrates that this is not a purely hypothetical question; such labor relations have been successful in constructing durable infrastructures.

Although cobblestone roads clearly supported incremental improvements in the lives of young men, these transformations were continually interrupted by delays between projects and payments. In some ways these disruptions are intrinsic to the nature of infrastructural work. They are also connected to relations between city governments and international lenders, and to GIZ's goal of using cobblestone to promote good governance. In 2015 Holyfield explained that there were currently sixty cobblestone companies in Jimma, where there had been only eleven a few years ago. Although the number of cobblestone projects had increased, with so much competition there were still far more gaps between contracts than in the past. He claimed that in some cases cobblestone associations resorted to using bribes to access contracts, but this was not as common as with other types of road construction, where the stakes were higher.

The lack of regular work was the most common grievance among cobblestone workers. Association members spoke of delays in payment, explaining that they often waited for months to be paid after completing a project. One association described a delay of seven months before being paid for their work. They struggled to budget their money to survive the occasional long dry spell between jobs. Irregular work made complete financial independence impossible, and most cobblestone workers continued to live with their parents. Holyfield had built a room within his family compound, but he was not prepared to purchase or rent his own property. Difficulties with disruptions were even greater for workers who do not receive a share of the profits from contracts.

Similar dynamics were present in Ethiopia's Universal Rural Roads Access Program (URRAP). Through this program, the Ethiopian government gave contracts to build roads in rural Ethiopia to small companies headed by recent engineering graduates. Like cobblestone, the construction process for the roads was intentionally labor intensive to provide jobs for rural communities. One URRAP engineer explained, "If the program worked properly it would be wonderful. Now, you work but the money does not reach your hand, even if you are working properly. You just sit and wait. The problem is politics. Administrators are afraid that they will be punished if they do not handle the money correctly, so they do nothing. Sometimes I think it would be better for me to leave this job and find something where I will be paid for my work." In other interviews, URRAP engineers praised the opportunity to learn skills and start a small business, but they complained that problems with regular payments made it difficult to work and complete projects in a timely manner.

Managing and distributing funds has been a challenge for both city administrators and cobblestone associations. The city administrator responsible for cobblestone in Hawassa explained, "Each payment can only be made after the completion of a phase of work. Strict guidelines are in place to be sure that the work is done properly. Cobblestone associations complain, but we cannot loosen our regulations. It is necessary to be very careful to ensure that all funds are used appropriately. Experienced associations are able to budget correctly so that they do not run out of funds before a project is complete." This is not to say that corruption and bias do not exist in the cobblestone sector. In Hawassa I often heard claims that cobblestone roads are distributed to particular neighborhoods on the basis of ethnicity. When I asked the city administrator why a neighborhood with relatively little vehicle traffic had been given cobblestone roads, he responded indirectly, explaining that at times a few very influential people may influence the location of cobblestone roads, but the municipal government is attempting to promote more discussion and to distribute roads equitably among neighborhoods. Although in practice, guidelines for the distribution of roads were quite vague, it was clear that regulations regarding payments were far more stringent.

For GIZ, these sorts of strict guidelines were a key part of one of its primary goals for the cobblestone program: creating good governance. GIZ documents praised a rigorous process in which a four-person committee must provide approval before a cobblestone company is paid (German Development Cooperation Office 2012, 14). A combination of outsourcing, increased competition, and standardization of practices created good governance (German Development Cooperation Office 2012, 9). As the cobblestone program developed, rather than rely on fixed prices, different aspects of the cobblestone construction process were outsourced to groups that could provide the most competitive bids. The payment system and quality control for contractors was regularized so that at each step in the process, work was consistently assessed before payments were made. GIZ argues that this process helps local administrators learn to handle increasingly large contracts effectively and efficiently, at the same time that cobblestone associations learn to manage all aspects of the construction process, including procuring materials, transportation, and labor. In the case of larger infrastructural development projects, management is generally outsourced because it is too complex for local administrators; therefore the process of learning and accountability associated with cobblestone is not present (German Development Cooperation Office 2012, 11). Even with strict guidelines in place, in interviews with GIZ administrators they argued that corruption was a major problem for cobblestone construction. One GIZ administrator claimed, "You just have to see the infrastructure to know where the corruption is," implying that poorly constructed roads were enabled by corrupt officials who did not enforce standards in exchange for bribes.

As in my analysis of the Bajaj system in the previous chapter, competing interests are at play here. Corruption is a major concern within the construction sector, and international collaborators such as GIZ fear that substandard work will be paid for. Therefore GIZ advocates multiple checks and assessments before cobblestone associations are paid. Checks and balances represent an administrative process that is intended to grow local governance in the sense that urban administrations establish both the credibility and the skill to govern. GIZ and the Ethiopian state believe that they are promoting a more just and fair form of governance. On the other hand, the young people who form cobblestone associations perceive these checks and balances as barriers to their own growth. Irregular work prevents the income and investments that they need to reposition themselves within relations of reciprocity. The state is denying their ability to mature and move toward adulthood.

To some extent, such breaks in work are intrinsic to jobs created through infrastructural development. Infrastructure construction is, by its nature, temporary. Projects begin, they are completed, and workers must move on. For young men working on asphalt roads, this creates a cycle of movement between the social categories of youth and adult, as they shift between positions of dependence and providing support for others (Mains 2012b). Cobblestone creates a different dynamic. The relatively slow and inexpensive nature of cobblestone construction is intended to create long-term employment opportunities. The case of Holyfield demonstrates that some young men are able to achieve extended growth in their own lives, but attempts to produce good governance fill this process with breaks and disruption as well.

Cobblestone and Relations with the State

Holyfield considered his work with the cobblestone association to be government work. The state had given him this work, and the exchange of his labor for income implied a qualitative shift in his relationship to the government. To some extent Holyfield had become part of the state. Although much of the funding for the construction of cobblestone roads came from GIZ and the World Bank, Holyfield and other young men consistently spoke of the roads as government projects. In Ethiopia, government work implies a relationship between various individuals who are differently positioned within a hierarchy of power that extends beyond the workplace, but relations of power in the private sector, particularly for those who are self-employed in the informal economy, are generally isolated to the moment of exchange (Mains 2012b). This distinction is an important factor behind the relatively high status of government employment and low status of self-employment.

For cobblestone workers such as Holyfield, road construction created desirable relations of exchange with the state. These were not the personal patron–client relations that individuals often sought to cultivate with state representatives. Here, the relationship is with a much more abstract and impersonal state. In exchange for one's allegiance the state provides infrastructure or, more important for Holyfield, paid work. That the state is offering a desirable good is not the only significant thing here. Like many young men, Holyfield had worked for a private company, but in discussing this work he made no assumption that the relationship with the company shifted his identity. State employment signified the presence of a qualitative relationship between the worker and an abstractly conceived "government." State employees often assumed that this relationship extended far beyond the workplace to encompass more personal social interactions. Young male cobblestone workers were becoming part of the state, and many of them were willing to put aside their cynicism about the ruling party in exchange for such a relationship. I was surprised, however, to hear Holyfield say that in building cobblestone roads he was not only creating progress in his own life, he was creating progress for his country. "Simply sitting will not help my country," he said. I did not hear similar expressions of patriotism from other cobblestone workers, but Holyfield's statement demonstrates the presence of a vision in which one simultaneously builds one's own life and one's nation—a nation that the state seeks to imagine through the lens of infrastructural development.

For young men such as Holyfield, the sense of membership associated with state employment is linked to class. Holyfield's position is based in aspiration. In my earlier research, unemployed young men consistently voiced a desire to attain government employment. Such employment not only brought a steady income; it also immediately inserted one into a complex and qualitatively desirable web of relationships. In the absence of traditional government jobs, cobblestone offers an acceptable alternative. Rather than a monthly salary, cobblestone workers are paid by the piece or contract, benefits are nonexistent, and they are always uncertain whether the work will extend beyond the duration of the current project. Underemployed young men, however, still find hope in this work. For the moment it is possible for them to assert a relationship with the state that, despite its dubious economic value, has historically been associated with the urban middle class in Ethiopia. Over the years I have observed a marked decline in the interest of young Ethiopians in accessing government work, but a relationship with the state continues to be valuable. In the case of cobblestone associations, the state provided numerous small benefits that were essential to the workers taking on the normative responsibilities of adults.

Cobblestone association members' relationships with the state extend to more concrete interactions and forms of support. In 2012 I was surprised when Holyfield and another member of his association, whom I had known for many years, were able to guide me through the confusing bureaucracy of Jimma's municipal administration and arrange an interview with the head of the cobblestone office. Just a few years ago, these young men were known primarily for the immense amount of time they spent hanging out on the street corner, but now they received polite greetings as they entered the municipal compound. In the past they attempted to use me as a contact for accessing economic opportunities, but now they were in a position to facilitate my research with city administrators. Contacts within the municipality could easily extend to other areas of life and help with accessing licenses and permits for operating a business or completing a small construction project.

The state also provides significant direct financial assistance for cobblestone associations. Administrators distribute opportunities for cobblestone work, ensuring that members of associations that do not win contracts are still hired as laborers to assist with projects. In addition to giving the initial trainings in paving and the actual construction process, administrators, who often have training in civil engineering, provide advice on management and technical issues. The state also helps the cobblestone associations save money and access equipment. For example, the government will provide a 1.5-million-birr vehicle for companies that document savings of 500,000 birr. When possible, the state also provides access to construction materials such as rock and sand at prices lower than market value. Most importantly, of course, the state initiates the vast majority of all cobblestone projects. Quite simply, without the state and its international backers, there would be very little cobblestone work in Ethiopia.

The support that the state provides for cobblestone associations creates something of a relationship of dependency. The Ethiopian state views cobblestone as a tool for employing urban youth, undermining youth opposition to the ruling party, and defusing young men's explosive potential. City officials explained that cobblestone companies are expected to "graduate" and move on to other, more challenging and capital-intensive forms of work. Ideally they should begin constructing residential or commercial buildings, or participate in the state-funded program for constructing rural roads. Doing so would make room for other workers in the nearly saturated cobblestone business. Actually moving beyond cobblestone was quite difficult in practice. In Hawassa, only three of the approximately thirty companies operating in the city in 2014 had accomplished this. Part of the difficulty of moving beyond cobblestone is overcoming the challenge of operating without assistance from the state. The state provides a baseline of support for cobblestone associations that allows them to get by in an extremely challenging economic environment. It is unclear whether they would be able to succeed without this support.

The level of allegiance that cobblestone workers had to the EPRDF party was not completely clear. Party membership certainly was not a formal requirement for joining a cobblestone association, but Holyfield's previous involvement in youth associations probably provided an advantage for him in receiving his initial training in paving. Holyfield and other cobblestone workers were quite clear that no party affiliation was required, but Holyfield also noted that his association observed holidays celebrating the EPRDF's accomplishments, and other workers outside of the public sector generally ignored these holidays. In discussing young people who received support for starting small businesses through the youth organizations, Marco Di Nunzio (2014a) explains that they often combined private critiques of the EPRDF with public displays of support. Although many young people who received state support were critical of the EPRDF, even superficial allegiance to the state could serve to establish the legitimacy of EPRDF rule.

In one interview, a GIZ administrator directly connected cobblestone with the state's legitimacy. He explained that cobblestone was "probably the most important project" that emerged from the urban agenda after the 2005 election because of its role in supporting the "mandate and justification of the Ethiopian government." When I pushed him on this point and asked about the implications of justifying an autocratic government, he responded, "At the end you have to see what governance and what kind of government does the society need at a certain time of development. When I see that the Ethiopian government managed to produce wealth, and growth and job creation, over the last ten years quite sustainably . . . coping with a massive urbanization, coping with climate change, coping with ethnic conflicts, with really shitty neighbors, I'm quite impressed that this anchor state of Horn of Africa is continuing to exist so strongly. I attribute it to the government."

The GIZ administrator implied that the production of wealth and job creation are linked with the state's autocratic practices and human rights abuses. Throughout this book I have focused on specific instances of construction. In each of these cases it is apparent that building infrastructures that generate economic growth have very different implications for different people. The asphalt road (chapter 2), for example, that created new investment opportunities in inner-city Hawassa displaced long-term residents to the city's periphery. The cobblestone case demonstrates that a more useful approach to understanding governance, legitimacy, and construction is to consider the interplay between historical and vital materialisms. To the extent that cobblestone has contributed to the Ethiopian state's legitimacy, it is a result not of growth, conceived abstractly, but of the particular relationship between productive inequalities and cobblestone technology. The successes of cobblestone do not legitimize the abuses of the Ethiopian state. Rather, they demonstrate the positive potential that exists when the needs of workers who provision infrastructure are prioritized.

Conclusion

In terms of productive inequalities, the state ultimately has power over the product of cobblestone workers' labor. The state determines the timing and quantity of payments to cobblestone associations. In the case of cobblestone, however, this productive inequality generated few tensions between workers and the state. In contrast to struggles over transportation, in building cobblestone roads government administrators did not prioritize the image of the city. Instead, they and cobblestone workers shared a similar goal—the creation of jobs. Like Bajaj drivers, cobblestone workers sought to attain social maturation by repositioning themselves within relations of reciprocity. A key difference in the case of cobblestone is that the state assisted workers in this endeavor by providing generous support to cobblestone associations. The incremental progress that Holyfield experienced in his relationships with others would not have been possible without help from the state, and this was dependent on relationships with international organizations.

Cobblestone is quite different from the Bajaj system in that it has been supported by hundreds of millions of dollars in grants and loans, primarily from GIZ and the World Bank. The Bajaj system receives little state investment aside from the government administrators assigned to regulate transportation. The Bajaj system functions through the use of fares paid by passengers. Although government guidelines for cobblestone roads stated that residents living on the roads should cover approximately 20 percent of the cost, this was not common in practice, at least in Hawassa. Cobblestone roads were clearly a state-subsidized project, and this smoothed over many potential tensions between the state and the cobblestone workers.

It is not only the financing that distinguishes cobblestone from other infrastructural development projects. The stones and roads themselves have a very specific temporality. Relations between workers and the state are based in the particular qualities of cobblestone construction. The process of building cobblestone roads is a form of slow growth that depends on workers using their hands to fit rocks together to form roads. Cobblestone prevents the reliance on machines that is associated with asphalt construction, and in doing so it preserves jobs. State support for cobblestone is certainly important, but it is the temporality embedded in the stone that generates incremental growth for Holyfield and other cobblestone workers. In contrast to asphalt, for which few workers are needed and relatively large surfaces can be covered in a short time, hundreds of young people have spent years covering the dirt roads of Jimma and Hawassa with cobblestone—and many roads remain uncovered. The slow process of cobblestone road construction supports both the state's desire to engage with disenfranchised urban youth and young people's desires to gradually take on many of the normative social responsibilities of adults.

Perhaps most important is that many cobblestone workers are organized into profit-sharing cooperatives, thereby eliminating a key productive inequality that is associated with construction. The laborers who build roads have a great deal of control over the product of their labor. In building cobblestone roads they secure opportunities to invest in education, family farms, and small-business opportunities. Cobblestone was introduced after the contentious 2005 election in part to bring young people back into the state. The materials create work for urban residents, and the organization of labor allows them to benefit from their work. To the extent that productive inequalities between state and labor have been reduced, the process of connecting citizens with the state has been successful.

Productive inequalities still exist, and at times they do result in tensions. For GIZ and the Ethiopian state, a key goal for cobblestone construction is good governance. To the extent that achieving this goal necessitates slowing payments to cobblestone workers, conflict is created. In these cases, the state uses its power over the product of cobblestone workers' labor to directly threaten the workers' livelihood. For the most part the state's first priority in cobblestone construction is job creation, but when priorities shift, conflicts over productive inequalities become apparent. When I last saw Holyfield in 2017 he complained that payments to cobblestone associations had been limited and the number of associations in Jimma had increased. He had not given up on cobblestone, but he was spending more and more time driving his Bajaj. Holyfield was having difficulty making the 100 birr daily payment to his savings association, and his plans for the future were facing constraints. Cobblestone work in the private sector was becoming more profitable than government contracts, but little work was available. Elsewhere I heard that limits on state payments were a result of corruption. Limiting payments to cobblestone associations made it more difficult for the associations to kick money back to government officials in exchange for overlooking low-quality work. In other words, administrators believed that paying cobblestone associations less would actually increase the quality of roads by removing opportunities for corruption. Regardless of the impacts on corruption, this demonstrates the ongoing presence of productive inequalities. Although laborers have a great deal of control over profits generated from their work, the state can intervene to limit these profits in ways that disrupt the cobblestone sector.

In this chapter I have artificially narrowed the scope of my analysis to relations between cobblestone associations and the state. Other productive inequalities and vital materials are certainly key to understanding cobblestone construction. Cobblestone road construction involves relationships between quarriers, chiselers, pavers, foremen, and others. Each of these groups is compensated differently for its labor, creating class hierarchies within the construction process. In terms of materials, Ethiopia is rich in basalt, a high-density stone that is ideal for cobblestone construction, but many cities are not located near basalt reserves. A lack of basalt can slow construction or lead to a reliance on locally available materials such as limestone, which quickly break down under the weight of heavy vehicles (Aschalew 2013). Ultimately, cobblestone demonstrates the value of a synthesis between historical and vital materialisms. At every stage in the construction process the specific technology of cobblestone is interwoven with relations between labor and the state. Labor, materials, and the state continually interact to build roads, and in this process citizen/state relations are both made and unmade.

CONCLUSION. The Time of Construction

In Hawassa, a new asphalt road in the city center created lucrative business opportunities for some and destroyed the homes and livelihoods of others. To allow the Gibe III dam to move water from the Omo River to sugarcane plantations and create major opportunities for investors, the state forcibly resettles farmers to villages. Road construction in Jimma continually stopped and started, leaving residents unsure about the future of their city. In this context of continual unexpected transformation, scholars have good reason to argue that twenty-first-century Africa can usefully be conceptualized in terms of temporariness (Goldstone and Obarrio 2016, 14; Mbembe 2016). Achille Mbembe explains that temporariness is an "encounter with indeterminacy, provisionality, the fugitive, and the contingent," and that daily experience for many is characterized by "uncertainty and turbulence; instability and unpredictability; and rapid, chronic, and multidirectional shifts" (2016, 222–23). There should be no doubt that temporariness describes the lived experience of many, not only in Ethiopia but globally. In many ways, however, the concept of temporariness raises more questions than it can potentially answer. Within this context of turbulence, what directions and interests are privileged over others? How do the past and the future affect the experience of the present as temporary? How do specific materials and technologies shape shifting relations of power, particularly those between citizen and state?

Construction, as both a site for research and an analytical framework, offers a means of answering these questions. Construction as an analytical framework necessarily involves change, contingency, and instability, but in contrast to temporariness it is not without directionality. It is a means of understanding change that does not get lost in the turbulence of temporariness. The construction of infrastructure is based on long-term plans for the future and expectations of growth. Construction involves incremental change and a return to an analysis of the "near future," which Jane Guyer (2007) claims has recently been absent from both theory and popular rhetoric. The spectacular fantasy of the future is highly important in images of the Grand Ethiopian Renaissance Dam, but the dam does not exist only in an imagined distant future. The dam is under construction, and the process of construction is accompanied by plans, hopes, and struggles for specific goals in the near future. Construction is a bridge between the uncertainty of the present and the distant future.[1]

The Ethiopian state would not invest billions of dollars in building roads and hydroelectric dams without a strong belief that these projects would continue to have value for many years to come. In Hawassa, government administrators were building roads not only to meet demand for movement and transportation in the present, but to fulfill the needs of a large, vibrant city in the future. The failure of road construction in Jimma reveals the continual potential for instability and unforeseen outcomes. Planning is key to the construction process, but plans are constantly unsettled. Such instability is not the same as the chronic uncertainty of temporariness. The process of construction provides structure for understanding conflict and change. In this conclusion I review the primary arguments I have developed with the intent of advancing construction as an analytical framework in which states, labor, and materials collide to both build and destroy.

States of Construction

At the time of this writing the Grand Ethiopian Renaissance Dam is still under construction. The dam is more than 60 percent finished, but much work remains, and it is uncertain from where the financing for the project will come. The GERD highlights the peculiar role of the state in producing plans and uncertainty during the time of construction. Construction is a reminder of both the power and limits of states. The GERD would not exist without the Ethiopian state, and the state has staked much of its legitimacy on the project. As the poster I discussed at the outset of this book demonstrates, the Ethiopian state advances a narrative in which hydropower, national renaissance, and the EPRDF-led government are inseparable. From the Ethiopian state's perspective the time of construction is in part a time of state-led progress toward an Ethiopian renaissance.

The Ethiopian state, however, can only build the GERD by working with various actors that bring layers of contingency to the time of construction. The actual construction of the dam is managed by Salini Impregilo, the same Italian company that has received billions of dollars from the Ethiopian government for the construction of other dams. A portion of the financing comes from China, with the stipulation that funds be spent on Chinese-made equipment. An even greater portion of funding comes from the sale of bonds. Many of these bonds are sold within Ethiopia, but many are also sold to the diaspora. This is a national project, and one must be an Ethiopian citizen or of Ethiopian descent to purchase bonds. Government officials travel the world to meet with community leaders from the diaspora and encourage the sale of bonds. The Ethiopian diaspora also provides much of the support for the political opposition within Ethiopia, creating a complex contradiction in which the same community that the government relies on for state building is the source of much of the opposition to the ruling party.

In the time of construction the state depends on relationships with private institutions to advance its agenda. These public/private relationships generate opportunities for corruption. All of the projects I have discussed in this book, from the multibillion-dollar hydropower dams to the relatively inexpensive cobblestone roads, were targets of accusations of corruption. When the state awards contracts for construction or changes urban transportation policies, it creates an opportunity for collusion between private interests and public officials. Indeed, beyond an abstract vision of a renaissance, construction is motivated in part by these opportunities. The time of construction offers a chance to access unprecedented levels of wealth, and nepotism is a key tool for winning the competition for contracts. Successful construction companies have further opportunities to shape public life. In Hawassa, the owner of one of the major construction companies built a monument to his father, Woldeamanuel Dubale, who was an important leader for the Sidama people from the 1970s through the early 2000s. The monument stands at a major intersection of one of Hawassa's new asphalt roads and signifies the power of construction companies to shape imagined futures and pasts.

The power of the state is great, but it faces severe constraints. This is the time of construction—state plans for a renaissance encounter so many actors and variables that uncertainty prevails. Even if the GERD is finished, engineers have raised questions about its potential to generate the promised level of power (Beyene 2013). This is not temporariness; a plan exists and it provides direction as construction moves forward in incremental stages. The dam is under construction. The state is also under construction as it seeks to convince citizens that it is leading the nation toward a renaissance. The ultimate outcome of this construction, however, is uncertain and highly unstable.[2] Unplanned aspects of construction—contracts with private companies, the sale of bonds to citizens, displacement, and environmental consequences—will quite possibly have more far-reaching consequences than the actual dam.

Improvisation and Regulation

In many ways a condition of temporariness produces improvisation. When conditions constantly change and the future is uncertain, improvisation is necessary. Yet, improvisations are not temporary. The improvisations used by residents of the Taddesse Enjore neighborhood were developed through years of living and working together. Like an experienced group of jazz musicians, Taddesse Enjore residents knew how to improvise together. Asphalt road construction disrupted long-term patterns of improvisation, but it also introduced new regularities. As a temporal narrative, construction supports a conceptualization of the present in terms of uncertainty and long-term planning, improvisation and regulation, and conflict and stability. In construction the temporary and improvisational are closely tied to regularities associated with planning. The successful road construction that supported growth in Hawassa depended on the ability of city administrators to improvise. Road construction transforms, but it is not disconnected from the past. New roads interact with longstanding ethnic and class-based hierarchies that have been built into the city (Mains and Kinfu 2016). Roads that were constructed through improvisation extend into the future and provide the foundation for further planning and development.

Conflicts over public transportation in Hawassa were also based in the relationship between improvisation and regulation. Bajaj drivers responded to changes in the price of fuel by improvising—increasing passenger fares, using long-term relationships to access fuel on the black market, negotiating cheaper leases with vehicle owners, and defying government regulations by going off route. At the same time, drivers demanded state intervention. They sought changes in state regulation that would make transportation more stable and predictable, for both themselves and their passengers.

Regulation and improvisation are not intrinsically in conflict with each other. Rather, the tensions that emerge from the encounter between regulation and improvisation at the time of construction are based in inequalities of power. In the case of asphalt roads in Hawassa, the improvisations of powerful administrators supported road construction and destroyed the improvisational livelihoods of inner-city residents. Not all improvisations are equal, and the process of construction placed them in opposition to each other. It is in this sense that the improvisation–regulation dynamic connects construction and destruction. As improvisations and regulations interact, construction and destruction are produced. In the process of building the city, certain people are excluded and marginalized. In Hawassa they were literally resettled from the city center to the periphery beyond the chicken farm, a place where it was very difficult to form new, improvised livelihoods.

Feeling the State

An affective politics assumes that perceptions of the state's legitimacy are not necessarily based on consciously weighing the advantages and disadvantages associated with various policy alternatives. An affective politics involves communication through signs that are felt rather than read. Construction brings affect and legitimacy together. It is through construction that urban Ethiopians feel the state. The dust of construction irritates one's eyes and nose. Slippery mud demands particular techniques for walking. Cobblestone roads replace dust and mud with a new texture of bumpy movement. It is not only through sensory experience that the state is felt. Affective relationships with the state are formed as infrastructure is built. When construction drags on for years and the city cannot function people feel rejected by the state. As my friend in Jimma put it, "The government treats Jimma like a stepchild."

It is in the relation between affect, infrastructure, and legitimacy that the connection between construction and destruction emerges. This is partially a result of the disruptive effects of construction. Mud, dust, and power and water outages are unsettling and continually remind urban residents of the problems of construction. The distribution of the benefits of infrastructures is inevitably unequal, and this also creates bonds and divisions between citizens and states. At a deeper level, however, affect has the power to bring citizens into the state as they embrace narratives of progress and renaissance through infrastructure.

It was faith in progress that initially motivated Jimma residents to donate money to road construction and to at least tentatively embrace state-led development. Although most urban Ethiopians doubt the ability of the EPRDF regime to make good on its promises of a renaissance, they do not dispute the underlying assumption that state-led development is a desirable possibility. They have embraced the idea of a developmental state, just not this particular regime. It is here that the destructive potential of an affective politics is greatest. The potential for legitimacy through construction of infrastructure exists, and many urban Ethiopians buy into this vision. However, it is almost inevitable that the imagined renaissance will not be realized. Even when particular projects are finished there is often a sense that construction is not complete. Like progress, construction is a process. To the extent that both construction and progress depend on continual movement, they cannot be completed. There is no standard measurement for evaluating progress. Claims of having achieved progress are always questioned. Some groups are always left out, marginalized, or simply not satisfied with what has been built. Like the young men I described in chapter 3, there are always those who feel that what has been built is hollow. It is progress's inevitable discontents that undermine the state's legitimacy. In seeking to create affective bonds, the state pulls citizens into narratives of progress that inevitably produce feelings of dissatisfaction and alienation. A better future is possible in the time of construction, but at least in Ethiopia it has been very difficult for the state to convince citizens that it can guide them beyond the present.

In contrast to construction, temporariness, as an analytical framework, masks the importance of the past for feelings about a changing present. Jimma residents described their encounters with mud and failed road construction as one step forward and two steps back. Such statements demonstrate the slippery and unstable nature of infrastructural development, but they also reveal assumptions about directionality. There is a forward and a backward. Both citizens and states have expectations about the outcomes of construction. Roads are built for a reason—to move forward. Affective attachments to places, things, and the state are shaped by this sense of direction and movement, even within a context of overwhelming temporariness.

The process of construction involves conflict and instability, but it also offers clear direction for exploring the roots of this instability. Construction does not occur without intensive engagement with materials, technologies, and networks of human labor. Specific infrastructural technologies introduce limits and possibilities that shape the tension between instability and planning that is essential to the construction process. The Bajaj brought a flexible mobility to urban transportation that threatened Hawassa city administrators' visions of a modern and legible city. Asphalt roads increased the speed of inner-city movement in ways that supported commerce and speculative investment. However, the construction of these same asphalt roads depended on negotiating changing municipal budgets, soil conditions, weather, and preexisting structures. The materials themselves constantly introduce both the possibility of incremental movement toward near future goals and sudden unexpected transformation, such as the collapse of tunnels at the Gibe II hydropower project.

Objects have particular affective dimensions that are often rooted in their temporality. The conflict between the Ethiopian government and International Rivers was based in part on differing feelings for the temporal dimensions of big dams. Flow and modernization are very different ways of thinking about the passage of time. The progressive change associated with big dams conflicts with the sense of flow that is valued by some anti-dam activists. Cobblestone and asphalt roads have very specific temporal dimensions as well. They differ in terms of both the speed of travel and the speed of construction.

The particular qualities of materials are important, but they do not act on their own. In building infrastructure and constructing a renaissance, the state depends on massive quantities of labor. The Bajaj system depends on drivers, vehicle owners, and city administrators. Cobblestone road construction depends on people to work in quarries, chisel rocks, and pave roads. The fantastic infrastructures that appear in state propaganda cannot exist without these people. This dependency creates tension. The state has an incentive to extract as much labor as possible in order to rapidly provision infrastructure at a low cost. The state also utilizes that labor to advance its own vision of a renaissance. Regulation of the Bajaj system was driven by state visions of a modern city. The state pushes to control the products of infrastructural labor both materially and symbolically. In many cases it separates laborers from the income generated by their work and the meaning that this work has in building the imagined city and nation. The people who work to provision infrastructure have little voice in the construction of an imagined Ethiopian renaissance.

Technology and materials are essential to this process. Regulations that limit the abilities of Bajaj drivers to earn incomes are based in part on administrators' perceptions of the modernity of Bajaj technology. Cobblestone—both the material and the system of constructing roads—shapes the productive inequalities between citizen and state. The case of cobblestone demonstrates that the process of construction does not necessarily create conflict between the interests of states and labor. By using infrastructure to support job creation and livelihoods rather than spectacular monuments to an imagined renaissance, the state eases tensions and reduces the potential for destruction. Beyond the specifics of the Bajaj and cobblestone cases, a synthesis between vital and historical materialisms offers an analytical tool for exploring the destructive potential implicit within the process of construction.

Constructing Destruction?

I write this at a time when in Ethiopia a future of destruction seems as likely as one of construction. The state of emergency that began in October 2016 continued until July 2017. A new state of emergency was issued in February 2018 after Ethiopia's prime minister, Hailemariam Desalegn, announced his resignation. Public protests were banned under the state of emergency, leading many urban Ethiopians to voice their discontent by simply staying home and in some cases refusing to open shops and other small businesses. The state of emergency was a response to ongoing popular protests against the ruling EPRDF party, most of them associated with the Oromo and Amhara ethnicities. For the most part, the government met the protests with violence. From the beginning of the protests in 2014 until the appointment of Abiy Ahmed as prime minister in April 2018, government forces killed over one thousand peaceful demonstrators (Horne 2018).

At a time like this it may be inappropriate to conceptualize life in Ethiopia in terms of construction. In contrast, the state's destruction of lives represents an abrupt end to human growth—and the introduction of chaos and instability for the family members of those who were killed. Yet this destruction is very much a product of construction. The uprisings are in part a result of the top-down plans for development through infrastructure that have recently dominated political life in Ethiopia. Protests began in 2014 in response to plans to expand the administrative boundaries of Addis Ababa into the Oromia region. Protestors are also inspired by so-called land grabs, in which the state pushes farmers off land in order to lease it to large agribusiness companies. They ask who is left out and who is included as the nation is built. It is no coincidence that protests have been strongest in the Oromia region. Oromos comprise Ethiopia's most populous ethnic group, and Oromos have historically been kept at the margins of economic and political power.

My colleagues in Ethiopia have expressed a great deal of optimism regarding Ethiopia's new prime minister, Abiy Ahmed. Abiy is Ethiopia's first Oromo prime minister and has already addressed some of the Oromo people's grievances. He quickly negotiated peace with some of the militant resistance groups and took significant steps toward ending the conflict between Oromos and Somalis. He has released many political prisoners and punished armed forces that direct violence toward protestors. It is too early to fully assess, but early signs indicate that Abiy will be a transformative leader. Certainly at the time of this writing he has far greater popular support than previous prime ministers. However, the relationship between construction and destruction goes beyond ethnicity. Abiy might be able to reduce the rising turmoil in Ethiopia, but the destruction that is intrinsic within construction cannot be addressed with only a change in political leadership. Under Prime Minister Abiy the Ethiopian state has continued to pursue rapid economic growth through massive state investments in infrastructure. In October 2018 the government announced $7 billion of new investments in roads and power generation. Ethiopia is still under construction.

Construction generates destruction through disconnection. Brian Larkin explains that "infrastructures are matter that enable the movement of other matter" (2013, 329). Beyond this, infrastructures create connections and disconnections (Anand 2017). That infrastructures such as roads and public transportation create connections between people and neighborhoods, and between present and future visions of the city, is somewhat obvious. However, these same infrastructures disconnect. For example, asphalt roads displace people from their homes and in some cases create barriers to walking. Disconnection is not the same as the absence of connection (Ferguson 1999; see Anand [2017] on disconnection and infrastructure). Disconnection, like abjection, involves a sense of loss and being cast out (Ferguson

1999). Jimma residents who experienced years of failed road construction and unprecedented problems with electrical blackouts were disconnected. The experience of disconnection is exacerbated when one observes others with connections to more desirable futures.

Construction's destructive potential increases through the dynamics I discussed in previous chapters. When infrastructural development is associated with a center that benefits from exploiting the periphery, as in the case of Ethiopia's hydropower projects, destruction becomes more likely. When administrators struggle to improvise techniques for dealing with complex and changing conditions as they oversee the construction of urban asphalt roads, then the possibility of destruction also emerges. When residents feel that they are mired in the mud of corruption, unable to access what they consider to be basic services—roads, electricity, water—then destruction is possible. When conflicts emerge between the state and the people who provision infrastructure, as in the case of the Bajaj, then destruction is likely. None of these areas of tension are organized strictly along the lines of ethnicity, and they are unlikely to disappear under Abiy's leadership.

These tensions are compounded by the near impossibility of development actually meeting the desires and needs of the majority of the population. Despite possessing one of the fastest-growing economies in the world, Ethiopia's per capita GDP remains below $2 per day. When one is starting from the bottom, even rapid growth is often not enough. Combined with high levels of inflation and an increased awareness of living standards in the U.S. and Europe, it is not surprising that many Ethiopians are frustrated and angry.

This anger is generally directed at the state. The Ethiopian state has staked its legitimacy on development, and when development does not, or cannot, occur, then uprisings and protests are created. Change is assessed not only in terms of infrastructure projects that demonstratively improve people's lives, but in regard to maintaining a positive affective relationship with the state. Because of government corruption, incompetence, and the numerous contingencies and challenges associated with the construction process, many urban Ethiopians do not believe the state operates in their interests. These feelings of suspicion and distrust undermine the state's legitimacy and again create a dynamic in which construction is directly related to destruction. This dynamic is exacerbated when the state responds to instability with violence. Although these human rights abuses have been greatly reduced under the new prime minister, construction will still generate tensions and conflict. A state that bases its claims to legitimacy on development and construction will necessarily experience a degree of instability because of the nature of the construction process.

This does not mean that destruction is inevitable. Rather, as I have argued in relation to construction as a temporal narrative, the time of construction is necessarily filled with tension and contradictions. Infrastructure, *meseret limat*, is the foundation for development in Ethiopia. Therefore, as a developmental state, Ethiopia rests on an intrinsically unstable foundation. But in many ways it is a necessary foundation, and even under Prime Minister Abiy Ethiopia's identity is closely tied up with construction. Construction of infrastructure offers a base for growth, but it is a base that is constantly moving and transforming. Destruction is not a certainty, but instability is inevitable.

Although a degree of instability is unavoidable, my analysis in the preceding chapters demonstrates clear possibilities for reducing construction's destructive potential. When the state prioritizes the livelihoods of urban residents, tensions are eased. What if the same model of worker cooperatives used in the construction of cobblestone roads is applied to other cases of infrastructural development? What if the profits from the construction of billion-dollar dams were shared among the workers who built them? What if technologies of development, such as cobblestone, were consciously selected with the intent to support slow growth? What if the state applied the same rigor it demonstrates in regulating the Bajaj system to regulating the relationship between Bajaj owners and drivers, or to increasing the minimum wage for construction workers? What if the immense value for commercial development generated by new asphalt roads was distributed among neighborhood residents? At the time of construction, possibilities are opened and closed. By pursuing some of these openings, the Ethiopian state might reduce the destruction that is implicit in the process of construction.

NOTES

INTRODUCTION

1. The World Bank defines a country as middle income if it has an annual per capita gross national income of $1,026 up to $12,475 (World Bank, n.d., "The World Bank in Middle Income Countries"). Ethiopia's per capita income in 2016 was $660, and if growth continues at the current rate of more than 10 percent, the country could reach middle income status by 2025 (World Bank, n.d., "The World Bank in Ethiopia").

2. In the Ethiopian case, international aid was primarily limited to military support from the Soviet Union during the Marxist Derg regime (1974–91). International aid increased dramatically beginning in the early 2000s, and between 2010 and 2013 Ethiopia received more than $3 billion annually in international support (World Bank, n.d., "Data"). However, with a 2013 population of more than 90 million and a GDP less than $50 billion, resources continue to be stretched very thin.

3. Scholars have used the Ethiopian state to support or refute different models of development. Tim Kelsall (2013) argues that Ethiopia demonstrates the importance of a strong interventionist state for creating economic growth. For Peter Radelet (2016), Ethiopia represents an exceptional case in which economic growth has occurred despite constraints on markets and the absence of democracy. My interest in Ethiopia as an exemplar is not to bolster one political economic theory of growth over another. Rather than fitting Ethiopia into a set of prepackaged assumptions, I explore what conclusions can be drawn from this encounter between authoritarianism and massive investments in infrastructure.

4. This argument builds on the insights of others, particularly Livingston (2012), Mbembe and Nuttall (2004), Ananya Roy (2009), Simone (2004), and Tsing (2015).

5. There is a vast literature on the informal sector, a concept first developed by Keith Hart (1973). I have found Breman (2016), Rizzo (2017), and Ananya Roy (2009) to be particularly useful in summarizing earlier discussions of informality and offering new perspectives.

6. Ananya Roy (2009) argues that the value of informality as an analytical category is partially because the term is strategically deployed by the state. Roy explains that the state often uses "informality as an instrument of both accumulation and authority" (81). To label a settlement or practice as informal is to legitimize arbitrary state intervention. Although I agree with Roy that close attention to state discourse and practice concerning informality is essential, the arbitrary deployment of the term is precisely what undermines its value as an analytical category. It is possible to explore how the state deploys the concept of informality without accepting that it is in fact a useful descriptive term.

7. Julie Livingston (2012) also invokes the relationship between improvisation and precarity in her analysis of a cancer ward in Botswana. Livingston contrasts improvised medicine with biomedicine that is based in a global system of knowledge and practice. All forms of biomedicine involve degrees of improvisation, but when equipment and supplies are lacking and training varies, greater levels of improvisation are necessary.

8. Ruth Leys (2011) has convincingly called into question much of the neuroscience that contemporary affect theorists use to support their claims regarding the gap between sensation and cognition. Emily Martin (2013) draws on Ludwig Wittgenstein's *Philosophical Investigations* to question the analytical value of a black box of experience that is somehow presocial and preconscious. Put simply, it is certainly possible that experiences and sensations exist outside of language, but the possibilities for investigating this nondiscursive realm are highly limited. Although I reject notions of affect as strictly nonconscious or asocial, affect still has great value in that it draws attention to sensation, intensity, resonance, and other forms of experience that lurk on the boundaries of representational language. The challenge for anthropologists is to explore how affective communication is incorporated into what Wittgenstein (1953) called "language games."

9. See Connolly (2002) and Thrift (2004, 2008) on affect and politics.

10. My analysis of the relationship between feeling infrastructure and feelings for the state emerges out of conversations with my colleague Peter Soppelsa.

11. James Ferguson (1997) explains that modernization theory and its emphasis on linear stages had much in common with the late nineteenth-century anthropological theory of E. B. Tylor and Lewis Henry Morgan.

12. See Etienne Balibar (2017) for a discussion of the complex relationship between the mystical and material dimensions of the commodity within Marxist thought.

13. Unless otherwise noted, all interviews and conversations were in Amharic.

CHAPTER 1. CONSTRUCTING A RENAISSANCE

1. The Grand Ethiopian Renaissance Dam (GERD) was originally called the Ethiopian Millennium Dam. Because of its unique calendar, Ethiopia celebrated its millennium in 2007. At the time of the millennium, Prime Minister Meles Zenawi began making specific references to an Ethiopian Renaissance and the concept of *hidase* (Orlowska 2013, 302).

2. Lori Pottinger worked for IR for nearly twenty years before moving on in 2015,

and she was involved in different campaigns concerning African rivers, including the Omo and the Nile.

3. The notion of skipping over certain technologies that are no longer desirable also comes up in discussions of automobiles; scholars have suggested that developing countries follow the lessons of some cities in the U.S. that are now trying to replace automobile traffic with bicycles (Vargo and Patz 2014).

4. Bonds are sold only to Ethiopian citizens and foreign nationals of Ethiopian descent. Interest on bonds is paid at Libor plus 1–2.5 percent, depending on how long the bond is held. To put that rate in perspective, the value of the U.S. dollar in relation to the Ethiopian birr approximately doubled between 2008 and 2012 and increased by 25 percent between 2012 and 2016.

5. See Johnson (2014) and Jones (2014) regarding the role that access to cheap energy played in supporting rapid economic growth in the United States.

6. I follow the Ethiopian convention of referring to Ethiopians by their given name rather than their patronymic name. Therefore I refer to Prime Minister Meles rather than Prime Minister Zenawi. However, I cite authors and list references by the writer's second name in order to maintain consistency and avoid the difficulty of determining if international scholars of Ethiopian descent prefer to be referred to by their first or second name.

7. As is the case with much of Ethiopia's history, ethnic boundaries are blurry here. Amhara ethnicity seems to have been particularly flexible, and local populations were able to "become" Amhara through assimilation—learning Amharic, converting to Orthodox Christianity, and intermarriage (Donham 1986). In terms of the popular memory, this expansion is generally conceived of in terms of the Amhara moving south and oppressing local ethnic groups.

8. It is likely that ethnic federalism has solidified what were previously loose and flexible boundaries. Particularly in the case of smaller ethnic groups, the historic reality of these boundaries has been highly disputed. See Markakis (1998) for an excellent description of disputes over ethnic identity and regional boundaries that have developed as a result of ethnic federalism.

9. Ethiopia's dam boom is not confined to the south. Salini received a no-bid contract worth nearly a half billion dollars to build the Tana Beles project in northern Ethiopia. Chinese contractors built the Tekeze Dam in northern Ethiopia.

10. *Rivergods* (Bangs and Kallen 1985) is a coffee table book that combines *National Geographic*–style photography of indigenous people and river landscapes with photos and accounts of American men white-water rafting in far-flung locations. The photos and stories of the bearded white American men braving powerful river rapids makes me wonder whether they are intended to be the "gods" in the book's title. Their stories are juxtaposed with those of European explorers such as David Livingstone, which also adds to the neocolonial feel of the text.

11. The identities of the panel members are not provided in the document.

12. As James Ferguson (2006) has discussed, anthropologists dislike labeling one group as more modern or advanced than another. This may explain why anthropologists so often quote from Meles's speech, highlighting his labeling of pastoralists as

backward. It is a categorization that immediately repulses many anthropologists, including myself. To put anti-dam activists in the position of labeling others as backward unsettles the cultural relativist sensibilities of many anthropologists. It forces them to acknowledge how hierarchies of modernity that they have long since rejected continue to shape their critiques and analyses.

13. "The one percent" refers to people in the top percentile of wealth.

14. The World Bank estimates that inflation in Ethiopia was more than 10 percent in 2015 (World Bank, n.d., "The World Bank in Ethiopia"), and Ethiopia's central bank devalued the birr by 15 percent in 2017.

CHAPTER 2. ASPHALT ROADS, REGULATING INFRASTRUCTURES, AND IMPROVISED LIVES

1. For overviews of the anthropology of roads see Dalakoglou (2010), Dalakoglou and Harvey (2012), Knox and Harvey (2011), and Masquelier (2002).

2. Following Simone, I use *human infrastructure* to refer to networks of people that accomplish many of the same tasks associated with material infrastructures. In this sense, the relationship I examine in this chapter is not strictly between material and human infrastructures. Often, social networks more broadly interact with material infrastructures, but framing the relationship in terms of human and material infrastructures is helpful in clarifying how closely the social and material are intertwined.

3. Woldeamanuel was a leader of the Sidama Liberation Front that resisted the rule of the Marxist Derg regime and shifted between resisting and collaborating with the EPRDF. A large statue of Woldeamanuel sits in the center of a roundabout at the end of WED Road. Woldeamanuel's son, Zelalem, is the owner of a major construction company that has been involved with some of the road construction in Hawassa.

4. The state owns all land in Ethiopia and therefore it is the physical structures and the lease to the land that are sold.

5. In contrast, Jimma is located in the Oromia region, but much of the urban population is not of Oromo descent. Furthermore, the size and diversity of the Oromo population made targeted interventions on behalf of the Oromo people much more difficult. In the early 2000s many of the municipal administrators in Jimma were Oromo, but they tended to be Christians from Shoa rather than Muslims from Jimma. This dynamic has shifted, but in Jimma I never encountered claims that infrastructures were built to benefit specific ethnic or religious groups.

6. Irregularities in both the initial election and revote led newly elected opposition party members to refuse to take their seats in the Parliament. The federal government accused the opposition of inciting unrest, imprisoned opposition members, and eventually appointed EPRDF members to take their places. Opposition party members were never able to take their seats, and there was almost no opposition party participation in the subsequent 2010 and 2015 elections.

7. Of the ethnic groups found in the SNNPR, the Wolayta have had the largest population in urban Hawassa since the 1970s. Everyday discussions contain a great deal of talk about tensions between Wolayta and Sidama, and therefore many Ethiopians view replacing Hailemariam Desalegn as president of the SNNPR with a Sidama as

a highly symbolic move. Hailemariam became prime minister of Ethiopia after Meles Zenawi died in 2012; Hailemariam ruled until 2018, when he resigned.

8. In contrast to Hawassa, in Jimma the bulk of road construction occurred within the ethnically diverse central city and was not intended as a pulling strategy to bring Oromo Muslims from the periphery into the city.

9. Another pastor also referenced Abraham's story in explaining how God had blessed Hawassa with growth and prosperity.

10. Paul Gifford (1987, 1994) has critiqued Reinhard Bonnke's evangelism in Africa, arguing that Bonnke depoliticized poverty by focusing on personal salvation as a path to wealth and implicitly supported authoritarian political leaders such as former Kenyan president Daniel arap Moi.

11. Although the pastor was highly critical of Muslims providing economic support to other Muslims in order to start small businesses, he explicitly noted that creating this type of economic network is a useful strategy for supporting Pentecostalism in Hawassa.

12. Churches are also major sites of construction and frequently located on new asphalt roads. The buildings are often very large, representing significant construction contracts and shifting neighborhood dynamics.

13. In 2013, $1 equaled approximately 18 Ethiopian birr.

14. This was shortly after a major currency devaluation and $1 equaled around 28 birr.

15. Over time, Doro Arbata residents left their old idders and formed idders with their new neighbors. Nearly all of the residents I spoke to in 2017 were no longer active in their old idders.

16. Ursula Rao's (2013) discussion of resettlement in India reveals similar intersections between the formal and informal.

17. Conversations with the Progress working group at Leibniz-ZMO have been essential for developing my thoughts on possibility and contingency.

CHAPTER 3. FEELING CHANGE THROUGH DIRT AND WATER

1. Ezana Weldeghebrael (2017) describes similar ETV broadcasts that connected infrastructure with an Ethiopian renaissance. Weldeghebrael convincingly argues that urban growth and a construction boom became symbols for progress and an Ethiopian renaissance.

2. I follow Leys (2011) and Lutz (2017) in not assuming that affect precedes cognition and avoiding a strict divide between affect and emotion. Cognition and affective experience are certainly blurred in the sense that much of what is felt is not immediately translated into representational language. Rather than try to pry open an opaque box of unconscious feeling, however, I necessarily focus on discursive representations of affective experience.

3. As I detailed in the introductory chapter, my approach to affective politics is more discursive than those of others who have addressed the topic (Connolly 2002; Thrift 2004). The categories of temporality, sensation, and exchange are in some ways artificial, because the three are inseparable. Despite a degree of simplification,

I believe these categories have analytical utility and avoid the vague abstractions that plague some analyses of affective politics.

4. I also made a brief research visit to Jimma in 2017, but I do not discuss those results in this chapter.

5. Government workers eventually tired of being strongly encouraged to donate their salaries to development projects, and I encountered no support for the state's requirement that they purchase government bonds for the Grand Ethiopian Renaissance Dam.

6. Jon Abbink (2006a, 2006b) and Tobias Hagmann (2006) have debated the value of political culture, particularly neopatrimonialism, for understanding contemporary citizen/state relations in Ethiopia. Hagmann (2006) critiques Abbink's use of neopatrimonialism to analyze the contentious 2005 national election, correctly noting that scholars rarely operationalize political culture in a meaningful way. In response, Abbink explains that political culture and neopatrimonialism offer "essential pointers towards a contextual explanation" (2006b, 613). In other words, rather than a definitive causal explanation for political practices, political culture suggests possibilities and relationships for further exploration. I agree with Abbink that neopatrimonialism is a useful concept for understanding the contemporary Ethiopian state as long as it is accompanied by a rigorous empirical analysis of contemporary citizen/state relations. There is certainly evidence that citizens' perceptions of the state's ability to provide resources and public goods influence their political opinions (Arriola 2008; Lefort 2007; Mains 2012a).

7. Another election joke that comes from a different group of friends: At an internet café in the year 2014 in Addis, a sign says, "We can show you the results of the 2013 Diversity Visa Lottery [this is quite common]." Below that is another sign that says, "We can show you the results of the 2015 national election."

8. Abiy Ahmed became prime minister of Ethiopia in 2018. At the time of this writing, after nearly one year in power, Abiy continues to enjoy a high level of popular support, including from longtime critics of the state such as Tafiq. It remains to be seen how support for Abiy will interact with perceptions of new infrastructural development projects.

CHAPTER 4. GOVERNING THE BAJAJ

1. Injera is the Ethiopian flatbread that is the basis of most meals in urban Ethiopia, but in this context it implies money.

2. State-financed construction of asphalt roads was essential for the rise of the Bajaj as a form of urban transportation, but this was never acknowledged by Bajaj drivers and owners.

3. In many African countries the bulk of urban transportation is provided by what is sometimes called "paratransit," a system of transport that parallels public transportation (McCormick et al. 2013). How states regulate paratransit varies widely, but it is common for tensions to exist between states and private transportation providers (Rasmussen 2012; Rizzo 2011; Tripp 1997).

4. Rosalind Fredericks's (2014) discussion of trash collection in Dakar is an excel-

lent example of an analysis based in the intersection between the state, vital things, and infrastructural labor.

5. Rizzo (2017, 4–6) belittles Simone's notion of people as infrastructure. Although Rizzo's critique of celebrations of open-endedness is useful, he overlooks the potential to combine a conception of people as infrastructure with the Marxian approach he advocates. Class relations are important for infrastructural labor, but this labor also serves the public good, and for this reason it is caught up in citizen/state relations. When people function as infrastructure, the state has a particular interest in regulating labor, and this has a major impact on class relationships.

6. Donham also provides an essential analysis of the relation between Marxist theory and twentieth-century anthropology.

7. This dynamic is not isolated to Ethiopia. In San Francisco, government administrators justified labor reform for public transit workers with claims that it was necessary to achieve a particular vision of urban livability (Fleming 2016).

8. The social history of the three-wheeled motorcycle deserves more exploration. The roots of Bajaj's production of three-wheelers seem to go back to a relationship with the German company Tempo, and the Tempo Hanseat three-wheeler that was built for carrying light loads. Such German-Indian manufacturing collaborations were common in the mid-twentieth century (Tetzlaff 2017). Today the African continent is one of the biggest markets for Bajaj exports.

9. This plan was eventually enacted, and in 2017 Bajaj were not permitted on the main road connecting Lake Hawassa with the piazza neighborhood and the city's bus station.

10. Government administrators seemed to view the 100 birr charge for leasing a Bajaj as a given. They never mentioned the possibility of regulating this charge, and when I directly raised the issue, they quickly dismissed the idea. My impression is that in contrast to the heavy regulation of the movement of the Bajaj, administrators did not believe regulating the relationship between owner and driver was within their purview.

11. Attempts to modernize taxis in Mumbai (Bedi 2016) were similar in that state endeavors to create a particular type of city conflicted with the needs of networks of taxi drivers and owners.

12. Marco Di Nunzio (2014b) explains that minibus workers have been criminalized in Addis Ababa, often in relation to political conflicts.

13. Particularly in rural areas, Ethiopian passengers are very reluctant to open windows on moving vehicles. This is largely a result of beliefs regarding wind and exposure to illness.

14. The connection between the Bajaj and job creation is not unique to Ethiopia. The Bajaj company website features a section called "Dreams." It links to videos of individual Bajaj owners in India, describing how the Bajaj has allowed them to achieve their dreams and be successful entrepreneurs. "Bajaj RE Dreams," accessed January 1, 2017, http://www.bajajauto.com/bajajre/owners-review.html.

15. In Amharic, *mengist aychelem*.

16. The fuel crisis also draws attention to technopolitical relationships between

multiple forms of infrastructure. Journalists reported that to reduce its dependence on Sudan for benzene, the Ethiopian government was increasing mandated levels of blended ethanol in fuel (Sisay 2011). Ethanol was produced from sugarcane in newly expanded state-owned refineries. The sugar itself was grown with the support of irrigation, made possible by state investments of well over $1 billion in the large dams discussed in chapter 1.

17. Taxi and minibus drivers staged a three-day strike in protest of police violence after the contentious 2005 Ethiopian election, and minibus touts were rewarded with connections to the state after helping end the strike (Di Nunzio 2014b).

CHAPTER 5. WHAT CAN A STONE DO?

1. Stone roads in Ethiopia are technically made from setts, a stone that is, unlike cobble, quarried and shaped into a regular size. However, I adopt the term *cobblestone*, as this is the word used by both Ethiopians and the international funders that support the road construction.

2. In some ways cobblestone roads emerged out of a struggle among development practitioners during the twentieth century to identify "appropriate technologies" (Schumacher 1973). A volume sponsored by the World Federation for Mental Health, titled *Cultural Patterns and Technical Change* and edited by Margaret Mead (1955), advocated introducing new technologies in ways that would minimize disruptions to culture. From this perspective technologies had the potential to create severe mental distress when introduced without consideration for cultural context. In his influential book *Small Is Beautiful*, E. F. Schumacher advocated an "intermediate technology" that is "vastly superior to the primitive technology of bygone ages but at the same time much simpler, cheaper, and freer than the super-technology of the rich" (1973, 145). Paul Farmer has famously critiqued appropriate technology, quoting a priest he met in Haiti, who claimed that appropriate technology meant "good things for the rich and shit for the poor" (1999, 21). The case of roads, however, is quite different from the medical technology that concerns Farmer. Where medical technology may be evaluated in terms of implications for maximizing patient health, no such single variable for evaluation exists in the case of roads. Roads are not necessarily intended to maximize the speed of travel, and therefore more variability exists in what is appropriate.

3. A comparison may be made with James Smith's (2011) analysis of the temporality of coltan in the Democratic Republic of Congo. Smith argues that the material qualities of coltan serve to both undermine and support local communities' engagements with incremental time.

4. Although women are involved in cobblestone road construction, I build off of my previous research with urban young men to focus primarily on the experience of young male workers.

5. Date: 27 January, 2004. Proclamation No. 384/2004. Title: A Proclamation to Provide for Controlling Vagrancy.

6. The Togolese government stopped building cobblestone roads because of the potential for protestors to use the stones in combat with police (Charles Piot, pers. communication).

CONCLUSION

1. I differ from Caroline Melly on this point. Melly (2016, 45–46) argues that the futuristic highways and massive urban redevelopment in Dakar are indicative of the gap between everyday life and long-term projections for change. Fantastic future projections are certainly important in conditioning the experience of the present, but the roads and the city that Melly describes are under construction. Dakar's citizens are engaging with the realities of near-future plans for a linear process of construction. My sense is that Melly's insightful discussion of "bottlenecks" actually has important connections with temporalities of the near future.

2. The mysterious death of Simegnew Bekele, lead engineer for the GERD, in July 2018 is an example of this uncertainty. Although police ruled that Simegnew's death was a suicide, many Ethiopians believe he was assassinated.

REFERENCES

Aalen, Lovise. 2011. *The Politics of Ethnicity in Ethiopia: Actors, Power, and Mobilisation under Ethnic Federalism*. Leiden: Brill.

Abbink, Jon. 2006a. "Discomfiture of Democracy? The 2005 Election Crisis in Ethiopia and Its Aftermath." *African Affairs* 105 (419): 173–99.

Abbink, Jon. 2006b. "Interpreting Ethiopian Elections in Their Context—A Reply to Tobias Hagmann." *African Affairs* 105 (421): 613–20.

Abbink, Jon. 2012. "Dam Controversies: Contested Governance and Developmental Discourse on the Ethiopian Omo River Dam." *Social Anthropology* 20 (2): 125–44.

Africa Development Bank. n.d. "Ethiopia Economic Outlook." Accessed June 20, 2016. http://www.afdb.org/en/countries/east-africa/ethiopia/ethiopia-economic-outlook/.

Anand, Nikhil. 2011. "Pressure: The PoliTechnics of Water Supply in Mumbai." *Cultural Anthropology* 26 (4): 542–64.

Anand, Nikhil. 2017. *Hydraulic City: Water and the Infrastructures of Citizenship in Mumbai*. Durham, NC: Duke University Press.

Appel, Hannah, Nikhil Ananda, and Akhil Gupta. 2015. "The Infrastructure Toolbox." Theorizing the Contemporary, *Cultural Anthropology*, September 24, 2015. Accessed December 18, 2018. https://culanth.org/fieldsights/725-the-infrastructure-toolbox.

Arriola, Leonardo. 2008. "Ethnicity, Economic Conditions, and Opposition Support: Evidence from Ethiopia's 2005 Elections." *Northeast African Studies* 10 (1): 115–44.

Aschalew, Melkame. 2013. "Cobblestone's Rocky Road." *Addis Fortune* 13 (678). Accessed April 4, 2018. https://addisfortune.net/articles/cobblestonesrocky-road/.

Avery, Sean. 2012. *Lake Turkana and the Lower Omo: Hydrological Impacts of Major Dam and Irrigation Development*. Oxford: University of Oxford African Studies Centre.

Ayele, Anteneh. 2004. "How Can We Tackle Vagrancy without Addressing the Social and Economic Problems of Youth?" *The Reporter* (Addis Ababa).

Balibar, Etienne. 2017. *The Philosophy of Marx*. London: Verso.

Bangs, Richard, and Christian Kallen. 1985. *Rivergods: Exploring the World's Great Wild Rivers*. San Francisco: Sierra Club Books.
Barata, Data. 2012. "Minority Rights, Culture, and Ethiopia's 'Third Way' to Governance." *African Studies Review* 55 (3): 61–80.
Bardeen, Sarah. 2016. "Dancing with Rivers: A Meditation for Earth Day." *International Rivers*. Accessed June 22, 2016. https://www.internationalrivers.org/blogs/433-23.
Barry, Andrew. 2013. *Material Politics: Disputes along the Pipeline*. Chichester, UK: Wiley-Blackwell.
Bedi, Tarini. 2016. "Taxi Drivers, Infrastructures, and Urban Change in Globalizing Mumbai." *City and Society* 28 (3): 387–410.
Bennett, Jane. 2010. *Vibrant Matter: A Political Ecology of Things*. Durham, NC: Duke University Press.
Beyene, Asfaw. 2013. "Why Is the Hydroelectric Dam on the Blue Nile, the Grand Ethiopian Renaissance Dam (GERD), Sized for 6000 MW?" *Finfinne Tribune*. Accessed April 13, 2018. http://gadaa.com/oduu/index.php/20303/2013/06/19/why-is-the-hydroelectric-dam-on-the-blue-nile-the-grand-ethiopian-renaissance-dam-gerd-sized-for-6000-mw/.
Blackbourn, David. 2006. *The Conquest of Nature: Water, Landscape, and the Making of Modern Germany*. New York: W. W. Norton.
Breman, Jan. 2016. *At Work in the Informal Economy of India: A Perspective from the Bottom Up*. Oxford: Oxford University Press.
Bromber, Katrin, Jeanne Feaux de la Croix, and Katharina Lange. 2014. "The Temporal Politics of Big Dams in Africa, the Middle East, and Asia: By Way of an Introduction." *Water History* 6: 289–96.
Bromber, Katrin, Paolo Gaibazzi, Franziska Roy, Abdoulaye Sounaye, and Julian Tadesse. 2015. "The Possibilities Are Endless: Progress and the Taming of Contingency." *Zentrum Moderner Orient Programmatic Texts* 9: 1–10.
Broussard, Nzinga, and Tsegay Gebrekidan Tekleselassie. 2012. *Youth Unemployment: Ethiopia Country Study*. Working paper 12/0592. London: International Growth Centre.
Bürge, Michael. 2011. "Riding the Narrow Tracks of Moral Life: Commercial Motorbike Riders in Makeni, Sierra Leone." *Africa Today* 58 (2): 58–95.
Caldeira, Teresa, and James Holston. 2005. "State and Urban Space in Brazil: From Modernist Planning to Democratic Interventions." In *Global Assemblages: Technology, Politics, and Ethics as Anthropological Problems*, edited by Aihwa Ong and Stephen Collier, 393–416. Malden, MA: Blackwell.
Chalfin, Brenda. 2014. "Public Things, Excremental Politics, and the Infrastructure of Bare Life in Ghana's City of Tema." *American Ethnologist* 41 (1): 92–109.
Chu, Julie. 2014. "When Infrastructures Attack: The Workings of Disrepair in China." *American Ethnologist* 41 (2): 351–67.
Clapham, Christopher. 2002. "Controlling Space in Ethiopia." In *Remapping Ethiopia: Socialism and After*, edited by W. James, D. Donham, E. Kurimoto, and A. Triulzi, 9–30. Oxford: James Currey.

Cole, Jennifer, and Lynn Thomas, eds. 2009. *Love in Africa*. Chicago: University of Chicago Press.
Connolly, William. 2002. *Neuropolitics: Thinking, Culture, Speed*. Minneapolis: University of Minnesota Press.
Dalakoglou, Dimitris. 2010. "The Road: An Ethnography of the Albanian-Greek Cross-border Motorway." *American Ethnologist* 37 (1): 132–49.
Dalakoglou, Dimitris, and Penny Harvey. 2012. "Roads and Anthropology: Ethnographic Perspectives on Space, Time, and (Im)mobility." *Mobilities* 7 (4): 459–65.
De Boeck, Filip. 2011. "Inhabiting Ocular Ground: Kinshasa's Future in the Light of Congo's Spectral Urban Politics." *Cultural Anthropology* 26 (2): 263–86.
De Waal, Alex. 2013. "The Theory and Practice of Meles Zenawi." *African Affairs* 112 (446): 148–55.
Di Nunzio, Marco. 2014a. "'Do Not Cross the Red Line': The 2010 General Elections, Dissent, and Political Mobilization in Urban Ethiopia." *African Affairs* 113 (452): 409–30.
Di Nunzio, Marco. 2014b. "Thugs, Spies and Vigilantes: Community Policing and Street Politics in Inner City Addis Ababa." *Africa* 84 (3): 444–65.
Di Nunzio, Marco. 2015. "What Is the Alternative? Youth, Entrepreneurship and the Developmental State in Urban Ethiopia." *Development and Change* 46 (5): 1179–200.
Donham, Donald. 1986. "Old Abyssinia and the New Ethiopian Empire: Themes in Social History." In *The Southern Marches of Imperial Ethiopia: Essays in History and Social Anthropology*, edited by D. Donham and W. James, 3–50. Cambridge: Cambridge University Press.
Donham, Donald. 1999a. *History, Power, Ideology: Central Issues in Marxism and Anthropology*. Berkeley: University of California Press.
Donham, Donald. 1999b. *Marxist Modern: An Ethnographic History of the Ethiopian Revolution*. Berkeley: University of California Press.
Donham, Donald. 2018. *The Erotics of History: An Atlantic African Example*. Berkeley: University of California Press.
Economist. 2011. "Africa's Impressive Growth." Accessed December 19, 2018. https://www.economist.com/graphic-detail/2011/01/06/africas-impressive-growth.
Ekbladh, David. 2010. *The Great American Mission: Modernization and the Construction of an American World Order*. Princeton, NJ: Princeton University Press.
Elyachar, Julia 2002. "Empowerment Money: The World Bank, Non-Governmental Organizations, and the Value of Culture in Egypt." *Public Culture* 14 (3): 493–513.
Elyachar, Julia. 2012. "Next Practices: Knowledge, Infrastructure, and Public Goods at the Bottom of the Pyramid." *Public Culture* 24 (1): 109–29.
Escobar, Arturo. 1995. *Encountering Development: The Making and Unmaking of the Third World*. Princeton, NJ: Princeton University Press.
Ethiopian Central Statistical Agency. 2010. *Population and Housing Census Report–Country–2007*. Addis Ababa: Central Statistical Agency.
Evren, Erdem. Forthcoming. "Tenses of Violence: Ruination and Accumulation along the Çoruh Valley." In *Reverberations: Violence across Time and Space*, edited by Yael Navaro et al. Philadelphia: University of Pennsylvania Press.
Fantini, Emanuele, and Luca Puddu. 2016. "Ethiopia and International Aid: Develop-

ment between High Modernism and Exceptional Measures." In *Aid and Authoritarianism in Africa: Development without Democracy*, edited by Tobias Hagmann and Filip Reyntjens. London: Zed Books.

Farmer, Paul. 1999. *Infections and Inequalities: The Modern Plagues*. Berkeley: University of California Press.

Ferguson, James. 1994. *The Anti-Politics Machine: Development, Depoliticization, and Bureaucratic Power in Lesotho*. Minneapolis: University of Minnesota Press.

Ferguson, James. 1997. "Anthropology and Its Evil Twin: 'Development' in the Constitution of a Discipline." In *International Development and the Social Sciences: Essays on the History and Politics of Knowledge*, edited by Frederick Cooper and Randall Packard, 150–75. Berkeley: University of California Press.

Ferguson, James. 1999. *Expectations of Modernity*. Berkeley: University of California Press.

Ferguson, James. 2006. *Global Shadows: Africa in the Neoliberal World Order*. Durham, NC: Duke University Press.

Ferguson, James. 2015. *Give a Man a Fish: Reflections on the New Politics of Distribution*. Durham, NC: Duke University Press.

Fisher, William. 1997. "Development and Resistance in the Narmada Valley." In *Toward Sustainable Development: Struggling over India's Narmada River*, edited by W. Fisher. Armonk, NY: M. E. Sharpe.

Fleming, Mark. 2016. "Mass Transit Workers and Neoliberal Time Discipline in San Francisco." *American Anthropologist* 118 (4): 784–95.

Fourie, Elsje. 2015. "China's Example for Meles' Ethiopia: When Development 'Models' Land." *Journal of Modern African Studies* 53 (3): 289–316.

Fratkin, Elliot. 2014. "Ethiopia's Pastoralist Policies: Development, Displacement and Resttlement." *Nomadic Peoples* 18 (1): 94–114.

Fratkin, E. M., and E. A. Roth. 2005. *As Pastoralists Settle: Social, Health, and Economic Consequences of the Pastoral Sedentarization in Marsabit District, Kenya*. New York: Kluwer Academic–Plenum.

Fredericks, Rosalind. 2014. "Vital Infrastructures of Trash in Dakar." *Comparative Studies of South Asia, Africa and the Middle East* 34 (3): 532–48.

Freeman, Dena. 2012. "The Pentecostal Ethic and the Spirit of Development." In *Pentecostalism and Development: Churches, NGOs and Social Change in Africa*, edited by Dena Freeman, 1–38. London: Palgrave Macmillan UK.

Gandy, Matthew. 2005. "Learning from Lagos." *New Left Review*, no. 33: 37–52.

Gebresenbet, Fana. 2016. "Land Acquisitions, the Politics of Dispossession, and State-Remaking in Gambella, Western Ethiopia." *Africa Spectrum* 51 (1): 5–28.

GERD National Panel of Experts. 2014. "A Proxy Campaign against Ethiopia? A Response by GERD National Panel of Experts (NPoE)." *EIPSA Communicating Article* 1 (3): 1–9.

German Development Cooperation Office (GIZ). 2012. *Making Good Governance Tangible: The Cobblestone Sector of Ethiopia*. Bonn, Germany: GIZ.

Gifford, Paul. 1987. "'Africa Shall be Saved': An Appraisal of Reinhard Bonnke's Pan-African Crusade." *Journal of Religion in Africa* 17 (1): 63–92.

Gifford, Paul. 1994. "Reinhard Bonnke's Mission to Africa, and His 1991 Nairobi Crusade." *Wajibu* 9 (1): 13–19.

Gizachew, Andnet. 2014. "Curses of Big Development Projects: Development-Induced Displacement and Its Socio-Economic Impacts on the Displaced People in the Case of Tekeze Dam." In *Culture, Technology, and Development: Urban Development, Resettlement and Education in Ethiopia*, edited by Daniel Mains, 101–22. Hawassa: Hawassa University.

Goldstone, Brian, and Juan Obarrio. 2016. "Introduction: Untimely Africa?" In *African Futures: Essays on Crisis, Emergence, and Possibility*, edited by Brian Goldstone and Juan Obarrio. Chicago: University of Chicago Press.

Gregg, Melissa, and Gregory Seigworth. 2010. *The Affect Theory Reader.* Durham, NC: Duke University Press.

Guyer, Jane. 2007. "Prophecy and the Near Future: Thoughts on Macroeconomic, Evangelical, and Punctuated Time." *American Ethnologist* 34 (3): 409–21.

Hagmann, Tobias. 2006. "Ethiopian Political Culture Strikes Back: A Rejoinder to J. Abbink." *African Affairs* 105 (421): 605–12.

Hagmann, Tobias, and Jon Abbink. 2013. "The Politics of Authoritarian Reform in Ethiopia, 1991 to 2012." In *Reconfiguring Ethiopia: The Politics of Authoritarian Reform*, edited by Jon Abbink and Tobias Hagmann, 1–16. London: Routledge.

Hanlon, Joseph, Armando Barrientos, and David Hulme. 2010. *Just Give Money to the Poor: The Development Revolution from the Global South.* Sterling, VA: Kumarian Press.

Harms, Erik. 2016. *Luxury and Rubble: Civility and Dispossession in the New Saigon.* Berkeley: University of California Press.

Harsin, Jill. 2002. *Barricades: The War of the Streets in Revolutionary Paris, 1830–1848.* New York: Palgrave.

Hart, Keith. 1973. "Informal Income Opportunities and Urban Employment in Ghana." *Journal of Modern African Studies* 11 (1): 61–89.

Harvey, David. 1985. *The Urbanization of Capital.* Oxford: Blackwell.

Hathaway, Terry. 2008. *What Cost Ethiopia's Dam Boom? A Look inside the Expansion of Ethiopia's Energy Sector.* Berkeley: International Rivers.

Henshaw, Amber. 2005. "Anguish over Ethiopia's Disappeared." *BBC News.* Accessed September 9, 2016. http://news.bbc.co.uk/2/hi/africa/4110630.stm.

Hoben, Allan. 1970. "Social Stratification in Traditional Amhara Society." In *Social Stratification in Africa*, edited by Arthur Tuden and Leonard Plotnicov, 187–224. New York: Free Press.

Hoben, Allan. 1973. *Land Tenure among the Amhara of Ethiopia.* Chicago: University of Chicago Press.

Hochschild, Adam. 1998. *King Leopold's Ghost: A Story of Greed, Terror, and Heroism in Colonial Africa.* Boston: Houghton Mifflin.

Holston, James. 1989. *The Modernist City: An Anthropological Critique of Brasília.* Chicago: University of Chicago Press.

Horne, Felix. 2018. "US Resolution on Ethiopia Passes." *Human Rights Watch.* Accessed April 13, 2018. https://www.hrw.org/news/2018/04/10/us-house-resolution-ethiopia-passes.

Human Rights Watch. 2002. "Ethiopia: Police Firing on Unarmed Protestors." Accessed June 16, 2016. http://www.hrw.org/news/2002/06/10/ethiopia-police-firing-unarmed-protesters.

Hurd, Will. 2015. "US, UK, World Bank among Aid Donors Complicit in Ethiopia's War on Indigenous Tribes, Opening the Way to International Agribusiness." *Global Research*. Accessed July 10, 2017. http://www.globalresearch.ca/us-uk-world-bank-among-aid-donors-complicit-in-ethiopias-war-on-indigenous-tribes-opening-the-way-to-international-agribusiness/5467738.

Hurd, Will. 2016. "Surviving the Second Conquest: Emperor Menelik and Industrial Plantations in Ethiopia's Omo Valley." *Solutions* 7 (1): 68–73.

International Rivers. n.d. "Healthy Rivers." Accessed June 22, 2016. https://www.internationalrivers.org/healthy-rivers.

International Rivers. n.d. "Problems with Big Dams." Accessed June 22, 2016. https://www.internationalrivers.org/problems-with-big-dams.

International Rivers. n.d. "Rivers and Biodiversity." Accessed June 22, 2016. https://www.internationalrivers.org/rivers-and-biodiversity.

International Rivers. 2013. *The Downstream Impacts of Ethiopia's Gibe III Dam: East Africa's 'Aral Sea' in the Making?* Berkeley, CA: International Rivers.

Isaacman, Allen, and Barbara Isaacman. 2013. *Dams, Displacement, and the Delusion of Development: Cahora Bassa and Its Legacies in Mozambique, 1965–2007*. Athens: Ohio University Press.

Johnson, Bob. 2014. *Carbon Nation: Fossil Fuels in the Making of American Culture*. Lawrence: University Press of Kansas.

Jones, Christopher. 2014. *Routes of Power: Energy and Modern America*. Cambridge, MA: Harvard University Press.

Jones, Will, Ricardo Soares de Oliveira, and Harry Verhoeven. 2013. *Africa's Illiberal State-Builders*. Working Paper Series No. 89. Oxford: Refugee Studies Centre, University of Oxford.

Joon-seung, Lee. 2014. "GM Korea Relaunches Damas and Labo." Yonhap News Agency. Accessed July 7, 2017. http://english.yonhapnews.co.kr/business/2014/08/26/1/0501000000AEN20140826007752320F.html.

Kamski, Benedikt. 2016. "Briefing Note 1: The Kuraz Sugar Development Project. Omo-Turkana Basin Research Network." Accessed July 13, 2016. http://www.arnold-bergstraesser.de/sites/default/files/field/pub-download/ksdp_briefing_note_omo_turkana_basin_research_network_1.pdf.

Kebede, Kassahun. 2009. "Social Dimensions of Development-induced Resettlement: The Case of the Gilgel Gibe Hydroelectric Dam." In *Moving People in Ethiopia: Development, Displacement and the State*, edited by Francis Piguet and Alula Pankhurst, 49–65. London: James Currey.

Kebede, Zeleke, and Serkalem Alemayehu. 2007. *History of Hawassa (1952–1999 E.C.)*. Hawassa: Hawassa City Administration.

Kelsall, Tim. 2013. *Business, Politics and the State in Africa: Challenging the Orthodoxies on Growth and Transformation*. London: Zed Books.

Klineberg, Eric. 2006. *Heat Wave: A Social Autopsy of Disaster in Chicago*. Chicago: University of Chicago Press.

Knox, Hannah, and Penny Harvey. 2011. "Anticipating Harm: Regulation and Irregularity on a Road Construction Project in the Peruvian Andes." *Theory, Culture and Society* 28 (6): 142–63.

Lamont, Mark. 2013. "Speed Governors: Road Safety and Infrastructural Overload in Post-Colonial Kenya, c. 1963–2013." *Africa* 83 (3): 367–84.

Larkin, Brian. 2008. *Signal and Noise: Media, Infrastructure, and Urban Culture in Nigeria*. Durham, NC: Duke University Press.

Larkin, Brian. 2013. "The Politics and Poetics of Infrastructure." *Annual Review of Anthropology* 42 (3): 327–43.

Larkin, Brian. 2016. "The Form of Crisis and the Affect of Modernization." In *African Futures: Essays on Crisis, Emergence, and Possibility*, edited by Brian Goldstone and Juan Obarrio, 39–50. Chicago: University of Chicago Press.

Latour, Bruno. 1993. *We Have Never Been Modern*. Cambridge, MA: Harvard University Press.

Lee, Rebekah. 2012. "Death in Slow Motion: Funerals, Ritual Practice and Road Danger in South Africa." *African Studies* 71 (2): 195–211.

Lefort, Rene. 2007. "Powers—*Mengist*—and Peasants in Rural Ethiopia: The May 2005 Elections." *Journal of Modern African Studies* 45 (2): 253–73.

Lefort, Rene. 2012. "Free Market Economy, 'Developmental State' and Party-State Hegemony in Ethiopia: The Case of the 'Model Farmers.'" *Journal of Modern African Studies* 50 (4): 681–706.

Lefort, Rene. 2013. "The Theory and Practice of Meles Zenawi: A Response to Alex de Waal." *African Affairs* 112 (448): 1–5.

Leys, Ruth. 2011. "The Turn to Affect: A Critique." *Critical Inquiry* 37 (3): 434–72.

Limbert, Mandana. 2001. "The Senses of Water in an Omani Town." *Social Text* 19 (3): 35–55.

Limbert, Mandana. 2010. *In the Time of Oil: Piety, Memory, and Social Life in an Omani Town*. Stanford, CA: Stanford University Press.

Livingston, Julie. 2012. *Improvising Medicine: An African Oncology Ward in an Emerging Cancer Epidemic*. Durham, NC: Duke University Press.

Lutz, Catherine. 2014. "The U.S. Car Colossus and the Production of Inequality." *American Ethnologist* 41 (2): 232–45.

Lutz, Catherine. 2017. "What Matters." *Cultural Anthropology* 32 (2): 181–91.

Mahajan, Vijay. 2009. *Africa Rising: How 900 Million African Consumers Offer More Than You Think*. Upper Saddle River, NJ: Prentice Hall.

Mains, Daniel. 2004. "Drinking, Rumour, and Ethnicity in Jimma, Ethiopia." *Africa* 74 (3): 341–60.

Mains, Daniel. 2012a. "Blackouts and Progress: Privatization, Infrastructure, and a Developmentalist State in Jimma, Ethiopia." *Cultural Anthropology* 27 (1): 3–27.

Mains, Daniel. 2012b. *Hope Is Cut: Youth, Unemployment, and the Future in Urban Ethiopia*. Philadelphia: Temple University Press.

Mains, Daniel. 2015. "Reconnecting Hope: Khat Consumption, Time, and Mental Wellbeing among Unemployed Young Men in Jimma, Ethiopia." In *Global Mental Health: Anthropological Perspectives*, edited by Brandon Kohrt and Emily Mendenhall, 87–102. Walnut Creek, CA: Left Coast Press.

Mains, Daniel, and Eshetayehu Kinfu. 2016. "Making the City of Nations and Nationalities: The Politics of Ethnicity and Roads in Hawassa, Ethiopia." *Journal of Modern African Studies* 54 (4): 645–69.

Mains, Daniel, and Eshetayehu Kinfu. 2017. "Governing the Bajaj: Technology, Markets and the State in Urban Ethiopia." *American Ethnologist* 44 (2): 263–74.

Markakis, John. 2011. *Ethiopia: The Last Two Frontiers*. Oxford: James Currey.

Markakis, John. 1998. "The Politics of Identity: The Case of the Gurage in Ethiopia." In *Ethnicity and the State in Eastern Africa*, edited by M. A. Hohamed Salih and J. Markakis, 127–46. Uppsala, Sweden: Nordiska Afrikainstitutet.

Martin, Emily. 2013. "The Potentiality of Ethnography and the Limits of Affect Theory." *Current Anthropology* 54 (S7): S149–58.

Marx, Karl. 1976. *Capital: A Critique of Political Economy, Volume I*. London: Penguin.

Masquelier, A. 2002. "Road Mythologies: Space, Mobility, and Historical Imagination in the Postcolonial Imagination." *American Ethnologist* 29 (4): 829–56.

Massumi, Brian. 1995. "The Autonomy of Affect." *Cultural Critique*, no. 31: 83–109.

Massumi, Brian. 2002. *Parables for the Virtual: Movement, Affect, Sensation*. Durham, NC: Duke University Press.

Mbembe, Achille. 2016. "Africa in Theory." In *African Futures: Essays on Crisis, Emergence, and Possibility*, edited by Brian Goldstone and Juan Obarrio, 211–30. Chicago: University of Chicago Press.

Mbembe, Achille, and Sarah Nuttall. 2004. "Writing the World from an African Metropolis." *Public Culture* 16 (3): 347–72.

McCormick, Dorothy, Winnie Mitullah, Preston Chitere, Risper Orero, and Marilyn Ommeh. 2013. "Paratransit Business Strategies: A Bird's-Eye View of Matatus in Nairobi." *Journal of Public Transportation* 16 (2): 135–52.

McMichael, Philip. 1996. *Development and Social Change: A Global Perspective*. Los Angeles: SAGE.

McShane, Clay. 1994. *Down the Asphalt Path: The Automobile and the American City*. New York: Columbia University Press.

Mead, Margaret. 1955. *Cultural Patterns and Technical Change*. New York: New American Library.

Melly, Caroline. 2013. "Ethnography on the Road: Infrastructural Vision and the Unruly Present in Contemporary Dakar." *Africa* 83 (3): 385–402.

Melly, Caroline. 2017. *Bottleneck: Moving, Building, and Belonging in an African City*. Chicago: University of Chicago Press.

Miescher, Stephan. 2014. "'Nkrumah's Baby': The Akosombo Dam and the Dream of Development in Ghana, 1952–1966." *Water History* 6 (4): 341–66.

Mignolo, Walter. 2011. "The Global South and World Dis/Order." *Journal of Anthropological Research* 67 (2): 165–88.

Mitchell, Timothy. 2002. *Rule of Experts: Egypt, Techno-politics, Modernity.* Berkeley: University of California Press.

Mosley, Jason, and Elizabeth Watson. 2016. "Frontier Transformation: Developmental Visions, Spaces, and Processes in Northern Kenya and Southern Ethiopia." *Journal of Eastern African Studies* 10 (3): 452–75.

Nehru, Jawaharlal. 1958. "Temples of the New Age." In *Jawaharlal Nehru's Speeches.* Vol. 3 (March 1953–August 1957). New Delhi: Ministry of Information and Broadcasting, Government of India.

Newell, Sasha. 2018. "The Affectiveness of Symbols: Materiality, Magicality, and the Limits of the Antisemiotic Turn." *Current Anthropology* 59 (1): 1–22.

Oakland Institute. 2011. *Understanding Land Investment Deals in Africa, Country Report: Ethiopia.* Oakland, CA: Oakland Institute.

Oakland Institute. 2014. *Engineering Ethnic Conflict: The Toll of Ethiopia's Plantation Development on the Suri People.* Oakland, CA: Oakland Institute.

Oakland Institute. n.d. "DFID and USAID Investigation Recordings." Accessed February 28, 2018. https://www.oaklandinstitute.org/dfid-and-usaid-investigation-recordings.

Olopade, Dayo. 2014. *The Bright Continent: Breaking Rules and Making Change in Modern Africa.* New York: Houghton Mifflin Harcourt.

Orlowska, Izabela. 2013. "Forging a Nation: The Ethiopian Millennium Celebration and the Multiethnic State." *Nations and Nationalism* 19 (2): 296–316.

Oqubay, Arkebe. 2015. *Made in Africa: Industrial Policy in Ethiopia.* Oxford: Oxford University Press.

Packard, Randall. 1997. "Visions of Postwar Health and Development and Their Impact on Public Health Interventions in the Developing World." In *International Development and the Social Sciences,* edited by F. Cooper and R. Packard, 93–115. Berkeley: University of California Press.

Parr, Joy. 2010. *Sensing Changes: Technologies, Environments, and the Everyday, 1953–2003.* Vancouver: University of British Columbia Press.

Piot, Charles. 2010. *Nostalgia for the Future: West Africa after the Cold War.* Chicago: University of Chicago Press.

Poggiali, Lisa. 2016. "Seeing (from) Digital Peripheries: Technology and Transparency in Kenya's Silicon Savannah." *Cultural Anthropology* 31 (3): 387–411.

Poluha, Eva. 2004. *The Power of Continuity: Ethiopia through the Eyes of Its Children.* Uppsala, Sweden: Nordiska Afrikainstitutet.

Pottinger, Lori. 2013. "A Tale of Two Dams: Comparing Ethiopia's Grand Renaissance to Hoover." Berkeley, CA: International Rivers. Accessed June 21, 2016. https://www.internationalrivers.org/blogs/229/a-tale-of-two-dams-comparing-ethiopia's-grand-renaissance-to-hoover.

Pritchard, Sarah. 2011. *Confluence: The Nature of Technology and the Remaking of the Rhone.* Cambridge, MA: Harvard University Press.

Radelet, Steven. 2010. *Emerging Africa: How 17 Countries Are Leading the Way.* Washington, DC: Center for Global Development.

Radelet, Steven. 2016. *The Great Surge: The Ascent of the Developing World*. New York: Simon and Schuster.

Rao, Ursula. 2013. "Tolerated Encroachment: Resettlement Policies and the Negotiation of the Licit/Illicit Divide in an Indian Metropolis." *Cultural Anthropology* 28 (4): 760–79.

Rasmussen, Jacob. 2012. "Inside the System, Outside the Law: Operating the Matatu Sector in Nairobi." *Urban Forum* 23 (4): 415–32.

Redfield, Peter. 2016. "Fluid Technologies: The Bush Pump, the LifeStraw and Microworlds of Humanitarian Design." *Social Studies of Science* 46 (2): 159–83.

Rizzo, Matteo. 2011. "'Life Is War': Informal Transport Workers and Neoliberalism in Tanzania 1998–2009." *Development and Change* 42 (5): 1179–205.

Rizzo, Matteo. 2017. *Taken for a Ride: Grounding Neoliberalism, Precarious Labour, and Public Transport in an African Metropolis*. Oxford: Oxford University Press.

Rodney, Walter. 1981. *How Europe Underdeveloped Africa*. Washington, DC: Howard University Press.

Rollason, William. 2013. "Performance, Poverty and Urban Development: Kigali's Motari and the Spectacle City." *Afrika Focus* 26 (2): 9–29.

Rostow, W. W. 1960. *The Stages of Economic Growth: A Non-Communist Manifesto*. Cambridge: Cambridge University Press.

Roy, Ananya. 2009. "Why India Cannot Plan Its Cities: Informality, Insurgence and the Idiom of Urbanization." *Planning Theory* 8 (1): 76–87.

Roy, Arundhati. 2001. *Power Politics*. Cambridge, MA: South End Press.

Sachs, Jeffrey. 2005. *The End of Poverty: Economic Possibilities for Our Time*. New York: Penguin Random House.

Sahle, Eden. 2011. "Court Freezes Part of DMC's Assets." *Addis Fortune* (Addis Ababa). Accessed June 27, 2016. http://allafrica.com/stories/201107270798.html.

Salini Impregilo. n.d. "Grand Ethiopian Renaissance Dam Project." Accessed June 30, 2017. https://www.salini-impregilo.com/en/projects/in-progress/dams-hydroelectric-plants-hydraulic-works/grand-ethiopian-renaissance-dam-project.html.

Schumacher, E. F. 1973. *Small Is Beautiful: Economics as if People Mattered*. New York: Harper and Row.

Schuman, Michael. 2014. "Forget the BRICS; Meet the PINES." *Time*. Accessed January 6, 2016. http://time.com/22779/forget-the-brics-meet-the-pines/.

Schwenkel, Christina. 2015a. "Sense." Theorizing the Contemporary, *Cultural Anthropology* website, September 24, 2015. Accessed May 7, 2018. https://culanth.org/fieldsights/721-sense.

Schwenkel, Christina. 2015b. "Spectacular Infrastructure and Its Breakdown in Socialist Vietnam." *American Ethnologist* 42 (3): 520–34.

Scott, James. 1998. *Seeing Like a State: How Certain Schemes to Improve the Human Condition Have Failed*. New Haven, CT: Yale University Press.

Serneels, Pieter. 2007. "The Nature of Unemployment among Young Men in Urban Ethiopia." *Review of Development Economics* 11 (1): 170–86.

Simone, AbdouMaliq. 2004. "People as Infrastructure: Intersecting Fragments in Johannesburg." *Public Culture* 16 (3): 407–29.

Sisay, Desalegn. 2011. "Ethiopia Braces for Oil Shortage as Sudan Shuts Pipes." *Afrik-News*, February 10. Accessed June 27, 2016. http://www.afrik-news.com /article18929.html.

Smith, James. 2011. "Tantalus in the Digital Age: Coltan Ore, Temporal Dispossession, and 'Movement' in the Eastern Democratic Republic of Congo." *American Ethnologist* 38 (1): 17–35.

Sopranzetti, Claudio. 2014. "Owners of the Map: Mobility and Mobilization among Motorcycle Taxi Drivers in Bangkok." *City and Society* 26 (1): 120–43.

Squires, Gregory, and Chester Hartman. 2006. *There Is No Such Thing as a Natural Disaster: Race, Class, and Hurricane Katrina*. New York: Routledge.

Star, Susan. 1999. "The Ethnography of Infrastructure." *American Behavioral Scientist* 43 (3): 377–91.

Stevenson, Edward, and Lucie Buffavand. 2018. "'Do Our Bodies Know Their Ways?': Villagization, Food Insecurity, and Ill-being in Ethiopia's Lower Omo Valley." *African Studies Review* 61 (1):109–33.

Stewart, Kathleen. 2007. *Ordinary Affects*. Durham, NC: Duke University Press.

Strang, Veronica. 2013. "Going against the Flow: The Biopolitics of Dams and Diversions." *Worldviews: Global Religions, Culture, and Ecology* 17 (2): 161–73.

Survival International. 2016. "Catastrophic Dam Inaugurated Today in Ethiopia." Accessed February 28, 2018. https://www.survivalinternational.org/news/11544.

Szwed, John. 1997. *Space Is the Place: The Lives and Times of Sun Ra*. New York: De Capo Press.

Tadesse, Kirubel. 2013. "Ethiopia: Big Nile Dam Could Ease Africa Power Failures." *Christian Science Monitor*. Accessed June 20, 2016. http://www.csmonitor.com /Environment/Latest-News-Wires/2013/0703/Ethiopia-Big-Nile-dam-could-ease -Africa-power-failures.

Tetzlaff, Stefan. 2017. "Revolution or Evolution? The Making of the Automobile Sector Industry in Mid-20th Century India." In *Cars, Automobility, and Development in Asia: Wheels of Change*, edited by Arve Hansen and Kenneth Bo Nielsen, 62–79. New York: Routledge.

Thagesen, Bent. 2004. "Soil Investigation." In *Road Engineering for Development*, edited by Richard Robinson and Bent Thagesen, 137–61. London: Spon Press.

Thompson, Marnie Jane. 2014. "Mud, Dust, and Marougé: Precarious Construction in a Congolese Refugee Camp." *Architectural Theory* 3 (19): 376–92.

Thrift, Nigel. 2004. "Intensities of Feeling: Towards a Spatial Politics of Affect." *Geografiska Annaler, Series B: Human Geography* 86 (1): 57–78.

Thrift, Nigel. 2008. *Non-Representational Theory: Space, Politics, Affect*. London: Routledge.

Tilt, Bryan. 2015. *Dams and Development in China: The Moral Economy of Water and Power*. New York: Columbia University Press.

Toggia, Pietro S. 2008. "The State of Emergency: Police and Carceral Regimes in Modern Ethiopia." *Journal of Developing Societies* 24 (2): 107–24.

Traugott, Mark. 2010. *The Insurgent Barricade*. Berkeley: University of California Press.

Tripp, Aili. 1997. *Changing the Rules: The Politics of Liberalization and the Urban Informal Economy in Tanzania*. Berkeley: University of California Press.
Truitt, Allison. 2008. "On the Back of a Motorbike: Middle-class Mobility in Ho Chi Minh City, Vietnam." *American Ethnologist* 35 (1): 3–19.
Tsing, Anna. 2015. *The Mushroom at the End of the World: On the Possibility of Life in Capitalist Ruins*. Princeton, NJ: Princeton University Press.
Turton, David. 2010. "The Downstream Impact." Paper presented at the Royal Africa Society Meeting on the Gibe III Dam, School of Oriental and African Studies, University of London, London, November 10, 2010.
Ulimwengu, John, Sindu Workneh, and Zelekawork Paulos. 2009. *Impact of Soaring Food Price in Ethiopia: Does Location Matter?* Washington, DC: International Food Policy Research Institute.
Vargo, Jason, and Jonathan Patz. 2014. "On the (Bike) Path to Prosperity: Why Banning Bikes Is Bad for Kolkata." *Huffington Post*. Accessed June 29, 2017. http://www.huffingtonpost.com/jason-vargo/kolkata-bike-ban_b_4157234.html.
Vaughan, Sarah. 2011. "Revolutionary Democratic State-Building: Party, State and People in EPRDF's Ethiopia." *Journal of Eastern African Studies* 5 (4): 619–40.
von Schnitzler, Antina. 2008. "Citizenship Prepaid: Water, Calculability, and Techno-politics in South Africa." *Journal of Southern African Studies* 34 (4): 899–917.
von Schnitzler, Antina. 2013. "Traveling Technologies: Infrastructure, Ethical Regimes, and the Materiality of Politics in South Africa." *Cultural Anthropology* 28 (4): 670–93.
von Schnitzler, Antina. 2016. *Democracy's Infrastructure: Techno-Politics and Protest after Apartheid*. Princeton, NJ: Princeton University Press.
Weber, Max. [1930] 2001. *The Protestant Ethic and the Spirit of Capitalism*. Translated by Talcott Parsons. London: Routledge Classics.
Weldeghebrael, Ezana Haddis. 2017. "Aspiring 'Developmental' State's Spatial Strategy towards Slum for Accumulation and Hegemonic Purposes: The Case of Addis Ababa." Paper presented at Inside a Construction Boom: Politics, Responsibility and the Temporalities of Urban Development Workshop, Brussels, Belgium, November 14.
Wells, Christopher. 2012. *Car Country: An Environmental History*. Seattle: University of Washington Press.
Wittgenstein, Ludwig. 1953. *Philosophical Investigations*. Malden, MA: Blackwell.
World Bank. 2013. "Ethiopia: Second Economic Update: Laying the Foundations for Achieving Middle Income Status." Accessed November 26, 2018. http://documents.worldbank.org/curated/en/885721468031488091/Ethiopia-Second-economic-update-laying-the-foundation-for-achieving-middle-income-status/.
World Bank. n.d. "Data: Net Official Development Assistance and Official Aid Received." Accessed January 6, 2016. http://data.worldbank.org/indicator/DT.ODA.ALLD.CD.
World Bank. n.d. "The World Bank in Ethiopia." Accessed August 24, 2018. http://www.worldbank.org/en/country/ethiopia/overview.
World Bank. n.d. "The World Bank in Middle Income Countries." Accessed August 24, 2018. http://www.worldbank.org/en/country/mic.

World Bank Group. 2017. "Global Economic Prospects: A Fragile Recovery." Washington, DC: World Bank.

"The World's Fastest Growing Economy?" 2011. *African Business* 379 (October 16): 57–60.

Zenawi, Meles. 2011a. Speech during 13th Annual Pastoralists' Day Celebrations, Jinka, Ethiopia, January 25, 2011.

Zenawi, Meles. 2011b. "States and Markets: Neoliberal Limitations and the Case for a Developmental State." In *Good Growth and Governance in Africa*, edited by Akbar Noman, Kwesi Botchwey, Howard Stein, and Joseph Stiglitz, 140–74. Oxford: Oxford University Press.

Zewde, Bahru. 1991. *A History of Modern Ethiopia, 1855–1991*. Oxford: James Curry.

INDEX

Page numbers followed by *f* indicate illustrations.